Remembering Awatovi

Peabody Museum Monographs • Number 10

PEABODY MUSEUM OF ARCHAEOLOGY AND ETHNOLOGY

HARVARD UNIVERSITY • CAMBRIDGE, MASSACHUSETTS

Remembering Awatovi

THE STORY OF AN ARCHAEOLOGICAL EXPEDITION
IN NORTHERN ARIZONA, 1935–1939

Hester A. Davis

with contributions by
Brian Fagan
Eric Polingyouma

PEABODY MUSEUM PRESS
HARVARD UNIVERSITY • CAMBRIDGE, MASSACHUSETTS

Editorial direction by Joan K. O'Donnell
Copyediting by Jane Kepp
Design and composition by Mary Sweitzer
Index by Thomas Kozachek and Mary Lynn Kennedy
Production management by Donna Dickerson
Printed and bound in Canada by Friesens

ISBN 978-0-87365-912-3 (cloth)
ISBN 978-0-87365-911-6 (paper)

Library of Congress Cataloging-in-Publication Data:

Davis, Hester A., 1930-
Remembering Awatovi : the story of an archaeological expedition in northern Arizona, 1935–1939 / Hester A. Davis ; with contributions by Brian Fagan and Eric Polingyouma
p. cm. — (Peabody museum monographs ; no. 10)
Includes bibliographical references and index.
ISBN 978-0-87365-912-3 (cloth : alk. paper) — ISBN 978-0-87365-911-6 (pbk. : alk. paper)
1. Hopi Indians—Arizona—Awatovi—Antiquities. 2. Excavations (Archaeology)—Social aspects—Arizona—Awatovi. 3. Excavations (Archaeology)—Arizona—Awatovi. 4. Awatovi (Ariz.)—Antiquities. I. Peabody Museum of Archaeology and Ethnology. II. Title.
E99.H7D377 2008
979.1004'97458—dc22

2008030906

Frontispiece: Diorama of an Awatovi Expedition scene, with Jo Brew, Bill Claflin Jr., and a member of the crew. The diorama, made by the Pitman and Guernsey Studio between 1935 and 1950, was a gift to the Peabody Museum from Helen Claflin Spring. Dimensions: 56 x 76.1 x 37.2 cm. Photo by Mark Craig © the President and Fellows of Harvard College.

To Penny and Mott,
for their never-ending interest,
support, and enthusiasm.

Ode To A Batch Of Cinnamon Rolls

(Sent by Air-post from Quemado, N.M., to Bass River, Mass., 1951)

In the dark backward abysm of time [1]
It's so long ago, for sooth and for shyme,
I could scarce remember the gorgeous sensation,
When I sanketh my teeth in a Thompson creation.

Oh what a world of irle ill-favoured faults [2]
Has cometh and gone, like the old-fashioned waltz
Since the days in the West, when I ate with a grin,
A cinnamon roll, cooked uppeth by Lin.

I have no other than a womans reason, [3]
For not being out there with you-all this season.
I'd come if I could, but alas, and take heed,
For I speak of the boy that I grew from a seed!

A needy, hollow-eyed, sharp looking wench, [4]
With a hunger that only a c roll could quench.
And with hundreds of miles twixt me and Lin
I never did think that I'd taste one agin.*

England, bound in by the triumphant sea, [5]
Had nothing, but NOTHING, on the triumphant me,
When a package arrived from a faraway land,
Addressed by that well known "Smithsonian" hand.

To gild refined gold, to paint the lily [6]
Or to save a cinnamon roll, would be silly.
So I ate them all up, well covered with butter,
And when I was done not a sound could I utter.

—Penrose "Penny" Davis Worman

1. *The Tempest,* Act I, Scene II
2. *Merry Wives of Windsor,* Act III, Scene II
3. *Two Gentlemen from Verona,* Act I, Scene I
4. *Comedy of Errors,* Act V, Scene I
5. *King Richard,* Act II, Scene I
6. *King John,* Act IV, Scene I
* "I was not born under a rhyming planet," *Much Ado about Nothing,*
  Act V, Scene I

Contents

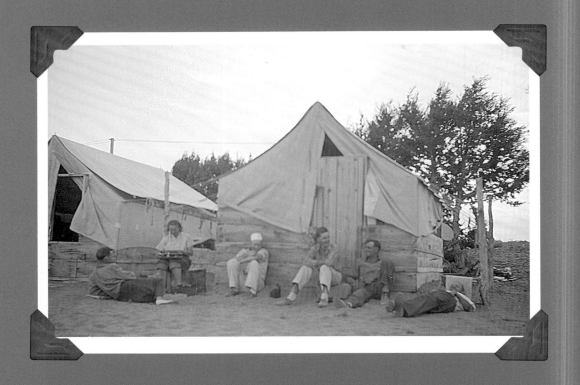

Recording Awatovi. Wat Smith, reclining at left, dictates to Penny Davis, with typewriter in her lap, the saga of the Nimmo-Brew wedding. Lin Thompson, Mott Davis, and Al Lancaster kibitz while Carlos García-Robiou snoozes at right, June 12, 1939.

Foreword

Remembering Field Camps

Brian Fagan

Excavation. The very word evokes images of spectacular discoveries and long days under the desert sun. Fieldwork is indeed the archaeologist's ambrosia, the cause of our most profound satisfaction. Most of us are happiest when in the field, unencumbered by classes, grades, bureaucracy, and all the impedimenta of academic life. Despite our denials to the contrary, there is still a sense of adventure about being in the field and making even the humblest of archaeological discoveries. We are, above all, discoverers. Archaeology is always about discovery, whether of a great city, a modest farming village, a Southwestern pueblo, or simply a scatter of stone tools.

Many of today's most interesting revelations come from air-conditioned laboratories rather than sun-dappled trenches, but we are still discoverers. For all the shift to the laboratory and microscope, much discovery still unfolds far from cities and towns, often in distant lands. Many of us still spend weeks and months living in remote field camps, often under canvas, sometimes in borrowed farm buildings, even in motels. Life in our camps is often lively, sometimes great fun, and sometimes, unfortunately, downright miserable. All the ingredients for human drama are there, but surprisingly, archaeologists rarely write about their field camps. Precisely why is a mystery. Perhaps project directors and staff members are exhausted from the effort of writing up their excavations. Luckily for readers of this book, some of the people who worked at the ruins of Awatovi Pueblo in Hopi country in the late 1930s did set down their camp experiences, which add an entirely new dimension to the research there. *Remembering Awatovi* is a unique celebration of a remarkable field camp in the American Southwest nearly three quarters of a century ago.

Reading this book evoked powerful memories from my own fieldwork. I remember some of my African excavation camps vividly—some for their locations, others for their smells, and still others because of the local people. I have camped on the edges of thousand-year-old village mounds in places where we had to carry in fresh water by truck for five miles. Invariably we lived under canvas, building camp kitchens, toilets, and showers from poles and thatch, just like our subsistence-farming neighbors. One camp sat high above the Zambezi River, where crocodiles lurked and a nest of black mambas thrived in the bank below us. I remember drinking gallons of tea after arduous, hot days of excavation—and a memorable occasion when the cook dropped the entire tray as a snake wriggled across the path in front of him. Once a mamba moved swiftly past me as I sat in a canvas bath by my tent. I have never sat so still in my life. Perhaps the most vivid memories of all were of moonlit nights when elephants came down to the river to drink and a surprisingly powerful scent of mud and dust assailed the nostrils. Late at night we heard lions on the other bank, roaring at the moon.

Over the years, memories of life in camp recede in the face of new discoveries and fresh archaeological experiences. Perhaps this helps to explain why few archaeologists ever write about their field camps. Some camps acquire reputations from gossip and brief recollections in autobiographies or diaries. Those run by the Egyptologist Flinders Petrie, for example, were notorious for their stinginess a hundred years ago. Generations of his helpers, such as Howard Carter of Tutankhamun fame, built their own huts and slept with finds stacked under their beds after dining from cans.

Another British archaeologist, Leonard Woolley, who excavated Ur, lived in style. Invariably he built an adobe field house for his few European companions. When he dug at the Hittite city of Carchemish on the Euphrates in 1912, his companion was T. E. Lawrence, later to achieve world renown as Lawrence of Arabia. Lawrence was responsible for the photography and pottery classification, tasks he performed somewhat erratically. The two men lived in an imposing excavation house constructed at a price of about $25, complete with mosaic floors, copper bath fittings, and red stucco walls. The house was always full of Arab and European visitors, arguing, gossiping, and engaging in political intrigue. For all its comforts, the house was a safe haven and a potential fortress against raiders. Woolley spent much of his time mediating disputes and trying to avoid trouble. His foreman, Sheikh Hamoudi, had started life as a bandit and became one of Woolley's closest friends. Woolley's *Dead Towns and Living Men* (H. Mitford, London, 1920) is a deeply engaging (if sometimes exaggerated) account of life at Carchemish.

One could go on about excavation camps, for they often figure, if inconspicuously, in famous excavations. The great 1925 earthquake at the Palace of Minos in Crete tossed Arthur Evans around in his palatial Villa Ariadne as local church bells tolled. The groaning earth reminded him of the legend of the Minotaur. Louis and Mary Leakey lived under canvas for years at Olduvai Gorge, surrounded by lions and rhinoceroses. Their excavations had none of the elaborate facilities taken for granted today. Louis was sick with the flu and in bed back in camp when Mary unearthed *Zinjanthropus* in 1959. Their tent was the stage for her breathtaking announcement of the discovery of "Dear Boy." There are times when the historian of archaeology wishes he or she could have been a fly on the wall at many of these field camps. The conversations would cast an entirely different light on the discoveries published in sober monographs years later.

Remembering Awatovi is the story of a field camp that remained in use in remote Hopi country for five years, between 1935 and 1939, during Harvard University's last pre–World War II expedition to the American Southwest. Hester Davis was only nine when her older brother and sister were invited to participate in the last season of excavations. She did not visit the site until 1991, a half century later, although she knew many of the participants personally. (She never knew the director, Jo Brew, however, and there I have the advantage over her, for I met him over lunch at Harvard in 1966.) Davis's family connections, and the instinct that researching the Awatovi Expedition would be fun, led Davis, herself an eminent archaeologist, into an entirely new kind of archaeological historiography based on primary sources. She asks fundamental questions. What was life at the excavation like? What effect did life in the field camp have on the research?

The result is a truly groundbreaking piece of archaeological history. At first glance, one might think that *Remembering Awatovi* is an obscure byway of archaeology, of interest only to the diminishing number of survivors and their families. Nothing could be farther from the truth. This meticulously researched book is a remarkable portrait of an era of Southwestern fieldwork that unfolded under unimaginably primitive conditions by today's standards. In its pages, some well-known (and some almost-forgotten) archaeologists come to life as people, which helps us better understand their archaeological work, much of which is still of fundamental value.

The Awatovi field camp was beautifully organized, a tribute to the administrative skills of Jo Brew, a somewhat unheralded figure in Southwestern archaeology. How good an archaeologist he was is a verdict for specialists, but he was certainly responsible for a well-fed, continually entertained, and happy field staff. That's what makes this book a precious rarity—its close look at the dynamics of the personalities that ebbed and flowed through the excavation. Brew recruited staff members whom he knew well and people with long experience of ranch life in remote places, among them an excellent cook, Lin Thompson, who acquired near mythic status in later years. People from all walks of life visited the camp—students, some of whom went on to forge major careers in archaeology; the great, among them A.V. Kidder and Earl Morris; and the soon to be great, such as Emil Haury. There were nonarchaeological visitors, too, a constant stream of outsiders who added spice to evenings in camp.

Through patient detective work and extensive interviews, Davis has compiled a delicious pastiche of a field camp where life was never dull and even the automobiles were beloved characters, among them a 1929 Model T Ford named "Pecos." These were the days before electronics and iPods, when people relied more heavily on one another for entertainment. We learn that the pottery tent was one of the centers of camp life, its easily opened sides providing a welcome draft on hot days. We learn, too, that the finds arrived every day in apple boxes, and floors were added to storage tents to keep out the pack rats. Life was not necessarily easy, but it was fun. How many present-day excavation camps can boast of a resident piano—and archaeologists who can play it? How many can also boast of a marriage, in this case between Jo Brew and Peabody Museum secretary Evelyn Nimmo?

Remembering Awatovi draws aside the veil of history that covers all excavations of this era, when outsiders could still come into the Southwest and do more or less what they liked, with the connivance of the Bureau of Indian Affairs. Despite this freedom, Brew and his colleagues maintained excellent relations with the local people who worked on the excavations, some of whom Davis interviewed for the book. She does not shy away from the emerging tensions over unearthing burials and other sensitivities that are now at the front of every Southwestern archaeologist's mind. This was very much a time of learning on both sides, when issues such as access to sites and treatment of the dead were growing concerns for everyone, at a matter-of-fact, sometimes seemingly unemotional level. Davis takes us behind the scenes to look at permit applications and negotiations with local Hopi communities at a time when the Indian Reorganization Act was first giving Native Americans the right to control excavations on their land. The Awatovi excavations ultimately ended not because of World War II but because local people could not agree which clan owned the site.

Davis throws light on logistics, too, the unspectacular part of fieldwork that archaeologists rarely describe or even want to dwell upon. We learn about the funding of the Awatovi Expedition and about relationships with local suppliers. We go behind the scenes as the camp becomes a more or less permanent one, and we learn what happened to the buildings when the excavation ended. Awatovi was carefully staffed with crewmembers for every niche, many of them recruited somewhat casually, and generally with success, for Brew apparently had an eye for the right people. In an era without instant communication, when excavating in the remoter parts of the Southwest was still a formidable undertaking, he seems to have been well aware of the importance of collegiality and compatible personalities. As a result, it must have been great fun to work at Awatovi, in a community, albeit a temporary one, where everyone pitched in, even if the cook firmly dismissed people from his kitchen. Everyone went out to push stranded visitors' automobiles out of the mud or sand. As far as training was concerned, it was training on the job, something very different from the field schools of today.

Every archaeologist, whether a Southwestern specialist or not, will find pleasure in Hester Davis's remarkable book. She reminds us that many things about field-work are still the same—the companionship, the importance of good food in camp, and the never-ending realities of logistics and provisions. Awatovi also reminds us that self-sufficiency and a sense of humor are ingredients of archaeology just as important today as they were in the late 1930s, when multidisciplinary research was in its infancy and computers lay in the future. *Remembering Awatovi* is no tiresome volume of obscure reminiscences. It is an affectionate and definitive examination of life in a field camp of the 1930s that holds many lessons for excavators today and in the future. Above all, it is a book about civility and mentorship, two fundamentally important ingredients of archaeology. Civility and professional mentoring are two things Hester Davis has taken seriously throughout her career, and this book is a fitting culmination to her many years of distinguished service to the past.

View of the Tallahogan Canyon, looking northwest from the top of Antelope Mesa, 1939.

Awat'ovi, A Hopi History

One morning a smoke arose from Antelope Mesa, as seen from Songòopavi village. Songòopavi (Shongopavi), the mother village, was the first village in the area to be settled, and it lay below Second Mesa rather than on the top where it is today. The smoke revealed the arrival on Antelope Mesa of the Kòokopngyam (Fire Clan) and Aasangyam (Mustard Clan) from the Chama drainage area, near what is now Santa Fe. These were the founders of Awat'ovi.

Awat'ovi (the Hopi spelling of the name) was one of the first villages built on the Hopi mesas. One cannot place a time or year on its founding, but there were settlements on Antelope Mesa as early as A.D. 700. But Awat'ovi, like neighboring villages of the time—Kawàyka'a (Kawaika-a), Tsakpahu (Chakpahu), Pink Arrow, Nesuftanga, Kòokopngyama (Kokopngyama), and Lölöqangwtukwi (Lululongturque)—was not a Hopi village. It was settled by Keresans. Later, clan groups from Homol'ovi arrived and joined those already living there. The settlement increased to several villages along the eastern edges of the mesa, each different from the others in language and cultural practices. Farming, the exchange of ceremonial dances, and foot races between the villages made the settlements prosperous. Their relationships with the nearby Hopi villages were good, some Keresans married into Hopi, and religious ceremonies were adopted that are still practiced today.

Shortly after A.D. 1000, the katsina people joined the Hopi mesas. By 1300 they were adopted by Awat'ovi and its neighbors, who changed their ceremonial calendars to accommodate the katsina ceremonies. Trade flourished between the villages on the mesas and pueblos to the east and north along the Rio Grande.

In the late 1200s, a great drought in the Southwest shifted the settlement of the mesas. Springs began to dry up, waters were rationed, and many villages on Antelope Mesa were abandoned as groups returned to their original homes to the east or to other places in the region that still had water, in the hope of finding a place to farm. The ensuing years were hard not only for Awat'ovians but also for other villagers on the Hopi mesas. Many religious and other important ceremonial activities died out due to the loss of important clans.

In the early 1500s, the Hopis heard of the arrival of strangers in the pueblos to the east, and the news raised interesting questions. The Hopi people traditionally await the arrival from the east of a "Paahana," a fair-skinned younger brother of the older and wiser Hopi, who will come to the Hopi people and ask and offer certain things. Some young Hopi men traveled to see the Paahana, and they returned with reports of a creature with a frightening, hairy face who was clothed in armor, carried a long lance, and behaved strangely. The Hopis waited, but the Paahana did not come. They were to learn from other Puebloan villages that the Spaniard came only to take and destroy. His arrival on the mesa was an incredible sight. When the Spaniards did arrive in 1540, they found only Awat'ovi still in existence on Antelope Mesa. They rode strange animals, carried unusual weapons, and ate different foods. This first group, the Coronado Expedition under Don Pedro de Tovar, came looking for precious metals. Finding none, they left, but later in the year another group came, again searching for stones and metals of value. Again finding nothing of use to conquer, the Spaniards left. Brief visits by the Europeans followed—Espejo in 1583, Oñate in 1598 and 1604. But it was not until 1628 that Father Alonso Peinado returned to build a house with a cross in the village of Awat'ovi. In 1629 missionary work was begun by three Franciscans to convert the residents of Awat'ovi and to put the province under the rule of the Spanish Crown. Their church was christened San Bernardino. Later, other churches were built at Hopi villages to the west.

To build the missions, Hopi people were enslaved. Many men became stonecutters; others were chained together and driven east to the Chuska Mountains to cut timber and pull the logs back to the villages, under the whips of the Spaniards. Many men died for lack of water and food. Indian women were also victims of the Spaniards and Moors. It is said that many children were born with goat eyes and goat hair (brown eyes and curly hair) and with light or black skin.

The Spaniards demanded that we Hopis live according to their way of life, a demand that caused a terrible shift in the lives of Awat'ovians and Hopis. The practice of Christianity was enforced. Religious leaders had to practice their ceremonies in secret, and some religious ceremonies began to die out. Spaniards entered our homes to collect religious items and then burned them. Our people opposed the Spaniards only to be killed.

The situation led to splits in families, clans, and villages. The settlement at Awat'ovi split in two, and members of the eastern village became strong followers of the

Catholic religion. Villagers from the western part tried to maintain their Hopi ceremonies and beliefs. Trade and visits with eastern Puebloan groups along the Rio Grande ceased as suspicion among the people grew, and anyone found not to belong in a village might be maimed or killed.

Then drought came again to the region. Leaders gathered to discuss the situation and met secretly with envoys from pueblos to the east. When Hopis heard of a plan to revolt against the Spaniards, they agreed to take part. On the designated day in 1680, the villagers destroyed the churches and killed the priests. But in the following years, their attempts to rebuild Hopi life were interrupted again by the arrival of Catholic fathers at Awat'ovi in 1700. Their arrival brought the Hopi villages together, and Hopis destroyed Awat'ovi in the fall of 1700. The village was abandoned permanently, and surviving families settled in other villages on the mesas.

Since the destruction of the village of Awat'ovi, it has been considered an evil place. No one at Hopi claims it. However, there has been a lot of interest in the village from the scientific community, who want to investigate it and learn who lived there and how they lived before it was destroyed.

In the 1930s, the Peabody Museum asked permission of the U.S. government to excavate portions of Awat'ovi and Kawàyka'a. They had the support of a Badger Clan leader from Mishongnovi (in Hopi, Musangnuvi) village, although it was understood that the Tobacco Clan were the leaders at west Awat'ovi at the time it was destroyed.

The excavation of Awat'ovi created a lot of opposition among Hopis. A destroyed village is a dead village. It is buried and should not be disturbed. Many bad events happened there, and bad memories should not be revived.

The Badger and Water clans from Mishongnovi initially agreed to the Peabody's excavations, and when the excavation began, several men from Walpi and Mishongnovi participated. When the museum asked for a renewal of the excavation permit, however, it was denied by the leader of the Tobacco Clan of Walpi, with support from other villages.

In its initial planning of the excavation, the Peabody did not include Hopis or rely on Hopi authority regarding the ownership and caretaking of Awat'ovi. Instead of involving the Hopi Tribe, the Peabody filed for a permit under the Antiquities Act, which was under the jurisdiction of the federal government. The expedition would thus be viewed as a federal issue and not be governed by tribal authority. The expedition took the position that the information from the dig would not be shared freely with the Hopi people.

Today there is an interest on the part of some Hopis in putting up a museum near the Awat'ovi site to house artifacts and display what was discovered in past excavations. It is known that the site was not founded by Hopis, and it is not considered a

Hopi village—but which eastern Pueblo groups lived there remains a question. The beautiful mural paintings from several rooms at Awat'ovi and Kawàyka'a villages depict the lives and lifestyles at the time of occupation, including the influence of katsinas, warfare, and the arrival of Spaniards.

After the destruction of Awat'ovi, members of the village were taken in or adopted by other Hopi villages. Some have married into other communities. Some of their descendants have taken active roles in their adopted villages, filling some of the ceremonial positions left by the original clans. Today the lands around Awat'ovi are still used by the descendants of the original Awat'ovians, but no one has ever claimed the village.

Eric Polingyouma
Blue Bird Clan, Shungopavi Village

Preface

In 1989 I realized that 50 years had passed since the end of the five years of excavations sponsored by Harvard's Peabody Museum of Archaeology and Ethnology on Antelope Mesa in northeastern Arizona. The Awatovi Expedition, as it was called, was the last and largest of the Peabody's pre–World War II expeditions. My brother Mott Davis and my sister Penny Davis had both been invited to be part of the expedition in its last summer, 1939—Mott as an archaeology student and Penny as a graphic artist. I was nine years old then, and although I did not visit the site until 1991, I eventually met most of the archaeologists involved, through Mott and Penny and my own career in archaeology. It would be fun, I thought, to make a record of what the people who were part of those five years remembered about their experiences on this last of the grand expeditions in the United States.

I was too late for some of them, of course. Most importantly, I missed John Otis Brew, known to everyone as "Jo," who directed the expedition; he passed away in 1988. But I was able to interview or correspond with about 20 people whose memories of Awatovi, even after 50 years, shone like shafts of light on the events of the time. (Some of them, too, have since died.) I had many talks with Mott and Penny as well as with Evelyn Brew, Jo's widow, and Dick Woodbury, an Awatovi staff member in 1938 and 1939. I also enjoyed personal interviews with staff members Watson Smith, Al Lancaster, Happy Foote, Ned Hall, and Dick Wheeler. Several other people contributed wonderful snippets of their experiences at Awatovi or memories of their visits there.

I was able to talk with two of the Hopi men who had worked on the crew: Gibson Namoki, in 1991 (he died the following year), and Patrick Coochnyama, in 2001. Other Hopis with whom I visited, mostly children of the men who worked at Awatovi, remembered their fathers and uncles talking about the project. Several of the children recalled visiting the field camp, and a few even remembered some of the archaeologists. Most of the professional archaeologists then working in the Southwest visited Awatovi at one time or another over those five years, and the surviving participants well remembered both the scientific and the social benefits of their stays in camp.

In August 1991 I visited Awatovi with Mott and Penny as part of my initial research into the story of the Awatovi excavations. Between 1989 and 1991, I went through most of the paper archives at the Peabody Museum and began writing as I accumulated information. I put together a long saga of the Peabody staff's effort to renew the museum's permit to excavate at Awatovi under the Antiquities Act. After a hiatus of eight years, in 1998 I received a Hrdy Fellowship from the Peabody Museum—and a challenge from Richard Meadow and Rubie Watson at the museum to finish what I had started. In 1999 I retired from the Arkansas Archeological Survey and went back to the manuscript in earnest.

Jo Brew never threw anything away. As a consequence, a wealth of information about the expedition lies in the archives at the Peabody Museum. Besides the field records, photographs, and maps, there are expense accounts and receipts, copies of telegrams, internal memos about planning and fund-raising, and saved correspondence. During the 1935, 1936, and 1937 field seasons, Brew wrote almost weekly to Donald Scott, the museum's director, describing the progress of the fieldwork and the doings in camp. In 1938 and 1939, when Evelyn Nimmo, one of the museum's secretaries (soon to be Jo's wife), joined the expedition, Jo dictated two daily journals to her, which she recorded in shorthand and then typed for the files. One journal dealt with the progress of the fieldwork, the other with everything else—from who came to visit and who won at pinochle to discussions with the Indian Service superintendent in nearby Keams Canyon about relations with the Hopi tribe. An additional written document is *One Man's Archaeology,* the autobiography of Watson Smith, another of the principals in the expedition. It offers almost 60 pages of Smith's memories of people and activities during the fieldwork at Awatovi and afterward, when he worked on analyses and reports.

The Peabody Museum's Awatovi archive holds probably 3,000 photographs, more than half of which are of people and the camp. Almost all the latter were taken by Hattie Cosgrove, who was in charge of the laboratory work and therefore was in camp most of the time. She tried to take a picture not only of every individual member of the staff and crew but also of each visitor.

Some of Jo Brew's papers and most of Watson Smith's are in the archives of the Arizona State Museum (ASM) at the University of Arizona in Tucson, and they contain some items concerning Awatovi. Smith must have had a personal camera, for his scrapbook of Awatovi photographs at ASM contains some images not in the Peabody files. The ASM archivist kindly copied all these for my use. Richard Ford, at the Museum of Anthropology at the University of Michigan, sent me photocopies of photographs in Volney Jones's archives from his time at Awatovi. Carlos García-Robiou also had a personal camera with him, as far as I can discern. There are many two-by-two-inch black-and-white pictures in the Peabody Museum's photo file with no negatives or negative numbers, which must be contact prints; Evelyn Brew believes these to be Carlos's. Some of them are used as illustrations in this book, and the credits indicate that he was the photographer. Would that I could have thanked him personally. Evelyn Brew also loaned me her personal photographs of people and events from 1938 and 1939; they are now in the Peabody Museum archives.

Mott Davis, Penny Davis Worman, Dick Woodbury, and Evelyn Brew all responded to my request for reminiscences with pages of information and informal comments, and I quote from these liberally throughout the book. Dick's and Evelyn's parents had saved all the letters they wrote from the field, which they each copied for my use. John Longyear's fiancée, later his wife, had saved all their correspondence as well, and John excerpted appropriate parts for me. One amazing bonus from John was about 15 minutes of eight-millimeter movie film. It included the historic occasion in September 1937 when Catholic mass was celebrated at the excavated Spanish mission altar at Awatovi. A copy of this film is now in the archives at Arizona State Museum. Helen "Haych" Claflin Spring cleared up a confusion about the name of the Model T Ford, "Pecos," which played an important role in the expedition. It had belonged to the Claflins and had no association with A.V. Kidder's project at Pecos Pueblo, New Mexico.

Kidder, a Southwestern archaeologist well known for his research in the 1920s at Pecos, kept personal journals for many years; they are now in the Harvard Archives in Widener Library. In one is a description of Kidder's first visit to Awatovi in 1917, and his journal for 1939 describes his week-long stay at the Awatovi camp that August. H. Warren Shepard, the father of staff member Anna Shepard, kept a short journal during their two-week visit in 1938, and these two pages are in the Peabody Museum archives.

In the written documents about the Awatovi Expedition, people's names are sometimes spelled creatively. Writers often addressed Jo Brew as "Joe," for example, and the camp cook, Lin (for Lindsay) Thompson, tends to show up as "Lyn." In quoted passages I have left the original spellings intact. The name Awatovi itself has been spelled in many ways over the centuries—Awatobi, Aguatubi, Ahua-tuby, A-wa-to-bi, Awat'ovi, and so on—and in direct quotations I have retained those versions, too. For place names, I have for the most part retained the spellings used in the Peabody's publications on Awatovi, which may differ from contemporary Hopi and other accepted spellings.

Writing this book has been a long journey, and I have asked the help of many friends, old and new. Everyone I contacted encouraged me in the project. My sister Penny was unfailingly enthusiastic and patient. She and her husband, Gene Worman, went to the Peabody from their home in Amherst, Massachusetts, in 1989 to see what kind of information the archives held. They discovered a bonanza of material and began taking notes. Gene actually started a draft narrative before his eyesight began to fail. Mott, Penny, Dick Woodbury, Evelyn Brew, and John Longyear all read at least one draft of the manuscript and corrected my errors of fact. Steven LeBlanc, director of collections at the Peabody, read a section and made useful comments. Ray Thompson, retired director of the Arizona State Museum, also read several sections, made corrections and comments that improved the manuscript, and looked up obscure things in answer to calls for help, for which I am grateful. Emil Haury, Eric Reed, Liz Morris, Ned Hall, Helen Claflin Spring, and Frank Hibben all wrote letters telling stories of camp life and people they remembered.

In 1997 I mentioned this project to Richard Meadow, chair of the Peabody Museum Publications Committee, who asked to see an outline and draft so far. He suggested that the story might fit with the committee's interest in having some of the museum's old projects written up. Rubie Watson, then director of the museum, offered me a Hrdy Fellowship, which allowed me to visit the archives at Arizona State Museum in Tucson and at the Museum of Northern Arizona (MNA) in Flagstaff. I am grateful to Alan Ferg, the ASM archivist, and Michael O'Hara, the MNA archivist, for their willing help.

While I was in Tucson, I met Leland Dennis, grandson of the Leland Dennis who was a Hopi member of the Awatovi crew. He gave me information about all five Dennis brothers who worked on the project and invited me to attend Emory Sekaquaptewa's Hopi language class, which he was taking. I knew Emory already, and he welcomed me graciously. At the end of class, he introduced me as a visitor. I mentioned why I was there and said that I would eventually be going to the reservation to try to find family members of the Hopi crew. Exclamations came from the front row—Anita Poleahla said she was the daughter of Evans Poleahla, and Marvin Lalo said he was a nephew of Erik Lalo, both crew members. Anita and Marvin were excited to hear of the project and helped me tremendously with introductions and genealogical information.

With the fellowship funds I was able to make two trips to the Hopi mesas. In 1994 I had made the acquaintance of Carolyn O'Bagy Davis, who was writing her biography of Hattie Cosgrove, *Treasured Earth: Hattie Cosgrove's Mimbres Archaeology in the American Southwest*. She, too, was enthusiastic about the project, and she knew many Hopi families from having given quilting workshops on the reservation. In March 2001 she took me to visit seven families of the Hopi men on the crew. Carolyn's friendship and help in this endeavor have been immeasurable.

I made the second trip at the invitation of the Hopi Cultural Preservation Office. In mid-August 2001 the Hopis were hosting a celebration of the 1680 Pueblo Revolt and asked if I could bring an exhibit of photographs of the Hopi men who participated in the excavations and talk with people coming to the Veterans Building for the ceremonies. I am grateful to Leigh Kuwanwisiwma, director of the Cultural Preservation Office, and Stewart Koyiyumptewa, tribal archivist, for their interest and support. Being a part of the celebration was a rewarding experience, and it allowed me to meet more families of the crew and others interested in Awatovi. The Peabody agreed to loan the portable photographic exhibit to the Hopi Cultural Museum for ongoing display.

The following archivists also provided access to their resources: Sarah Turner, American Institute of Architects (AIA); Clare Fleming, The Explorer's Club; Robert Leopold, National Anthropological Archives; Harley Holden, Harvard University Archives; and Brad Cole, curator of manuscripts at the Cline Library at Northern Arizona University. Special thanks go to Sarah Demb, archivist at the Peabody Museum until 2002, who bore the brunt of my visits and continual requests for more files and photographs. India Spartz, senior archivist, and Pat Kervick, associate archivist, at the Peabody took care of my many final requests for photographs, both photocopies and prints. Julie Brown, the Peabody's imaging services coordinator, scanned many of the prints, negatives, and documents reproduced here. Some of the prints were scanned by Jannelle Weakly from Wat Smith's photo scrapbook, now in the archives of the Arizona State Museum. I am grateful to Jannelle and to Alan Berg, archivist, for expediting this contribution to the manuscript. I also thank Rudy Busé, who went to great effort to find the photograph of A.V. Kidder at the Laboratory of Anthropology, Museum of Indian Arts and Culture, in Santa Fe.

The Internet put me in touch with Jane Motz, widow of staff member Fisher Motz, and with Vivian García-Robiou, daughter of Carlos García-Robiou. Both women greeted my questions with grace and interest. My search for information about Fisher Motz put me in touch with and in debt to Chris Downum at Northern Arizona University, who in turn put me in touch with Steve Hayden, whose mother was Fisher's first wife's cousin—the thread of connections in archaeology is long indeed.

Ben Smith, Watson Smith's son, when told of my impending visit, brought to the Arizona State Museum four large cartons of his father's papers, which proved to be a gold mine of Awatovi information. Anna Silas, who was director of the Hopi Cultural Museum when Penny, Mott, and I visited in 1991, took us on a memorable visit to Awatovi. Jenny Adams made available to me several tapes of her interviews with Al and Alice Lancaster, made while she was writing their biography, *Pinto Beans and Prehistoric Pots: The Legacy of Al and Alice Lancaster*. Archaeologists Kelley Hays-Gilpin and Dennis Gilpin read the manuscript, and Dennis steered me to the information about work at Awatovi by Charles Owen of the Field Museum in Chicago. Critical comments (in both senses of the word) of an anonymous reviewer saved me considerable embarrassment by pointing out errors of fact and suggesting some useful reorganization of chapters. Any errors that remain, of fact, attribution, or interpretation, are my own.

A near-final version of the manuscript was sent to the Hopi Cultural Preservation Office for review. Eric Polingyouma commented on several aspects. I thank him for his helpful remarks and particularly for generously providing a Hopi history of Awatovi. Finally, my good friend Brian Fagan graciously agreed to write a foreword, giving a more worldwide view of archaeological life, about which little has been written.

In 2002 Evelyn Brew invited me to stay for several days at her home in Cambridge, a short walk from the Peabody Museum, and insisted on feeding me as well. She is a most gracious hostess and friend. She went through more of Jo's files, loaned me her negatives, and sent correspondence and other information about both staff and crew. Her encouragement has been unfailing.

Joan K. O'Donnell, editorial director of the Peabody Museum Press, and Jane Kepp, copyeditor, have given me a world of lessons in writing English, making information clear, and expressing myself more effectively. Joan also took on the work of making the final decisions on which photographs to include. Donna Dickerson, project manager for the Peabody Museum Press, tackled all the technical and production matters necessary to ready a manuscript for the printer. Mary Sweitzer designed the book, with inspiration from Wat Smith's photo album.

A final heartfelt thank you goes to those who answered my plea for financial contributions to the press so a maximum number of pictures could be included. Alan Brew, Evelyn Brew, Richard and Nathalie Woodbury, and Edward C. Worman, on behalf of Penny Davis Worman, are the angels of *Remembering Awatovi*. To supplement their generous support, I was able to transfer unexpended funds from my Hrdy Fellowship to underwrite the cost of printing, for which I thank Sara Hrdy.

Finally, I am grateful for the support of the Arkansas Archeological Survey and Tom Green, its director. Among the perquisites of emeritus status have been the use of an office, a computer, and the copy machine and permission to bother other staff members when I need help. I owe a particular debt to Mary Lynn Kennedy, the Survey's editor, who read the manuscript with a keen eye and jumped in at the last minute to help refine the index. Debra Weddell, computer specialist for the Survey, and Lindi Holmes, the Survey's Sponsored Research Program's secretary, repeatedly got me out of technical trouble.

Hester A. Davis
Fayetteville, Arkansas
May 2008

Remembering Awatovi

The ruins of Awatovi in 1895, photographed by J. Walter Fewkes.

- 1 -

Awatovi's Turbulent History

Antelope Mesa is the easternmost of four flat fingers of land that jut out from the broad hand of Black Mesa in northeastern Arizona. On the south edge of Antelope Mesa sits Awatovi, a precontact and historic Hopi village that has been deserted for more than three hundred years. To the west of Antelope Mesa, the three mesa fingers known as First, Second, and Third Mesas host the contemporary Hopi villages. Empty today of human habitation, Antelope Mesa is sparsely covered by desert scrub and the occasional stunted juniper. Its most prominent features are its steep, rocky escarpments and rolling sand dunes. But the endless view of tablelands and canyons to the south and west has a grandeur that must have influenced the immigrants who came to the mesa some eight hundred years ago to choose this spot for their home.

In Hopi country, inhospitable as the landscape may appear, wherever there is water, there have been people. The valleys and mesas offer enough springs, seeps, and small, intermittent streams to have made settlement possible for centuries. On the slopes of Antelope Mesa, springs trickle out where the aquifer meets an underlying layer of impermeable rock. The people who built Awatovi had good reason for choosing this place: a large spring emerges just a few hundred yards away, on a path to Tallahogan Canyon, where their cornfields would have been.

Between about A.D. 1200 and 1250, a few Hopi families used locally available stone, adobe mud, and small timber to build the first rooms of the village that would come to be called Awatovi. Over the years the population grew, and residents built new rooms, often on top of old ones they had filled with trash and dirt. The complex began to sprawl, spreading to the north and east.

By sometime in the 1400s, the oldest group of rooms, which archaeologists would later call the Western Mound, had been abandoned for newer blocks of houses just to the east and north. This was the village visited by Spanish explorers in the sixteenth century.[1] The Spaniards' first few appearances at Awatovi were little more than short-lived annoyances. Ultimately, the changes they brought would prove catastrophic for

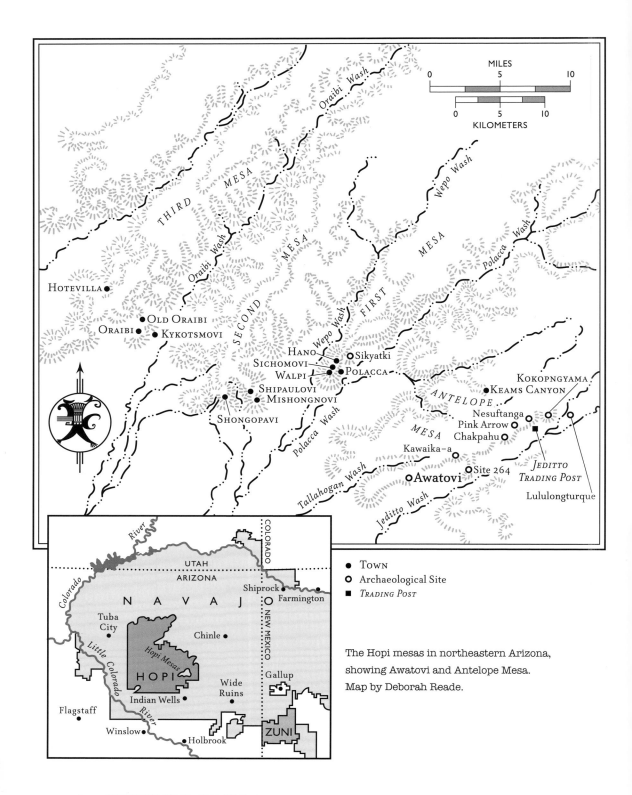

MILES

KILOMETERS

● Town
◉ Archaeological Site
■ *Trading Post*

The Hopi mesas in northeastern Arizona,
showing Awatovi and Antelope Mesa.
Map by Deborah Reade.

The south edge of Antelope Mesa. A wall of the mission is visible on the horizon at right.

the village. In 1700, conflict among the Hopis over whether or not to continue to welcome the Spaniards and their religion would bring Awatovi down in fire and slaughter.

In the summer of 1540, an army led by Francisco Vázquez de Coronado—the first Spaniards to explore northern New Spain—camped at Zuni in what is now west-central New Mexico. The Zunis told Coronado of several villages to the northwest in the *provincia* of "Tusayan," as the Spaniards called the Hopi homeland. Hoping to find a trail to the Pacific, Coronado sent Pedro de Tovar, Fray Juan de Padilla, and 20 soldiers to reconnoiter Tusayan.[2] Because Awatovi was the easternmost Hopi village occupied at the time, researchers have assumed that this was where Hopis and Spaniards first met. Spanish records fail to name the village visited by Tovar,[3] but he reported back to Coronado that the Indians he met told of a large river to the west—probably the Colorado. Shortly afterward, Coronado sent García López de Cárdenas in the same direction. Cárdenas stopped briefly at a Hopi village, again presumed to have been Awatovi, and went on to "discover" the Grand Canyon.

One chronicler of the Coronado expedition, Pedro de Castañeda de Nájera, wrote that the people of Tusayan—whom he described as "quarrelsome among themselves"—defied Tovar and his party with bows and arrows, shields, and wooden clubs, refusing to let the Spaniards advance toward their village. Tovar's men attacked and "knocked down many Indians," whereupon the residents of the pueblo "came out in peace with gifts" and the troop immediately disengaged.[4] Castañeda de Nájera was not an eyewit-ness to the event, but even if his secondhand account is accurate, the two appearances of Spanish soldiers and horses on Antelope Mesa lasted but a few days each and seem to have had little effect on the people or their daily lives. It would be another 43 years before Spaniards again visited the Hopi villages.

In 1583, Antonio de Espejo, on a long expedition from Mexico into Pueblo Indian territory, reached the Hopi villages with a few soldiers, servants, and a priest. His visit, too, was short. Juan de Oñate, the "first official and successful colonizer of New Mexico," reached the Hopi towns in 1598, but again the chroniclers mentioned no town of Awatovi by name.[5]

Although the Indians of Mexico had been ravaged by European diseases such as influenza and smallpox by 1600, Spanish documents make no mention of similar epidemics among the Hopis or other Pueblo villages in the sixteenth century.[6] This is hardly proof that none struck, but overall, neither historical nor archaeological evidence implies that the Hopis' early, brief exposures to Spaniards changed them in any significant way. This was not true in the early nineteenth century, when "epidemics struck Hopi several times."[7]

By 1609 the Spaniards had established their military and administrative headquarters in Santa Fe. Franciscan friars had already founded small missions in a few of the Rio Grande pueblos and at Pecos Pueblo to the east. Twenty-three friars were busy in New Mexico by the end of 1616.[8] In 1629, 30 Franciscan priests arrived in Santa Fe from Mexico City, doubling the number of missionaries and allowing them to reach the western pueblos of the Acoma, Zuni, and Hopi people.[9] On August 20, 1629, three Franciscans arrived at Awatovi to establish a mission. Because August 20 was the feast day of Saint Bernard of Clairvaux, the friars dedicated the mission to him, calling it "San Bernardo de Aguatubi."[10] Aguatubi is one of many spellings of the village name in the Spanish documents.

Father Francisco Porras, Father Andrés Gutierrez, and Cristóbal de la Concepción, a lay brother, came to stay at Awatovi, but the Hopis were no more welcoming than they had been of Pedro de Tovar. Father Porras died, perhaps of poison, in 1633. An inquiry by the Spanish authorities never established whether or not he was deliberately murdered by the local people.

Before his death, Porras planned the building of a great church ("Church 1"). In the 1930s, when archaeologists from the Peabody Museum of Archaeology and Ethnology excavated Awatovi, they uncovered its foundation. This church was never finished, and the excavators surmised that either Father Porras or the priest who followed him realized that the foundation was simply too big. Trees large enough to span the roughly 40-foot-wide building and support its roof probably grew nowhere near

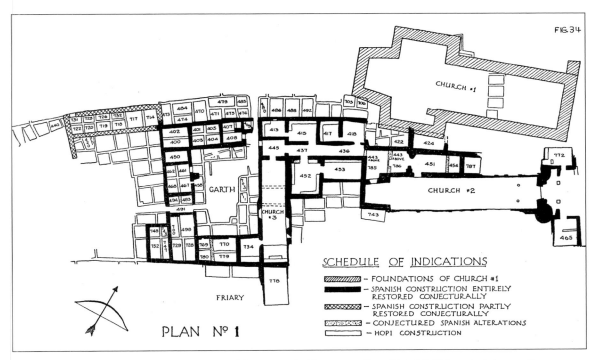

FIG.34

SCHEDULE OF INDICATIONS

▨▨▨ – FOUNDATIONS OF CHURCH #1
▬▬▬ – SPANISH CONSTRUCTION ENTIRELY RESTORED CONJECTURALLY
▨▨▨ – SPANISH CONSTRUCTION PARTLY RESTORED CONJECTURALLY
▨▨▨ – CONJECTURED SPANISH ALTERATIONS
▭▭▭ – HOPI CONSTRUCTION

PLAN Nº 1

Plan of the ruins of Churches 1 and 2 as revealed by excavation. This 1937 drawing shows all friary rooms, including the new Hopi walls for rooms that were reused historically.

Awatovi. The Spaniards had Hopi workers build a smaller church immediately south of the foundation of the first one. Only 25 feet wide but the same length as the first—100 feet—the second church was still an impressive structure. The priests also had native laborers build a friary, an intricate complex of rooms adjacent to the church on the west. This church and the friary served the mission for 50 years, until the Pueblo Revolt of 1680.

The Franciscans established two other small missions in Hopi villages, at Oraibi on Third Mesa and Shongopavi on Second Mesa. They made the village of Walpi, on First Mesa, a *visita*—a mission with no permanent friar. But the Hopis, like their Pueblo neighbors to the east, remained strongly resistant to Christianity and to the presence of Spaniards in general. In some of the pueblos along the Rio Grande, people tried to rebel during the years following the establishment of the missions, and the suspected poisoning of Father Porras in 1633 may itself have been an act of rebellion. At Zuni the year before, residents had killed two friars.[11] Until 1680, however, every attempt to rid the villages of Spaniards ended in failure.

That year, for the first time, all the Pueblos, from the Rio Grande to the Hopi mesas, planned a revolt together. Between August 10 and 13, the men in every village

View of Awatovi after excavation in 1939, looking south-southwest. The southern half of the foundation of the unfinished cruciform church (Church 1), extends across the middle of the photo, and the remains of Church 2 appear to the south of it. The friary rooms can be seen in the background at far right.

rose up, killed the local priests, in some places destroyed the churches, and drove the Spanish soldiers and settlers from New Mexico. The missions at the Hopi towns were not spared. So far as is known, Hopi warriors killed all four Spanish priests in their territory at the time.

At Awatovi, rebels largely destroyed the church but not the friary rooms, which the villagers took over for living quarters. They divided large rooms and corridors into small rooms and made doorways smaller, conforming to their traditional architectural style. It is possible that they continued to carry out Christian rituals in their own fashion, for archaeologists later found Christian-style burials dating after the revolt in the floor of Church 2.

The Pueblo Indians lived free of Spaniards for 12 years, but in 1692 Spanish forces returned from the south and retook New Mexico. In November of that year, Diego de Vargas, the new governor and captain-general, visited Awatovi and other Hopi villages.[12] The people of Awatovi, surprisingly, were reported to have been friendly, but those in other Hopi villages were not. Vargas departed after a short visit, leaving no soldiers or priests behind. The Spanish reconquest in Hopi land was incomplete, and Vargas's troops were too busy elsewhere to pay much attention to these distant villages. In 1693 and 1696, fighting broke out between Spanish soldiers and residents of pueblos along the Rio Grande. Some of the rebellious Indians fled to the Hopi villages, although Awatovi is not specifically mentioned as a place of refuge.

Awatovi was the closest Hopi village to Zuni, and people of the two pueblos often visited and traded with one another. When Spanish priests opened a new mission at Zuni in 1699, the Hopis are said to have volunteered "to return to Christianity, rebuild the churches, and receive missionaries," possibly "at the instigation of the inhabitants of Ahua-tuby."[13] In mid-May 1700, a Father Garaicoechea arrived at Awatovi, probably with one other priest. He immediately began to remodel the old friary rooms to suit his needs and had a few of them converted for use as a small chapel.[14] Archaeologists later found its altar stone and also uncovered what they interpreted as a barracks and stable north of the historic Hopi village. Father Garaicoechea had asked the Spanish governor in Santa Fe to quarter soldiers at Awatovi to protect the Christian Indians there (not to mention the priests) from warriors in the hostile Hopi villages. The soldiers never arrived, and there is no archaeological evidence that the barracks were ever occupied.

Unprotected, Father Garaicoechea was lucky to be away one terrible night in the late fall of 1700 or the winter of 1700–1701—the precise date is unknown. According to some Hopi oral histories, the chief of Awatovi headed a faction that considered Christianity to be witchcraft. The only way to purify his people of this evil, he believed, was for the village to be eradicated, and he secretly asked the hostile Hopis of other villages to attack Awatovi.[15] On that winter night, men from conservative villages on the other mesas stormed the village, reportedly trapping many men in the kivas, or underground ceremonial rooms, which they set afire. Although archaeologists have referred to this event as the "sacking of Awatovi,"[16] the oral histories say nothing about buildings being destroyed, other than the kivas being set ablaze.

A 1701 record by Pedro Rodríguez Cubero lends credence to the tales: "I certify to the King, our lord, through the royal *audiencia* of the City of Mexico, and the other judges and courts of his Majesty, on the matter of the campaign which I carried out during the months of June and July in the province of Moqui [Hopi] against the apostate Indians there, following the annihilation which they committed upon the converted Indians of the pueblo of Aguatubi . . . "[17]

Whatever happened at Awatovi that night, it effectively ended any effort by the Spaniards to convert or even control the Hopis. No one, either priest or Indian, ever returned to the mission of San Bernardo de Aguatubi, and the deserted village and church slowly began to crumble. The Spanish authorities largely left the Hopis alone. Their mesas were simply too far from Santa Fe to be policed, and in any case the Spaniards' settlement priorities lay in the more heavily populated Rio Grande valley, with its wealth of Indian laborers and its potential for irrigation agriculture. Hopi country offered neither attraction.[18] Unlike the more closely controlled Pueblo communities in New Mexico, the Hopis continued to practice their ancient culture relatively unhindered for another century and a half.[19]

The first account in English of the attack on Awatovi was written by Adolph Bandelier, a self-taught archaeologist who was one of the first to work in the Southwest. He published the story, which he had learned from Hopis, in his two-volume *Final Report of Investigations among the Indians of the Southwestern United States* in 1890 and 1892. Bandelier never visited the ruined village, most of which had, by his time, collapsed in on itself, melting back into the earth.

The first archaeologist to visit the site of Awatovi was Victor Mindeleff, an employee of the Smithsonian Institution's Bureau of American Ethnology. He inspected the ruins in 1884 and published a description of them in 1891 in his monograph *A Study of Pueblo Architecture in Tusayan and Cibola*. Although Mindeleff did no digging, he made a plan map and drawings of the "fragmentary walls of rough masonry [which] stand to a height, in some cases, of 8 feet above the debris."[20] These were probably walls of the mission.

It was the story of the massacre that lured the first archaeologist actually to excavate at Awatovi. In the decade following Mindeleff's visit, J. Walter Fewkes, another Smithsonian staff member, dug there twice, primarily to try to verify the tale. He was interested in Hopi ethnology and had recorded many myths and oral histories, one of which was about the destruction of Awatovi. "In the summer of 1892," he wrote, "I passed ten days in camp at the Tusayan ruin called by the Hopi, A-wa-to-bi, 'the place of the Bow people'; [and] by the Navajos, Talla-hogan, the 'Singing House.'" The Hopi name referred to the Hopi Bow Clan, and the Navajo name presumably alluded to the music the priests had sung during mass.

Fewkes continued: "At that time, accompanied by Mr. A. M. Stephen, I made a reconnaissance and a few excavations in order to acquaint myself with the ruin, but I was particularly anxious to test the story of its destruction, still repeated by the Hopi, and to gather from archaeological researches whatever data could be found to shed light on the disaster which overthrew one of the most populous of the Tusayan pueblos about two hundred years ago."[21]

Fewkes discovered what he believed to be a kiva, with "charred wood, ashes, and other evidences of fire" and, scattered in the dirt that filled the room, a "skull and other bones."[22] The bones were too few, however, "to answer the requirements of the

Drawing of the Awatovi site made by Victor Mindeleff during his 1884 visit. A comparison of the drawing with the 1935 photograph on page 175 shows how much the Spanish buildings had weathered during the following half century.

legend."[23] Because the Hopi men who worked for him appeared upset at finding the bones, Fewkes halted further excavation in the room.

Fewkes did not dig in the ruins of the mission during those first 10 days of work, but in 1895 he was back for another busy two weeks. He excavated in the mission, in the Western Mound, and particularly in the village ruins north of the mission, still seeking evidence to confirm the Awatovi massacre. He found ashes and small pieces of burned wood around the churches and scattered human bones in rooms southeast of the mission. One human skeleton lay on the floor of a room there, but Fewkes found no others in the main site. He identified a burial ground in the dunes southeast of the mission but said that relic hunters had already dug into it heavily. In the Western Mound, where he uncovered at least four stories of rooms, Fewkes found little corn, whereas in the rooms east and north of the mission he discovered "stacks" of corncobs and rooms filled with stored corn showing evidence of fire.

While Fewkes was digging, the *New York Herald* was feeding the public's fascination with the new science-cum-adventure of archaeology by publishing a sensationalized account of his work.[24] Headlines in the Sunday edition of October 20, 1895, trumpeted:

EXCAVATED TWO BURIED CITIES
Professor Fewkes' Discovery of the Abodes of a Race
That Once Flourished in Arizona

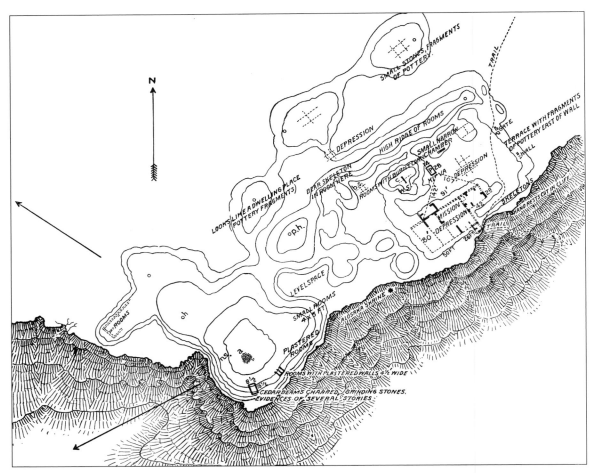

J. Walter Fewkes's map of Awatovi, indicating his areas of excavation in 1895. The main features visible at the time included the Western Mound, the mission area, and the historic pueblo rooms (the "high ridge of rooms" north of the mission).

THE ROMANCE OF AWATUBI
An Indian Chief Found Entombed in a City
Whose Inhabitants Were All Massacred

BEAUTIFUL POTTERY DUG UP

Fewkes's report on his work, published in the annual report of the Bureau of American Ethnology in 1898, was far more prosaic. It included illustrations and descriptions of pottery—mostly whole vessels—and bone tools. He described but did not illustrate stone tools and clay ornaments "in the form of birds and shells," as well as a little bell also made of clay. The bell came from a room in the pre-Hispanic Western Mound, and Fewkes believed it had seen use before the establishment of the mission.[25] Details like these gave Fewkes's colleagues a glimpse into what might lie under the eroded surface of the abandoned village, but in the end his excavations turned up nothing dramatic—and certainly no firm evidence for the fabled massacre. Fewkes himself admitted that he had failed to find proof.

The Bureau of American Ethnology wasn't the only institution to put Awatovi on its interest list in the late 1800s. With funding from Stanley McCormick, the son of Cyrus McCormick of International Harvester fame, the Field Museum in Chicago sponsored four seasons of archaeological work in Hopi country, from 1897 to 1900. The last of these, called the Fourth Hopi McCormick Expedition, was led by Charles Owen, an assistant curator at the museum. For eight months in 1899 and 1900 he excavated in "the ancient cemeteries of the ruins of Sikyatki, Awatovi, and Mishongnovi."[26] He was at Awatovi in August 1900, digging six rooms, probably in the Western Mound, and 55 graves. Apparently he got to Awatovi one step ahead of a rival. His notes for August 13 say, "Prepared to move to Awatobi. Made start with team in evening. Packed 2 burros and moved over in night to head off Russell."[27]

"Russell" was undoubtedly Frank Russell, who was in the area in 1900 conducting an "archaeological survey of the Little Colorado district, including Awatovi."[28] Apparently he was working for the Peabody Museum. Neither Owen nor Russell published anything about his explorations, but their collections are still at their respective institutions—150 catalogued items at the Field Museum and 25 at the Peabody.

Early in the new century, researchers gave Awatovi a rest. In 1901 Walter Hough, representing the Smithsonian Institution's U.S. National Museum, did fieldwork on Antelope Mesa as a part of the Museum-Gates Expedition, but he did not dig at Awatovi. Instead, he excavated at the ruins of Kokopnyama, Chakpahu, and Kawaika-a (now often spelled Kawaika'a or Kawàyka'a), later commenting that studying them was "attended with hardships because of the lack of water." Awatovi, he noted, "still has fine springs, and this fact, coupled with its accessibility, would sooner or later have led to its excavation." (He knew that parts of it had been dug previously.) "The lack of water," he added, "has not prevented the Navaho tearing the Jettyto [Jeddito Valley] ruins to pieces in search of pottery for the trader."[29]

To my knowledge, no archaeologist again visited Awatovi until 1917, when Alfred Vincent Kidder, at the beginning of his distinguished career as a Southwestern archaeologist, spent some time in Hopi country while waiting to be called up for duty in World War I. He wrote in his journal on July 9, 1917, that after setting out on horseback in search of ruins, he "spent about an hour" at Awatovi and then rode "along the mesa to Keams Canyon, 9–10 miles." Approaching the village site, he saw a "big spring

Alfred Vincent "Ted" Kidder and an unidentified child
examine a cache in Room 30 at Pecos Pueblo, 1920.

in the canyon 1/3 m[ile] N[orth] of ruin and another to the E[ast] up canyon. The ruin lies on the S[outh] edge of a fairly broad (1/4–1/3 mile) mesa and is very extensive."

In 1915, Kidder, who was known professionally as "A.V." and to his friends as "Ted," had begun the excavations at Pecos Pueblo for which he would become famous. He was keenly interested in the way pottery designs had evolved throughout ancestral Pueblo history. Archaeologists were becoming aware that because pottery designs changed over time, sites could be excavated in stratigraphic layers—more recent layers normally on top of older ones—and the potsherds might provide relative dates for each layer. Much of Kidder's description of Awatovi revolved around the pottery sherds he saw: "At about 400 yrds N of the ruin noticed much broken Sikyatki pottery in the sand blows and at one place a skel[eton] exposed and with it the remains of a bowl. Also saw some B & W [black-on-white painted] ware." Sikyatki Polychrome pottery, characteristic of the centuries from about A.D. 1400 to 1700, has designs painted in black and orange on the surfaces of yellow-glazed vessels. It is still possible to see many broken pieces of this brilliantly decorated pottery at Awatovi and other Hopi sites.

Kidder continued:

> The ruin itself is literally covered with sherds as are the S slopes of its rubbish. B & W of the generalized style (?), B & W Kayenta types, Little Colorado ware, Sikyatki and what might be called late Sikyatki or early historic Hopi [ware]. The latter seems to be coarser and heavier than Siky[atki] so runs to odd shapes (soup plates, etc), to very shallow dippers. On and about the mission church ruins, this ware seems to predominate and there also seems to be less corrug[ated ware, or plain cooking pottery] here than elsewhere. . . .
>
> There are distinct signs of stratified rubbish on the S slopes all along and the places where houses were built on old heaps. Almost no excav[ation] has been done and what there is is very shallow.
>
> Adobe walls to be seen in church ruins. Made a consid[erable] sherd coll[ection] of all styles, but time and transport forbade taking "test" lots.

All these pottery names meant something to Kidder and his colleagues, and his short description shows how far archaeological research in the Southwest had come in the 20 years since Fewkes's work. Researchers were now categorizing ceramic wares according to their decoration, shape, and technology. This allowed them to trace relationships between archaeological cultures and geographical areas by determining which people made similar wares and who traded pots with whom. Kidder's one-hour visit to Awatovi would also, years later, prompt him to encourage the Peabody Museum of Archaeology and Ethnology, in Cambridge, Massachusetts, to venture there in 1935.

✢

The Peabody Museum may have been a relative latecomer to Awatovi, but it had launched its archaeological research in the Southwest in southern Utah in the late nineteenth century. Between 1875 and 1877, "Dr. C. C. Parry excavated [for the Peabody] on the Santa Clara River in Southwestern Utah,"[30] and a Dr. Edward Palmer spent five years before 1881 digging and collecting in south-central Utah.[31] Peabody expeditions to northeastern Arizona began in 1914 and ran almost continuously until the end of 1939, except for the years of World War I. Samuel J. Guernsey and A.V. Kidder looked for archaeological sites and carried out "test excavations"—small, exploratory excavations—there in 1914. After the war, Guernsey was again in the field. Reporting on his research between 1920 and 1923, he wrote that he was in charge of the work each year, "with the exception of the last two weeks of the 1923 season, when the work was taken over by Mr. and Mrs. William H. Claflin, Jr., and Dr. A.V. Kidder."[32]

Bill Claflin was about to become a singular force behind the Peabody's work in the Southwest. In 1927 he was both curator of Southeastern archaeology at the museum and an important donor when he and Raymond Emerson, another Peabody supporter, traveled "into the wild country near the Colorado [River] below the mouth of the Escalante River, a region almost unknown archaeologically."[33] Excited by what they saw, the two men developed a plan for a grand archaeological survey of southeastern Utah west of the Colorado River. They and their wives generously established "an ample fund to enable the Peabody Museum to prosecute the plan" over five years.[34]

From 1927 to 1931, researchers for the Claflin-Emerson Expedition surveyed and test-excavated ruins in the canyons of all the major rivers in southern Utah, excluding only San Juan County in the extreme southeast corner. Except for Noel Morss's 1931 *Notes on the Archaeology of the Kaibito and Rainbow Plateaus in Arizona*, this research went unpublished until 1969, when James Gunnerson described the Fremont culture of the "northern Anasazi frontier," drawing on the fieldwork conducted more than 35 years earlier.

Although the Claflin-Emerson Expedition ended in 1931, the Peabody missed not a beat with its work in Utah. That same year the museum inaugurated its three-year Southeastern Utah Expedition, a project conceived by the light of "camp fires in the canyons" of the Green and Colorado rivers by museum director Donald Scott and a young graduate student named John Otis "Jo" Brew.[35] Kidder suggested Alkali Ridge to the pair as a likely location, and Brew spent November 1931 in the field there. He went back for four months in each of the following two years, with the goal of either defining what archaeologists called the Pueblo II period of ancestral Pueblo culture or eliminating it altogether from the chronology devised during a conference Kidder held at Pecos Pueblo in 1927. Brew did find evidence for a distinct Pueblo II period and wrote it up in his Ph.D. dissertation, published by the Peabody Museum in 1946 as *The Archaeology of Alkali Ridge*—still a classic in the field.

Meanwhile, in 1924 the museum expanded its geographic coverage of the Southwest by hiring two skilled amateur archaeologists, Cornelius "Burt" and Harriet "Hattie" Cosgrove, to record and excavate sites of the Mimbres culture in southwestern New Mexico. The Cosgroves spent four summers excavating the Swarts Ruin and then several years exploring caves in southern New Mexico and Arizona. In 1936 they would join the Peabody staff at Awatovi.

The first Awatovi field camp, near the Jeddito Trading Post, 1935.

Awatovi, 1935

In documents archived at the Peabody Museum, Bill Claflin gets the credit for conceiving the Awatovi project. No written records tell precisely how or why the subject first came up, but memos between Claflin and museum director Donald Scott in the early months of 1935 reveal that the two men had been talking about starting a major dig at the Awatovi ruins. One can easily imagine them hatching the plan over lunch at the Harvard Faculty Club.

Claflin had visited the Hopi Reservation as a teenager and was taken to Awatovi in the 1920s. He and A.V. Kidder did some excavating on Antelope Mesa in 1923 (Kidder mentioned it in his journal), but not at Awatovi. The story of the mission and of the double destruction of life, Spanish and Hopi, at Awatovi fascinated Claflin. He returned occasionally to visit his Hopi friends and by 1934 had seized on the notion of an archaeological project at Awatovi as a good way to provide work for some Hopi men during the Great Depression.[1] Besides, two years had passed since the end of the fieldwork on Alkali Ridge. It was time for the Peabody to think about organizing another expedition to the Southwest.

William H. Claflin Jr., like Burt and Hattie Cosgrove and many other archaeologists of their era, came to the profession through enthusiasm and field experience, not through formal training. In 1906, at the age of 13, the native of Swampscott, Massachusetts, read in a book called *Antiquities of the Southern Indians* an "eloquent eulogy" to the huge, precontact shell mound on Stallings Island in the Savannah River, between Georgia and South Carolina.[2] At the time, he and his family were in Augusta, Georgia, where the climate relieved Bill's asthma, and he visited the site.

Two years later young Claflin had the chance to dig on Stallings Island for two days, "with the aid of three negroes."[3] At 19 he spent his summer vacation in the Southwest, doing the adventurous things an Easterner might do, "such as hunting mountain lions and riding wild cows."[4] This was when he first visited the Hopi villages

William H. Claflin Jr.

and met a couple from Mishongnovi named Luke Kawanusea and Vivian Tewanyinima.[5] He might well have seen Awatovi at this time, because Luke Kawanusea had fields in nearby Tallahogan Canyon. He might also have heard the story of the destruction of the Franciscan mission of San Bernardo de Aguatubi.

Claflin graduated from Harvard in 1915 and joined the army, serving with the First Massachusetts Field Artillery during the Mexican border campaign of 1916–1917 and later, in World War I, as an artillery captain in France.[6] At war's end he plunged into the Boston financial world. A partner in the investment firm of Tucker, Anthony, and Company for 15 years, he also served for many years as president of the Boston Stock Exchange. In 1917 Claflin married Helen Atkins, whose father, Edwin F. Atkins, had headed the Soledad Sugar Company in Cuba since the 1880s. In 1926, upon the death of his father-in-law, Claflin became president of the company, which operated a sugar manufacturing plant and raised cattle on some 3,000 acres.

Meanwhile, his interest in archaeology never wavered. In 1925 Claflin went back to Stallings Island to dig again, this time for five days with seven workmen.[7] He was already using his wealth to support the Peabody Museum, and in 1927 he was named curator of Southeastern archaeology, a position he resigned in 1928 when he was

Louise and Donald Scott leaving the Awatovi camp in their town clothes, 1939. Their Packard was known as "the Behemoth."

appointed treasurer of Harvard College.[8] In 1929 Burt and Hattie Cosgrove spent three months excavating on Stallings Island, undoubtedly financed by Claflin. He himself wrote the report about what he had found in 1925 and about the Cosgroves' later work; the museum published it in 1931. It was during this heady time for Claflin that he and Raymond Emerson sponsored the Peabody's survey in southern Utah. Claflin's youthful excitement over his Utah adventure and his fondness for the Hopi country steered him toward promoting an excavation at Awatovi as the Peabody's next big project.

Claflin's friend Donald Scott, director of the Peabody Museum from 1932 to 1948, furnished the Awatovi project with the leadership vital to its success. Scott has been characterized as "a man of society and dedicated to propriety."[9] He was reserved, but after the end of the Awatovi expedition he invited many of the staff to his home in Cambridge to reminisce over picnic suppers. Born in New York in 1879, the Harvard graduate of 1900 began his career in the cotton merchandising business. By 1909 he was secretary and treasurer of the Century Company, a New York publishing house of which his father was president. Starting in 1913 Scott served as a director of Century, which became Appleton-Century and then Appleton-Century Crofts. He sat on the

War Trade Board and the U.S. Shipping Board during World War I. In 1919, with an associate, he purchased the *New York Evening Post* and was named vice president of the newspaper. Scott, like Claflin, was a businessman whose heart belonged to archaeology. During his vacations from work at the *Post*, he "conducted archaeological reconnaissance by pack train in the rugged canyon and mesa country of southeastern Utah."[10] In 1928, at the age of 49, he left the *Post* to pursue graduate studies in anthropology at Harvard. The following year he was named assistant director of the Peabody Museum, and in 1932, director. During his time as director, Scott "promoted expeditions in physical anthropology, ethnology, and archaeology to Middle and South America, Central Europe, Africa, the Near East, Southeast Asia, Australia, and Oceania." His collection of photographs and drawings of rock art was said to be "the most extensive in existence."[11]

It would be Scott's responsibility not only to provide overall direction for the Awatovi Expedition but also to raise the money for it. Luckily, with his friend and colleague Claflin on board, that would not be difficult.

As Scott and Claflin got serious about an Awatovi project, Scott asked Jo Brew to compile some information about Awatovi and the Hopis. Brew had never been to Hopi country, but his work at Alkali Ridge during the three field seasons of the Southeastern Utah Expedition had immersed him in Southwestern archaeology. And unlike Scott and Claflin, Brew had chosen archaeology as his profession from the beginning.

John Otis Brew, who signed himself "J. O." but was always called "Jo," was a native of Malden, Massachusetts, born in 1906. He developed an early interest in classical archaeology and graduated from Dartmouth College in 1928 with a bachelor's degree in fine arts. That fall he entered graduate school at Harvard, where he completed his residency requirements in 1931. His first experience of archaeological fieldwork came in the early summer of 1930 in Fulton County, Illinois, with the University of Chicago.[12] The following summer he was off to southern Utah as a member of the Claflin-Emerson Expedition. He performed so well there that Scott decided to have him head the museum's expedition to Alkali Ridge. In the summer of 1934 Brew was able to stretch his archaeological experience overseas when he accompanied Hugh Hencken and Hallam Movius on the Harvard Irish Expedition, "excavating a hill fort in County Clare and a lake dwelling in County Heath."[13]

That fall, while Brew was back at the Peabody writing his dissertation, Donald Scott enlisted him to help plan the Awatovi Expedition. On March 1, 1935, Brew gave Scott a memorandum in which he reviewed the relevant literature and described the site, the

J. O. "Jo" Brew at Awatovi, 1939.

area, the relations of previous archeologists and anthropologists with the Hopis, and the newly passed Indian Reorganization Act, which would affect the way the museum conducted its work. Unfamiliar with the Hopi Reservation, Jo got a few details wrong. For example, he identified the "nearest store" as being at "Polacca Wash, First Mesa." Later he amended this line with the handwritten note, "Jedito [sic] Springs trading post." Indeed, the post at Jeddito Springs sat much closer to Awatovi than did the Polacca post. It was to become the Awatovi Expedition's link to the outside world.

The outline of the memo, presumably responding to Scott's request for certain information, ran like this: Location; Nearest Town; Nearest Store; Road; The Site; Names of Site; Labour; Permission to Excavate; Relations with the Hopi. In planning any archaeological project, one must consider these types of factors before turning to practicalities such as where the archaeologists might live, who the supervisory personnel will be, and even how the work will be financed. The thrust of the information Scott wanted Brew to gather had to do with the site's potential to reveal new data about the Spanish mission and the earliest historic occupation in the eastern part of the Awatovi site and about the older, precontact village in the Western Mound.

Because Claflin was interested in the possibility of using Hopi labor, Brew sought information from Mischa Titiev at the University of Michigan, who had been doing ethnological studies in the Hopi towns. He asked Titiev about the Hopis' probable attitudes toward excavations at the site and whether a dig there would spark problems with the tribe. He reported in his memo: "Mr. Titiev . . . believes that with reasonable care there is no question that Awatobi could be excavated."

Brew surely consulted Kidder, too, about the archaeology of the area. Kidder, then chairman of the Division of Historical Research of the Carnegie Institution of Washington, working out of the Carnegie's Cambridge office, was the foremost Southwestern archaeologist of the time. He had worked for the Peabody early in his career, exploring for sites in northeastern Arizona with Samuel Guernsey in 1914, and had been curator for Southwestern archaeology at the museum from 1919 to 1931. His diary suggests that he took part in some of the early discussions about an expedition to Awatovi, for he expressed the satisfaction he felt in stimulating Scott and Claflin's interest in the site.[14]

One outcome of Brew's discussions with cultural anthropologists such as Titiev was that he and Scott recognized the unprecedented opportunity Awatovi offered for linking precontact Hopi settlement to what was known about historic Hopi life and thus to modern Hopi culture. In a cover note to his March 1 memo, Brew drafted a grand, perhaps grandiose, vision of the expedition's results. "Taken in conjunction with ethnological work and present and projected developments in physical anthropology," he wrote, "a carefully considered archaeological project lasting with sufficient funds over a period of years should produce in Northeastern Arizona the most complete Southwestern study yet attempted. It would be far fuller than work in the Zuni area, where sufficient advantage has not been taken of 'spade work' actually accomplished, and it would be more complete than Pecos [where Kidder had worked for 10 years] because it would go back much further and come down to the actual present in the time-scale."

If the goal was to look at deep chronology, then the whole of Antelope Mesa became subject to investigation: "The archaeological side of such a program would include not only the known post-Spanish and supposed just pre-Spanish levels at Awatobi, but all underlying periods at the site itself, the sites at the foot of the mesa (reputedly older) and an attempt to trace cultural development in the area back to Basket-maker [the earliest Puebloan culture] or whatever else may be." Brew concluded: "This would be a big job, but properly handled with sufficient time and funds it would be of inestimable value to Southwestern Prehistory."

The surviving documents may sound prosaic to readers today, but to Brew, Scott, Claflin, and others involved in the fall and winter of 1935, their discussions must have been exciting. Their commitment to a large, long-term project grew. An undated memo in the Peabody files—unsigned but almost certainly Brew's handiwork—elaborated the arguments for making the Awatovi project a big one. One enticement was "the possibility of procuring in a single site a stratigraphic sequence from the Basket-maker III period [ca. A.D. 600] to 1700 A.D." Another was "the certainty of tracing the story of cultural development from Pueblo III (the first large Pueblo period [1250–1300]) up to the present."

On April 24, 1935, Claflin and Scott had what nowadays would be called a power lunch at the Union Club in Boston. From it emerged a "Memorandum of Conversation" about what they called the "Awatobi Expedition." After discussing Brew's report of March 1, the two recorded, they "agreed that it was desirable to undertake excavations at Awatobi." They would ask Brew to "prepare a more detailed budget on the basis of test digging during the present year." This first season of work, "if satisfactory indications were secured," would be followed by "a serious excavation of the site over a period of several years." Finally, the memo noted, "Mr. Claflin agreed to contribute up to $2500.00 for this first year's work." Scott offered Jo Brew the position of field director as part of the museum's contribution.

Only one formal step remained before Brew could pack up and head west. Under the Antiquities Act of 1906, the museum had to obtain a permit from the Department of the Interior in order to conduct archaeological work on an Indian reservation.[15] Scott, Claflin, and Brew agreed that they would apply for only a one-year permit to do preliminary excavations at Awatovi and to reconnoiter the rest of the mesa. With some results in hand and a better understanding of the ruins, they could apply for a second permit covering additional years.

Scott wrote a letter to the secretary of the Interior in July 1935 summarizing what was planned for the work on Antelope Mesa. It is the nearest thing extant to what today would be called a research design. Scott requested permission to "conduct preliminary archaeological survey and test trenching upon Antelope Mesa, south and east [sic; west] of Keams Canyon Indian Agency, and along the Jeddito Valley to the east of Antelope Mesa and below it, and . . . to excavate and make intensive studies of the ruin of Awatovi at the southern end of Antelope Mesa." He continued:

> The aims and purposes of the work . . . are to obtain a detailed understanding of the cultural sequence from the period of the Great Pueblos or Pueblo III to the later periods after the coming of the white man, and to tie this knowledge in with the existing and living Hopi culture of today. The archaeological remains and particularly the pottery are

expected to show the diffusion and interrelation of the culture groups during this period. Dr. A.V. Kidder of the Carnegie Institution of Washington has examined his collections of sherds from this site [Awatovi] and gone over the problem with us and believes that a much needed addition to our knowledge of the Pueblo culture can be gained by this research. No other large Pueblo of this period has been thoroughly excavated, with the single exception of Pecos which lies upon the eastern horizon of the Pueblo area. It is hoped also that underlying the visible ruin there may be found stratified layers of earlier cultures which will be of great importance in increasing our understanding of the development through these periods. In general what is sought is knowledge as to cultural development and diffusion rather than the mere plan of a ruin and its rooms.

The decision to apply for a one-year permit would eventually bring the project to a premature end, owing to a new wrinkle in the permitting process. For the moment, getting an Antiquities Act permit meant simply submitting a form to the Department of the Interior, which consulted with the Smithsonian Institution. Scott did so in July 1935 and had no trouble getting his one-year permit. But the Indian Reorganization Act had been signed into law in 1934, giving Indian tribes greater autonomy over their affairs and their land. The days when archaeologists could dig almost anywhere they wished were about to end. Researchers were going to have to become more accountable to the people whose ancestors they were studying.

Scott had no intention of ignoring the Hopis, but he hoped he would be able to negotiate with them informally. He wrote to his friend Jesse Nusbaum, at the time director of the Laboratory of Anthropology in Santa Fe and consulting archaeologist for the Department of the Interior: "Naturally we realize that the Hopis will have to be dealt with no matter what permissions may be secured, and we are very well informed of their attitude. We believe, however, that this can be successfully handled with tact and fairness and that the definite employment which it will bring to them will be of considerable advantage."

Ultimately, tact and wages would be insufficient to sustain the goodwill of some influential Hopis. For the moment, however, the assistant secretary of the Interior, in a letter dated August 26, 1935 (a significant date for future renewals, as it turned out), approved the Peabody Museum's permit "with the privilege of renewal." It carried a few conditions. "Transportation in government automobiles," for example, could not be granted "except in such cases where no extra expense to the Government is involved." More significantly, it stipulated that no grave or burial ground abandoned for less than a century could be investigated "without permission of the governing council of the Indians involved." John Collier, the commissioner of Indian Affairs and a party in the issuing of permits, had a reputation as a champion of Indians, and this

Gibson Namoki (left) and Sylvan Nash unloading wood for the cook stove at the Awatovi camp, 1938.

stipulation likely resulted from his consultation with various tribes. Although the rule would not hamper the expedition's work—any graves the crew could expect to find would be more than a hundred years old—it did hint at the autonomy American Indians were beginning to recover and the hurdles Scott and his colleagues would face when they tried to renew their permit for later years.

Jo Brew spent April 1935 corresponding with three men whom he wanted to hire for the project: Al Lancaster, as field foreman; Alden Stevens, as surveyor and cartographer; and Lin Thompson, as camp cook. All three had worked with him at Alkali Ridge, and all agreed to participate. He also had to arrange to get the museum's equipment, left in storage at the Laboratory of Anthropology in Santa Fe at the end of the Alkali Ridge fieldwork, shipped to Jeddito Trading Post. The museum probably already owned much of what Brew would need on Antelope Mesa—tents, kitchen gear, shovels, trowels, and wheelbarrows. A few essential items would prove missing. On October 1, 1935, Brew appealed to the Peabody by telegram:

> PLEASE SEND TO HOLBROOK EXPRESS RUSH SIX TRENCH PICKS STOP THESE
> SHOULD BE IN THE MUSEUM EQUIPMENT BUT IF NOT CAN BE OBTAINED FROM
> ARMY NAVY STORE.

```
                    AWATOBI BUDGET 1935

   Tools and technical supplies . . . . . . . . . . . . $100
   Photographic supplies . . . . . . . . . . . . . . . . 100
   Medical supplies (4 antevenin @ $10) . . . . . . . . . 55
   Camp expenses (food, utensils, etc.) . . . . . . . . . 200
   Transportation to and from field . . . . . . . . . . 300
   Trans. In field (including purchase of car) . . . . . 600
   Hotel and restaurant in field . . . . . . . . . . . . 100
   Communications (postage, tel. & tel., exp. & freight) . 200
   Labour
        Lancaster 3 mos. @ $125 . . . . . . . . . $375
        Stevens 3 mos. @ $100 . . . . . . . . . . 300
        Cook (camp & gen. handy man @ $3 per day)  270
      * Labour @ $2.50 per day for 10 weeks
             $150 per man -- 6 men . . . . . . . . 900
   Total Labour . . . . . . . . . . . . . . . . . . . .1,845

                                        _____

   Total . . . . . . . . . . . . . . . . . . . . . . .$3,500.


   *  This does not include feeding labourers as it is expected
      they will provide own food.
```

The budget drawn up by Jo Brew for the 1935 field season.

Brew budgeted $3,500 for the 1935 season—more than Claflin had pledged, but the museum would make up the shortfall. In the end he tallied $4,013.21 in actual expenses. Among the unanticipated needs were a barbed wire fence, which was put up around the Awatovi site at the end of the field season, and four mattresses purchased to place on top of the canvas army cots when the weather got cold. Scott approved the additional costs from museum funds.

Permit in hand, staff recruited, and equipment organized, Brew traveled by train to Santa Fe that September, picked up a car he had stored at the Laboratory of Anthropology in 1933, arranged to ship the tools and equipment that had been stored at the lab, and, after a detour north to pick up Lancaster and Thompson in Colorado, headed for Antelope Mesa. Fall was the best time to work under the Arizona sun. The first Awatovi Expedition field season would run from September 24 to November 30, 1935, with another six days to send specimens back to Cambridge, store equipment, and pack up the camp. The first things Brew had to do upon arrival were to set up the field camp and hire a crew.

Left: Everett Harris leaning against what Jo Brew called the "power plant," where the generator was stored, 1939. Right: Alec (left) and Leland Dennis, 1937.

At Keams Canyon, Brew asked the Indian Service superintendent to recommend some Hopi men who might make good fieldworkers. He hired eight of them that first year. Gibson Namoki, Sylvan Nash, and Joe Thomas came from First Mesa, and Everett Harris, Alec Dennis, Leland Dennis, Cecil Calvert, and Jacob Poleviyuma, from Second Mesa. Calvert and Thomas worked on the project only in 1935, but the other six men returned for all the subsequent years. Brew also hired one Navajo, Woody Blacksheep—probably recommended by Chi Roberts, the trader at Jeddito Trading Post—for a short time in 1935 to help search for sites at the eastern end of the mesa, which was part of the Navajo Reservation.

Brew paid the Hopis $2.00 a day. None of them had any previous archaeological experience, but Brew later extolled their skills. On October 18, 1935, he wrote to Donald Scott that the Hopi excavators were so "familiar with the materials of the ancient constructions [at Awatovi] that they recognize plastered walls, adobe floors, etc., immediately. . . . They have sharp eyes, too, attested by the number of tiny square and other shaped pieces of turquoise we are getting which seem to have dropped out of turquoise mosaics."

Left: Cecil Calvert in one of the excavated rooms at the Awatovi site, 1935. Right: Jake Chong Poleviyuma.

To supervise the Hopi crew, Brew had already turned to his friend James Allen "Al" Lancaster, who had worked for him at Alkali Ridge. Lancaster, in his early forties at the beginning of the Awatovi Expedition, was short on formal education but long on experience and skill in field archaeology. He had grown up on a farm in southern Colorado and was fond of pointing out to educated Easterners that he was "just a bean farmer."[16] Pre-Hispanic sites around his home had always interested him. In the early 1920s he signed on with Paul S. Martin, a major figure in Southwestern archaeology, as foreman for excavations the Field Museum of Chicago was sponsoring at Lowry Ruin, not far from Lancaster's home. Thus began a career in archaeology spanning more than 40 years.

Lancaster's practical abilities, which he would bring to the Awatovi Expedition during each of its five field seasons, were almost endless. He could do everything from constructing floors and walls for the tent camp to teaching the Hopi crew excavation techniques. Jenny Adams, who wrote a biography of Lancaster and his wife, Alice, said that he seems to have been able to operate in several worlds—understanding and contributing to the interpretation of the archaeological research, translating

Al Lancaster, field director for the Awatovi Expedition, taking notes.

this information into terms the Hopis understood, and maintaining his home and family in Colorado.[17]

Lancaster's innate knack for managing people might have been honed during World War I. Brew's journal for July 21, 1938, mentions Lancaster's telling stories around the campfire about his experiences in the army's aviation Signal Corps. He had enlisted and was sent to Oregon to "work in the lumber mills turning out spruce lumber for airplanes. He described . . . the handling of the men in those camps with his usual amusing manner and attention to detail." Mott Davis, my brother and an Awatovi Expedition member in 1939, told me that "Al personified unassuming self-assurance and strength of personality, as well as physical strength, and he had piercing blue eyes. He knew where he stood, and everyone else, knowing where he stood, respected him and looked to him as a leader."

Lancaster was a consummate teacher, as dozens, perhaps even hundreds of present-day Southwestern archaeologists can testify. Richard Woodbury, who joined the Awatovi project in 1938, later recalled that Lancaster "started you off on something simple, explained a bit more as you went along, took the shovel or trowel or brush and 'demonstrated' by 'having a look myself.' With the Hopi workmen or the staff, he always sensed what everyone was doing and 'happened by' when it was suitable, but didn't hang over them when not needed. For the laggard he had a joke, sometimes unprintable, and for success he had appreciation and enthusiasm."

In the lists of staff members that appear in the prefaces to most of the Awatovi publications, Lancaster is listed as assistant director. In 1935, however, the proper Scott "could not see giving such a title to a bean farmer who had not gone past the eighth grade."[18] In the archival records Lancaster is called "assistant to the director." Watson Smith, another key Awatovi participant in later field seasons, summed up Lancaster and his contribution to the Awatovi Expedition this way: "Al's personality made possible, to a very large extent, the success of the whole operation. His personality vis-à-vis not only the Hopi employees but also the rest of the camp, his wit, his wisdom, his jollity, his good nature, were indispensable on all fronts. . . . He was a . . . wit, and he was capable, as some wits are not, of pointing the finger of jokery at himself."[19]

An archaeological crew must be well fed, or complaints will abound. As a consequence, one of the most important members of any archaeological field project is the cook. For the Awatovi Expedition, Brew hired one of the best—Lindsay C. "Lin" Thompson, a 48-year-old from Blanding, Utah. He had displayed his talents while cooking for Brew during the second year of the Alkali Ridge project, and like Lancaster he was an obvious choice. One of his talents was his ability to adapt to field conditions: he cut wood for the stove, kept meat and butter cool by wrapping them in wet burlap, ordered food and other supplies in bulk, and even did good carpentry. He could be gruff at times and did not appreciate people's invading his kitchen, but his sense of humor was always welcome during conversations at mealtimes and around the campfire.

Two other men rounded out the small staff hired for the 1935 season. Alden "Steve" Stevens began as surveyor and draftsman, assigned to make contour maps of the large sites on Antelope Mesa and to help lay out grids over all sites that were tested, so that the excavators could keep track of artifacts and other information room by room or square by square. Stevens had been working for the National Park Service but was temporarily out of a job. He welcomed Brew's offer of work for six weeks and indeed drafted the original maps of Awatovi and several other large sites on the mesa. Brew welcomed Stevens's car, too, paying him six cents a mile for the use of it, which was less expensive than buying a new one.

Lin Thompson, the expedition's famous cook, probably 1937.

Stevens seems to have had a good sense of humor, which must have added greatly
to evenings around the campfire. In the initial correspondence between him and Brew,
Jo asked Steve's advice about photography, particularly whether he thought it would
be good to have a darkroom at the camp, to make sure the photographs recording the
excavations were going to be good ones. Steve discouraged this idea immediately,
reminding Jo of the blowing sand that would seep into every crevice and the impossi-
bility of keeping chemicals cool in the Arizona summer. He did recommend that the
Peabody purchase for Jo's use a new-fangled piece of equipment—a new model of the
"Weston Photometer, which retails for a list [price] of $22.50 and appears notably
superior in many ways to the old model." Continuing his persuasion, he wrote: "It is
the only infallible exposure meter; it can be only a question of time until it saves its own
cost just in film, not to mention time and other expense involved in taking duplicate pictures. Its reputation everywhere is that it can't fail, never wears out, is very simple to use,
clears corners thoroughly, toasts evenly on both sides, will not buckle, rip, or embarrass
the ladies of the party, and has two spare tires and a bumper."

Alden Stevens with surveying equipment and camera, 1938.

Just before the field season ended, Stevens learned that a new Park Service job had come through, and he left in mid-November to work on exhibits for the new visitor's center at Shiloh Military Park in Tennessee. (He returned to Awatovi for the 1938 season, accompanied by his wife, Marian.) Brew then "borrowed a surveyor for two weeks" from Mesa Verde National Park to complete the maps Stevens had begun. The surveyor was Robert "Bob" Burgh, an archaeologist working at the time "on the Ruins Survey branch of the Park Service."[20] Burgh's association with the Awatovi Expedition was brief, but he continued a career in anthropology and years later, in Tucson in 1955, worked with another Awatovi participant, Watson Smith, on a specialized study of some of the pottery from the Western Mound.[21]

For himself, Lancaster, Thompson, and Stevens, Brew set up a tent camp under some shady piñon trees near the Jeddito Trading Post, at the eastern end of Antelope Mesa. It was a simple "fly camp," as he called it, with tents for sleeping, one for equipment and storage, and a sheltered area for cooking and eating. Soon he added two tents to be

Bob Burgh (right) with Al Lancaster at the wash stand in the camp near Awatovi, 1935.

shared by the Hopi crew. After a couple of weeks exploring the mesa, Brew found what he felt was a better place for the camp, about a mile east of Awatovi, and moved his tents and equipment there. This would become the permanent location for the Awatovi Expedition camp until the end of the project in September 1939.

The new camp was comfortable and the work went well. In his first letter to Donald Scott, dated September 28, Brew reported happily: "I have seen all of the large ruins and about 15 small ones. We already have a collection of arrow points from Awatobi, a whole pot, and a skeleton washed out by the recent rains. . . . I can only say this is the kind of thing I have been hoping for. It looks very, very good."

By October the weather was freezing at night, but Brew wrote to Scott on the eighteenth: "We are quite comfortable in camp, with stoves in the tents." Near the end of the field season, on November 16, Brew described to Scott what was going on around him: "[The camp] is the scene of great activity: men in the trench [at Awatovi]; engineering department [Alden Stevens] with plane table, range pole, pegs, and flags (of orange satin dress goods) all over the site; a crew digging fence post holes; a team [of Hopi horses or mules] and scraper; one Hopi making boxes; and the cook making cinnamon rolls, angel cake, and pun'kin pie (out of sweet potatoes)."

The 1935 field camp after it was moved nearer to the Awatovi ruins.

Although earlier researchers such as Hough and Kidder had found all of the six large sites on Antelope Mesa, no one knew much about the small sites. A primary goal during the 1935 season was to search them out, describe them, and collect the pottery sherds that littered their surfaces. Brew was especially interested in small sites that dated earlier in the area's cultural sequence than the known large sites.

Brew and his crew recorded 55 small sites on Antelope Mesa that fall. The pottery collected from them showed them to run the gamut from Basketmaker III times to the historic period (see table, page 39). This was an exciting find, because it showed that Brew had been right to predict that Antelope Mesa would be a choice place in which to study Puebloan culture over a great span of time. His field notes also mention ruins of Navajo hogans and small Hopi field houses near Tallahogan Springs, but he did not record them as archaeological sites or include them in the total number of sites found.

Potsherds found when the Hopi crew dug some test pits at a site near the trading post—a small ruin known simply as Site 4—revealed that people had lived there during at least four time periods: Basketmaker (BM) III and Pueblo (P) I, II, and III. Brew was delighted with this discovery and on October 10 wrote to Scott with obvious satisfaction: "In all their surveying [on Antelope Mesa], the Museum of Northern Arizona has no BM III [sherds] from the Jeddito area. We showed Lynn Hargrave [an archaeologist at MNA who had done much of the earlier survey work] four sites,

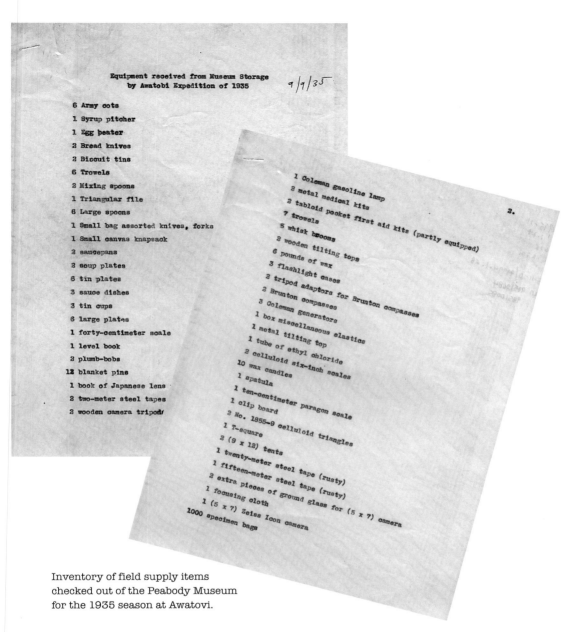

Equipment received from Museum Storage
by Awatobi Expedition of 1935   9/9/35

6 Army cots
1 Syrup pitcher
1 Egg beater
2 Bread knives
2 Biscuit tins
6 Trowels
2 Mixing spoons
1 Triangular file
6 Large spoons
1 Small bag assorted knives, forks
1 Small canvas knapsack
2 saucepans
2 soup plates
6 tin plates
3 sauce dishes
3 tin cups
6 large plates
1 forty-centimeter scale
1 level book
2 plumb-bobs
12 blanket pins
1 book of Japanese lens
2 two-meter steel tapes
3 wooden camera tripods

2.

1 Coleman gasoline lamp
2 metal medical kits
2 tabloid pocket first aid kits (partly equipped)
7 trowels
5 whisk brooms
2 wooden tilting tops
6 pounds of wax
3 flashlight cases
2 tripod adaptors for Brunton compasses
2 Brunton compasses
3 Coleman generators
1 box miscellaneous elastics
1 metal tilting top
1 tube of ethyl chloride
2 celluloid six-inch scales
10 wax candles
1 spatula
1 ten-centimeter paragon scale
1 clip board
2 No. 1855-9 celluloid triangles
1 T-square
2 (9 x 12) tents
1 twenty-meter steel tape (rusty)
1 fifteen-meter steel tape (rusty)
2 extra pieces of ground glass for (5 x 7) camera
1 focusing cloth
1 (5 x 7) Zeiss Icon camera
1000 specimen bags

Inventory of field supply items
checked out of the Peabody Museum
for the 1935 season at Awatovi.

two with house type exposed, and discovered three more while he was here. Also a
P I Black-on-White [site] of which he has no record."

The map begun by Stevens and completed by Burgh, drawn with contour intervals
of 20 meters, showed the location and number of each site recorded that first season.
Named on the map were the six large sites—from west to east, Awatovi, Kawaika-a,
Chakpahu, NeSheptanga (Nesuftanga), Kokopnyama (Kokopngyama), and
Lululongturqui (Lululongturque)—and one medium-sized site called Pink Arrow
because of a pink projectile point found there.

The long north–south trench across the Awatovi site excavated in 1935, looking north.

It was the site of Awatovi, of course, that had most interested Scott, Claflin, and Brew from the beginning of their discussions. During the 1935 season the crew dug a 2-meter-wide trench for a length of 233 meters across the narrow dimension of Awatovi, south to north. Brew thought he was putting the trench mostly through open areas, or plazas, and therefore through few rooms, but he soon learned otherwise. On October 18, after only four days of working on the trench, he wrote to Scott: "The small plaza I picked for preliminary excavation is purely a surface thing, the reoccupation in Mission times of an area which had served as a major mission dump. Beneath it is a mass of Sikyatki rooms [characterized by Sikyatki Polychrome pottery], many of which have restorable jars and other artifacts . . . on the floors."

The Pecos Classification, Used by Researchers on the Awatovi Expedition

DATES A.D.	PERIOD	CHARACTERISTICS
600–800	Basketmaker III	Dwellings are pithouses or slab houses. Pottery is made; cooking ware is plain, undecorated.
800–1000	Pueblo I	Cooking vessels have unobliterated coils or bands at neck; painted pottery appears. Villages are composed of aboveground, contiguous rectangular rooms of true masonry.
1000–1150	Pueblo II	Corrugations extend over entire exterior surfaces of cooking vessels. Small villages occur over a large geographic area.
1150–1300	Pueblo III	Very large communities; artistic elaboration and specialization in crafts.
1300–1540	Pueblo IV (protohistoric)	Artistic elaboration declines; corrugated wares gradually disappear, giving way to plain wares.
1540–1700	Pueblo V (historic)	Pueblos adopt and then discard some European vessel forms and designs.

SOURCES: Linda S. Cordell, *Prehistory of the Southwest* (San Diego: Academic Press, 1984), 55–56, 105, and table 3.5.; J. Jefferson Reid and Stephanie Whittlesey, *Grasshopper Pueblo: A Story of Archaeology and Ancient Life* (Tucson: University of Arizona Press, 1999).

NOTE: The traits listed here now apply largely to northern Arizona; other sequences and names have been identified for other areas of the Southwest. Dates are approximate.

What the excavators found in the test trench fulfilled all Brew's hopes for the scientific potential of the site. "We have a wealth of good stratigraphy," he told Scott in his October 18 letter, "both in refuse material and architecturally. Some of our Sikyatki floors are fifteen feet below the surface and the lowest of them are built on [human-deposited] fill. Some of our rooms are two storeys high already and will be higher or on top of other buildings. And all this in what appears on the surface to be one of the thinnest parts of the site." On November 16, referring to the test excavations at Awatovi, he wrote to Scott: "I have dreamed of this sort of thing for years but I never expected to get so much with such a small crew."

Altogether, Brew and his men excavated 106 rooms and five kivas at Awatovi that season. He reported that most of the buildings uncovered in the trench dated to the fifteenth and sixteenth centuries—the late precontact years.[22] The workmen found plaster well preserved on the walls of some rooms, "holding forth promise of wall paintings such as [those] found by Hough at Kawaiokuh [Kawaika-a]."[23] The rooms

LEGEND
Contour Lines
Sandstone Ledge
Areas of Low Relief
Areas of High Relief
Intermittent Watercourse
Excavated Rooms–1935 Season
Excavated Rooms–Prior to 1935
Unexcavated Rooms–Exposed Walls
Unexcavated Rooms–Standing Walls

JEDDITO EXPEDITION 1935
PEABODY MUSEUM
OF HARVARD UNIVERSITY
TOPOGRAPHIC MAP OF
AWATOBI
SHOWING TEST TRENCH

SCALE
0 10   METERS   100
0   50   FEET   300
Contour Interval–One Meter
Datum Arbitrarily Assumed
Topography by Robert Burgh

Map by Robert Burgh of all excavated areas at the Awatovi site, 1935.
The map's title calls the project the "Jeddito Expedition" because the decision
to concentrate on Awatovi had not yet been made. The area identified as
Jeddito Mesa on the map is, in fact, Antelope Mesa.

were filled with refuse—bone and stone tools, bone beads, shell ornaments, whole pottery vessels and sherds, squash and melon seeds, corn kernels and cobs, piñon nuts, and roof timbers.[24] The five kivas all lay at the southern end of the trench, nearest the edge of the mesa, and as luck had it, the first found was the most elaborate. Its contents proved it to have been in use, at least for a short time, after the arrival of the Spaniards.[25]

As the digging continued to unearth more and more information, Brew began thinking in terms of more than one future season of work there. In his last letter to Scott from the field, dated December 6, 1935, he expressed caution about what to attempt the following year: "As for next year at Awatobi, I think the best bet will be to make a start, at least, on the Great Western Mound. . . . I think I would rather leave the mission until later. The excavation of the mission should not be undertaken without considerable special preparation." He speculated that many of the "altar gadgets, etc., were homemade, and in their archaeological shape will be rather hard to recognize without considerable familiarity with that sort of gear. Consequently, I should like a bit of an opportunity to look these up before jumping into the Mission."

Although Brew's early thoughts were not entirely prophetic, the next two seasons of work did generally follow a sequence of excavating first in the Western Mound and then in the mission. Meanwhile, looking ahead to 1936, Brew left the bulk of the collections and the camping equipment at the Jeddito Trading Post and was back in Cambridge for Christmas. Somewhere along the way, the die had been cast for several returns to Awatovi.

The 1938 Awatovi staff. Front, seated: Lin Thompson, Dick Woodbury,
Evelyn Nimmo, Al Lancaster, Jo Brew, Marian Stevens, Haych Claflin, Alden Stevens.
Rear: Ross Montgomery, Jay Hooton, Watson Smith, Happy Foote, Hattie Cosgrove,
Carlos García-Robiou, John Hack, Kirk Bryan, Hal Winchester, Ned Hall.

- 3 -

Getting Ready

The popular media like the sound of the word *expedition*. It conjures up images of hectic preparations, vast crates and packing boxes, and arduous trips to far-off lands to excavate for "lost civilizations." Archaeologists seldom organize expeditions on that scale anymore—instead, they conduct "research projects." But they still need skilled and compatible personnel, safe and reasonably comfortable accommodations, food no one will complain about, the means to clean and store artifacts, and sufficient funds to cover salaries, accommodations, equipment, travel, and contingencies. None of these requirements has changed in the twenty-first century.

Jo Brew, Donald Scott, and their colleagues in Cambridge in the winter of 1935–1936 were hardly planning an adventure on the scale of a Hollywood epic, but the Awatovi Expedition still demanded a sizable cast of participants, a large camp, plenty of equipment, and of course money. It also required some large packing crates and long trips to a (relatively) strange land. For some of the Awatovi staff it was their first trip to the West and their first long journey by train.

Discussions again took place, but no correspondence or memos about them survive. Other than budget notes, nothing in the Peabody archives tells when or why the staff decided to request a permit to continue the work for another three years—which, as we will see, turned into four seasons of fieldwork. In any case, the Department of the Interior granted the request in a letter dated July 22, 1936. Because the previous permit ran to August 26, 1936, Scott and Brew assumed that the three years would end on August 26, 1939. They had planned to carry out fieldwork from approximately August through November each year, but the final permitted "year" included two field seasons: August to December 1938 and May to August 1939.

The impression one gets from the existing documents is that fund-raising for the expedition each year was at best informal, and sometimes the expedition's future seemed downright precarious. Scott relied on Bill Claflin for the majority of the funds.

The museum officially supplied less than half the needed money, though it always came through with supplements, and Scott may even have made personal contributions.

In the winter of 1935, Jo Brew prepared alternative budgets for three more years of work. One budget, for approximately $9,000 a year, was his "preferred budget," and another, at $9,500, his "wish list." A minimum figure of $7,500 per year reflected compromises between what he wanted to do and what might be financially possible. The savings, according to his notes, would be "obtained mostly through cuts in labor and staff"—and the cost of constructing the field camp would be extra. Estimating the time and money needed for archaeological research was, and still is, a tricky business. One cannot know exactly what lies under the surface of a site, and surprises happen.

By June 1, 1936, Scott had commitments for only $6,700 for that summer's work. Of that, the museum would put up as much as $2,500, Bill Claflin promised to donate $3,000, and he raised another $1,200 from Raymond Emerson and two other friends in the stock brokerage business. A "for the record" memo of July 1, 1936, observed that the approved budget of $6,700 allowed for a three-month field season, August through October, with the possibility of continuing work for a week or two into November. Moreover, the museum would "guarantee $500.00 for the erection of an enclosed work shed to contain a work room, an office, a supply storage room, and possibly a drafting room although this may be combined with the office." This building was never constructed, but the $500 was added to the budget anyway, bringing the total Brew had to work with to $7,200.

Jo Brew had never planned or run a large project before Awatovi, but his original budget projections proved accurate: $7,200 was insufficient. As it turned out, the 1936 field season lasted into the third week of November and cost a total of $8,196.68. A January 26, 1937, note in the archives says that "for the last month of work we advanced [Brew] $1500 more, making a total of $8200" and neatly covering the total cost known by that time. Jo's check for $3.32, made out to the museum, is attached to the memo. The treasurer of Harvard—who at the time happened to be Bill Claflin— had to have his books balance.

Actual expenditures exceeded estimates in all years after 1935, but always with Scott's approval. As far as I can determine, the museum always covered the overages. In most years the additional expenses arose largely from the need to stay longer than expected in the field—surprises indeed happened. Excavators found the first painted kivas midway through the 1936 season, and in the next two years the complexity of the mission ruins demanded extra time and supplies. Altogether, expenses for five field seasons—18 and a half months full-time—came to $43,936. If Brew's salary, paid by the museum, and the time of the many participants who volunteered their services in the field were figured in, the actual cost would be more than double that amount.

Archaeologist Cory D. Breternitz has estimated that financing one season of an equivalent project today—three full-time staff members for three months and eight "shovel hands" for 10 weeks—would run to about $135,000.[1]

Jo Brew proved adept at keeping expenses down by offering graduate students and even some of his professional colleagues a great experience, good food, and free camping at a fascinating archaeological site—without wages. A handwritten 1938 "Field Organization Chart" bears a penciled note saying "not paid by PM [Peabody Museum] 18; paid by PM 7 + 15 Hopis." Everyone had to find his or her own way to camp, but once there, out-of-pocket expenses were few—laundry, mail, meals during trips to Winslow, Holbrook, or Gallup, and gifts. As word of the tempting project and the congeniality of Brew's field camp spread through the anthropological grapevine, he found himself with no shortage of skilled volunteers and knowledgeable visitors.

✢

The people Brew enlisted or found serendipitously available to him for the 1936 field season brought with them a mix of talents, education, and experience. Luckily for the expedition, Al Lancaster and Lin Thompson agreed to come back that year and for all later field seasons. Two new key staff members, Hattie Cosgrove and Watson Smith, also signed on in 1936 and stayed with the project to the end.

Hattie Cosgrove served as what we would now call the laboratory supervisor. "In charge of the pottery tent" was Brew's description of her role. She and her husband, Cornelius Burton "Burt" Cosgrove, had spent their early married years in Atchison, Kansas, where Harriet Silliman had been born in 1877 and where Burt had lived since the age of 14.[2] Burt earned a law degree at the University of Nebraska but afterward went to work in Hattie's family's hardware store. Both Cosgroves were interested in archaeology and enjoyed spending Sunday afternoons finding sites around Atchison and collecting artifacts.

In 1907 the couple and their infant son, Burton Jr., moved to Silver City, New Mexico, where Burt worked for a year in his uncle's hardware store. When the uncle died, he went to work for a larger hardware company in town and stayed there until 1924. Burt and Hattie loved exploring, camping, hiking, and finding Indian sites in that beautiful country, and their explorations eventually focused on a Mimbres village near Silver City known locally as Whiskey Creek Ruin, but which they called Treasure Hill. The family often spent Sundays digging in the ruins.

By 1917 the Cosgroves had joined the Santa Fe chapter of the Archaeological Institute of America, through which they met the professional archaeologists of the area and visited some of the Pueblo ruins in northern New Mexico. In 1919 they

Hattie and Burt Cosgrove at Awatovi, 1936.

purchased the Treasure Hill site and began more orderly excavations there. They visited Frederick Webb Hodge, of the Southwest Museum, in 1920 at his summer field camp at Hawikuh (Hawikku), near Zuni, New Mexico. They also went to Pecos, where they met Ted Kidder, who would become a lifelong friend.

The Cosgroves improved their scientific techniques as they continued to work at Treasure Hill. By 1923 Kidder had visited that ruin and others in the Mimbres River valley with them. Impressed with their knowledge, interest, and enthusiasm, he asked them, in his position as a curator for the Peabody Museum, if they would direct a Peabody-sponsored survey of the Mimbres Valley. Both now in their mid-forties, the Cosgroves decided to make a dramatic career change.

Burt quit his job at the Cox Hardware store and went to work for the Peabody. It was another few years before Hattie began to receive a salary for her work. For four months during the years 1924–1927 they excavated at Swarts Ruin, one of the largest known Mimbres sites, essentially uncovering the whole village. Their report is still the most complete one on a site of that important pre-Hispanic culture.[3] With this dig finished, they continued to carry out projects for the Peabody in the Southwest, and in 1936 Brew asked them to join the Awatovi Expedition. Hattie was 59 that July, and Burt 61. Some of the staff thought the pair might act as "elder advisors" to Brew if he turned out to be a bit green for the task, and they could also serve as chaperones when single women became part of the crew.[4] Hattie, experienced in the study of ceramics, was to run the pottery tent, and Burt was to be a supervisor in the field.

Sadly, Burt Cosgrove fell ill and died in late October 1936. He got stomach cramps after supper one evening, and Hattie, Burt Jr., who was visiting, and Al Lancaster took him to the hospital in Keams Canyon. There he was treated and seemed to feel better but was advised to stay overnight. The other three returned to camp. Not long afterward, a Hopi appeared on horseback, bringing word that Burt had died suddenly. Donald and Louise Scott were in camp at the time, and along with everyone else tried to help Hattie deal with the blow. She took Burt's body to Atchison for burial and later that winter returned to work at the museum in Cambridge, processing artifacts from Awatovi.

Hattie was back in the field in 1937, and over the course of three seasons saw to the processing of more than "half a million potsherds [which] were excavated, washed, classified, and recorded."[5] She made individual drawings of some six hundred handles of vessels, a pet research project of her own. Because she was the senior woman in camp, Hattie also ended up playing the unofficial but vital role of camp hostess. She took it upon herself to greet all visitors and kept a running list of who they were. Even more fortunately for this story, she took myriad photographs of the staff and crew, most of the guests, and of scenes around camp.

Wat Smith relaxing in the Awatovi camp "plaza," 1938.

The second new staff member in 1936 who proved himself indispensable was Watson Smith—known always as Wat—a gentleman and a scholar in every sense. Like the Cosgroves and so many others in this story, he came to professional archaeology relatively late in life. Born in Cincinnati, Ohio, in 1897 to a relatively well-to-do family, he graduated from Brown University in 1919, having studied geology, history, literature, and philosophy. After a few years' work in industry, he entered Harvard Law School, graduated in 1924, and worked until 1929 for a law firm in Providence, Rhode Island. Finding that the law suited his temperament no better than business, Wat arranged that year to go to Turkey with the University of Cincinnati to excavate at Troy. The opportunity was thwarted by the deaths of both his parents and an aunt within a few months of each other. It took him three years to settle his relatives' estates, but in 1933, inheritance in hand, he was free to follow his enthusiasm for archaeology.

At the Field Museum in Chicago, Wat met archaeologist Paul Martin, who invited him to spend the summer of 1933 at Lowry Ruin in southwestern Colorado, then being excavated under Martin's direction. Wat returned to work at Lowry for the 1934 season as well. That experience and a winter at the University of California in Berkeley put him in touch with many other Southwestern archaeologists, one of whom was Ansel Hall. Hall asked him to join the Rainbow Bridge–Monument Valley Expedition (RBMVE), in which Wat participated in the summers of 1935, 1936, and 1937.[6]

In 1935, Wat and others from the RBMVE visited Brew's camp at Awatovi. Smith and Brew had first met in 1933, when Wat and others of the Lowry crew had toured Jo's excavations at Alkali Ridge. During the visit to Awatovi, Jo invited Wat to come and work there for the 1936 season, since the RBMVE was in the field early in the summer and the Awatovi Expedition would not begin until August. Years later Smith wrote of this opportunity, "I was naturally pleased at that prospect, but what it was to do for me in its fulfillment, I could not then have dimly foreseen. Perhaps I do not even now, in retrospect, fully comprehend it, because it became and remains a continuing and living experience."[7] The "living experience" began for Wat upon his arrival, just a few days after someone discovered the first painted wall in a kiva at Awatovi. As he told the story:

> Nothing had been done about the painted kiva walls at the time of my arrival, because everyone else in the group was engaged in his own operation, whatever that might be. The job of investigating those painted walls was, therefore, given to me. This rather meager and unpromising beginning turned out to be one of the bonanzas of the whole Awatovi expedition. In subsequent summers numerous painted kivas were discovered, some of them very, very elaborately decorated, and since I had undertaken that phase of the operation, I continued it, devoting almost all of my time for four years to it.[8]

The kiva murals of Awatovi turned out to be the most spectacular and information-rich finds of the entire dig.

Wat is mentioned in the Peabody archives as one of many volunteers on the expedition, which meant he received no salary. Although probably few of his colleagues knew it, he was quite a wealthy man and had the luxury of devoting his life to archaeology unpaid. He had his own car at Awatovi, and his generosity with it added greatly to his colleagues' ability to take trips, visit Hopi villages, and in general lessen their isolation. His intellect more than made up for his lack of advanced academic training in archaeology, and his unassuming nature, wit, and enjoyment of good conversation made him an asset to camp life. Jo Brew later said of him: "He became the anchor man of the Awatovi staff, our chief writer and editor, and a close personal friend."[9]

The Hopi men Brew had hired for the 1935 field season had proved a boon to the project, and he wanted them back. To line up crewmen for the 1936 and subsequent seasons, Brew turned to his friend Luke Kawanusea at Mishongnovi, who recruited the new crew members. Six of the crew from 1935 came back the next year, together

Luke Kawanusea, his wife, Vivian Tewanyinima, and one of their grandchildren.

with some new faces. Alec and Leland Dennis, for example, were joined by their brothers Emory and Elwood in 1936, and brother Chester joined them in 1938. (Elwood was called Hop-Along or Hoppy because he walked with a limp.) By the end of the fieldwork, 30 Hopis had been involved in the project, 15 from First Mesa and 15 from Second Mesa. As the workload grew and time slipped away, the actual numbers of Hopis on the crew each year increased, from 9 in 1935 to 15 in both 1936 and 1937, 16 in 1938, and 19 in 1939.

Most of the Hopis who worked on the project were in their mid-twenties at the time, a few slightly older, and a few in their late teens. Some were married with families, some were single. At any given time, approximately half the crew was from First Mesa and half from Second Mesa. (Third Mesa was too far away.) Many of the men were related by blood or clan, and undoubtedly some of them were related to Luke Kawanusea or his wife, Vivian Tewanyinima. Besides the five Dennis brothers from Second Mesa, there were four Namoki brothers from First Mesa. Cecil Calvert and

Jake Poleviyuma were brothers as well. Everett Harris was a cousin of the Dennis brothers, and Douglas Coochwytewa was Alec Dennis's brother-in-law. Roland Hunter was Luke Hovelo's son.

Brew's letters and journal say that he felt the men enjoyed the work, but my interviews with two of their families suggested that some of the men were wary of digging at Awatovi. Perhaps it was because of the legend of its destruction, perhaps because of the burials, perhaps because of the ceremonial artifacts and murals in the kivas—it was difficult to pin them down about why their fathers had felt reluctance. "My dad always said he knew it was wrong [to dig there]," one man told me, "but he needed the money to feed his family." The men also probably served their villages by telling the elders what was going on at the site and in camp.

The Hopi men ran or rode horses from their villages to the camp every Sunday evening and went home the same way the following Friday evening or Saturday noon, except during ceremonies and dances, when they did not work. The Peabody provided them with two living tents, one for the men from each mesa, and a communal tent where they cooked their meals during cold or wet weather. Sometimes people in the main camp could hear them singing in the evenings around their campfire, where they cooked when the weather was good. Brew provided them with some staples and canned goods, which they supplemented with rabbit meat. Penny Davis recalled seeing one or two of the Hopis riding back to camp at dusk with rabbits they had shot. Al Lancaster remembered that they collected pieces of cottonwood and in the evenings whittled small katsina dolls to sell to tourists. Often in the evenings they joined the rest of the staff in the cook shack or around the campfire.

The sizable Hopi crew was outnumbered by the Anglo staff—20 to 30 of them in any one year, although the majority of them did not actually stay for the whole field season. For a project of the scale planned for 1936–1939, Brew knew he would need a variety of specialists, excavation supervisors, and assistants. He began identifying likely candidates early in 1936 and recruited an eclectic group, from established university professors to first-time-in-the-field novice archaeologists, from scholars who went on to develop respected careers in archaeology to those who counted this as their only time on a dig. In museum publications about the expedition, Brew made sure everyone was recognized as contributing to the project, distinguishing only between "permanent staff" and people "associated with the expedition at one time or another in specialized capacities or as general assistants." So-called permanent staff, however, might well be volunteers or people who visited the site only briefly.

THE CREW WHO WORKED AT AWATOVI, 1936-1939

The five Dennis brothers at the Awatovi camp. Left to right: Elwood "Hoppy," Leland, Emory, Chester, Alec.

Patrick Coochnyama (Williams).

Randolph David, 1939.

Luke Hovelo.

Arthur Masayteva.

Max Namoki, 1939.

Fred Kinsley, 1939.

Larry Gallegos, 1939.

Dana Namoki.

Eric Lalo.

Left: Homer Philips, 1936. Right: J. C. Fisher Motz, 1937.

Of the people listed as "Excavation Supervisors, Surveyors and Topographers, Field Supervisor of Stone and Bone Artifacts, Physical Anthropologist, Cataloguer, Photographer, and General Assistants," none worked for more than two years, and several were in residence for only a few weeks. Each field season saw a new "surveyor/ topographer" on the job: Homer Phillips, a student at the University of New Mexico, in 1936; J. C. Fisher Motz, an engineer who had worked at other archaeological sites in Arizona, in 1937; Alden B. Stevens, from the 1935 season, again in 1938; and Bob Jones, another UNM student, in 1939. Kirk Bryan, an associate professor of physiography (now called physical geography) at Harvard who spent only a few days each year at Awatovi, was listed in the Awatovi publications as "consultant in geology." Charles "Happy" Foote, a teenage relative of Al Lancaster's who came in 1938 and 1939 to chop wood and help in the kitchen, stayed for the whole of those field seasons. Edward Pierrepont Beckwith, a member of the Explorer's Club of New York City who had done aerial photography for the RBMVE, volunteered his time over just one weekend in 1937. He contributed to the expedition immeasurably, however, by allowing Brew to fly with him to take aerial photographs of Awatovi and Antelope Mesa— a rare opportunity in those days.[10]

Left: Bob Jones, 1939. Right: Charles "Happy" Foote.

Rounding up his interdisciplinary team for 1936, Brew also enlisted the experience of Volney Jones, a professor of botany at the University of Michigan and creator of the university's Ethnobotany Laboratory. Jones came to Awatovi for three seasons—1936, 1937, and 1939—to collect samples of plants and seeds, through an agreement between the Museum of Anthropology at the University of Michigan and the Peabody. Brew was particularly interested in learning what plants Spaniards might have introduced into the mix of indigenous wild and cultivated plants the Hopis used. Jones experimented with "flotation," now an established field method in archaeology. He immersed adobe bricks in water, and as the adobe clay fell apart, the plant material inside it floated to the surface. There it could be scooped off and then dried and later identified in Jones's laboratory.

Brew also spoke to Kirk Bryan at Harvard about needing someone to study the geology and physical environment of Antelope Mesa. Bryan suggested John "Johnny" Hack, one of his graduate students. Hack would work all four seasons at Awatovi, gathering data about the natural environment, examining contemporary Hopi farming practices— research that would become classic in Southwestern archaeology—and studying the Hopis' precontact coal mining. Bryan himself visited the Awatovi camp every year to consult with Hack on his dissertation research and lend his expertise to discussions around the campfire. In his late forties at the time of his association with the Awatovi Expedition, Bryan had worked for some 15 years for the U.S. Geological Survey before joining the Harvard faculty. He was one of the first in his field to see the relationship between geology and archaeology, a specialty now known as geoarchaeology.

While Hattie Cosgrove processed the pottery the workers collected, someone was needed to clean and catalogue the tools and ornaments fashioned from stone and animal bone. Richard "Dick" P. Wheeler was a graduate student at Harvard when Brew invited him to take part in the Awatovi Expedition as "field supervisor of stone and bone artifacts." He would play that role during 1936 and most of the 1937 season, before a family crisis called him home to Ohio. Another Harvard student, Richard "Dick" B. Woodbury, replaced Wheeler the next two seasons in what they called the "Osteo-lapidarium," from the Latin words for "bone" and "stone." Woodbury later remembered that Dick Wheeler's full black beard "led the Hopis to call him 'Jesus' (presumably from the religious pictures they had seen), and when I succeeded him in the Stone and Bone tent, I was sometimes called 'Second Jesus.'"

Brew hired Don Watson, an archaeologist working at Mesa Verde National Park, as a "general assistant" for 1936, undoubtedly to help Lancaster supervise the Hopi crew. He knew he could count on members of the Peabody staff to fill out the work team, whether on official assignment or simply for pleasure. Donald Scott and his wife, Louise, traveled to Awatovi every summer and pitched in, Donald searching for and photographing rock art on the cliffs below the rim of Antelope Mesa and Louise working as another general assistant, wherever she could be of use. Bill Claflin and his wife, Helen, too, came out to Awatovi every season, usually staying in camp for at least a month. Helen helped Hattie Cosgrove in the pottery tent and assisted Wat Smith with the delicate task of scraping off layers of kiva murals after the images in each layer had been painstakingly drawn. Bill worked at the site and become particularly interested in burials as excavations progressed in the ruins of the mission church.

The Claflins brought their three children with them as well. Katherine "Kitty" Claflin, a young teenager at the time, got another of the "general assistant" titles when she came in 1937. Her older sister, Helen, known still as "Haych," helped in the pottery tent and with the mural scraping in 1938 and 1939. Haych had graduated from the Windsor School in Boston in 1937, and that fall Scott hired her to work on cataloguing artifacts and baskets at the Peabody. She worked there until the summer of 1938, when she went to Awatovi to help Hattie and Wat, and returned for the 1939 season as well. Bill Claflin III, referred to as "Young Bill," was a student at Harvard with an interest in archaeology but little if any field experience until Brew put him to work. First he helped John Hack, and later, often using one of the Hopis' horses for transportation,

Clockwise from top left:
Volney and Joyce Hedrick Jones; John Hack;
Dick Woodbury, 1939; Dick Wheeler, 1937.

Left: Four of the Claflin family in front of the Awatovi cook shack, 1938. Standing: William "Bill" H. Claflin Jr.; seated, left to right: Helen (Mrs. Claflin), daughters Helen "Haych" and Katherine "Kitty." Right: William H. "Young Bill" Claflin III.

he searched out and recorded sites on the mesa. He appears on the permanent staff list as being "in charge of reconnaissance."

People who joined the expedition in later seasons were just as varied as those Brew recruited in 1936. The 1937 season saw the addition of excavation supervisors Thomas Campbell, John M. Longyear III, and Charles "Charlie" Amsden, the last of whom would return through 1939. Harold P. Winchester held the same title in 1938. Campbell and Longyear were both graduate students in archaeology at Harvard, and Longyear had been working with Paul Martin at Lowry Ruin during the summer of 1937, when Brew invited him to come to Awatovi. He participated for only one month, but he remembered thinking that Brew was especially pleased to have him because he owned a movie camera and a car.

Charlie Amsden had been introduced to archaeology as a teenager in Farmington, New Mexico, where A.V. Kidder hired him as a camp helper in 1914.[11] After graduat-

Charles and Madeleine Amsden.

ing from Harvard in 1922 he joined the diplomatic corps, but while serving as U.S. consul in Sonora, Mexico, he contracted tuberculosis and had to return to the United States. He spent one summer season, probably in the mid-1920s, with Kidder at Pecos and in 1927 became a curator at the Southwest Museum in Los Angeles.

Amsden and his wife, Madeleine, visited Awatovi in 1936. Brew gave them a tour of the area, including Site 4, where no one was working that year. Amsden must have shown interest in it, because for the following three seasons he and Madeleine returned during their two to three weeks of vacation. In 1939 he concentrated on completing the excavation of that site and of Site 4A nearby. Although ill health prevented him from writing up and publishing this work, a later commentator pointed out that "his careful and detailed notes on the D-shaped kiva [at Site 4] were the basis of Watson Smith's published description of it. . . . The Smith-Amsden collaboration is probably the best report on a D-shaped kiva in the archaeological literature of the Southwest."[12] Madeleine Amsden helped Hattie Cosgrove in the pottery tent and Wat Smith in scraping kiva murals.

Amsden also contributed by recommending a friend of his as someone who might help Brew interpret what was being uncovered of the Awatovi mission. Ross G. Montgomery was a well-known ecclesiastical architect in southern California in the mid-1930s, with a special interest in Spanish mission churches. At Amsden's suggestion, he visited the site during the 1937 season and was fascinated. He and his wife, Elvira, came out to Awatovi every year through 1939, staying for several days at a time to advise Brew on where to dig and what to look for. Brew felt that Montgomery's comprehensive experience with the architecture of Spanish Catholicism gave him an almost uncanny knowledge of what the excavators would find, and his aid in interpreting the ruins proved indispensable to the expedition's success.

The 1937 season saw an influx of general assistants, too—some for the entire time, others for only short stays. George W. Brainerd, who came for a month after the RBMVE wrapped up that summer, brought prior archaeological experience. Fred Eggan was a professor of cultural anthropology at the University of Chicago, doing ethnographic research on the Hopis. He visited Awatovi for several weeks in both 1937 and 1938 and gave Brew a wealth of useful information about Hopi cultural and social organization. Jack Mineer was a local man from Keams Canyon. Kenneth D. MacLeish, son of the poet Archibald MacLeish, was one of the many Harvard graduate students Brew enlisted. He was working on his dissertation on the Hopi language in 1937 and helped out at Awatovi for a month. Two secretaries from the Peabody Museum, Dorothy Newton and Marion Hutchinson, also came out to Awatovi in 1937. Despite the common title "assistant," these people's assignments were multifarious. Brainerd helped prepare tree-ring samples to be sent to the University of Arizona for dating. MacLeish worked as an excavation supervisor, and Eggan, besides acting as a consultant, helped dig. Newton and Hutchinson aided Hattie Cosgrove with the cataloguing chores.

Another Peabody secretary, Evelyn Nimmo, who came out to Awatovi in 1938 and 1939, proved to be singularly important to the project, especially to its director. The recent college graduate, working at the Peabody as an office assistant, jumped at the chance to go to Awatovi to help with cataloguing. She also became secretary to Jo Brew and, providentially for this story, took daily dictation from him and typed up the daily field and camp journals. During the summer and fall of 1938, and continuing after their return to Cambridge at the end of the field season, Jo courted Evelyn, and they announced their engagement in February 1939. On June 11, in the pottery tent at the Awatovi camp, Nimmo and Brew were married.

Carlos García-Robiou was another bit of good luck that befell Brew and the expedition. A professor of archaeology at the University of Havana, he was traveling around the United States in 1938 on a Guggenheim Fellowship. He had visited the

Tom Campbell, 1936.

Ross G. Montgomery.

George W. Brainerd, 1937.

Fred Eggan.

Kenneth D. MacLeish, 1937.

Dorothy Newton, 1936.

Marion Hutchinson, 1937.

Evelyn Nimmo, 1938.

Carlos García-Robiou, 1938.

Harold P. Winchester, 1938.

Peabody and met Donald Scott, who told him about the work at Awatovi and assured him he would be welcome to visit. García-Robiou made his way to camp, and Brew, upon learning that among other things he was a photographer and a cartographer, invited him to stay. He did, for the remainder of that season and all of the 1939 season. His talent at the piano was only one of many qualities that made him a "beloved member of the party."[13]

✠

As other participants arrived in 1938 and 1939, they continued to follow the pattern set in 1936—a staff member for every niche, and every serendipitous opportunity seized upon. Again, some were young and inexperienced, such as Harvard undergraduate Harold P. Winchester and teenager Jay Hooton. Jay was the son of Earnest A. Hooton, a well-known professor of physical anthropology at Harvard, and Brew invited him to Awatovi for the 1938 season as a general helper around camp. Henry "Harry" Hornblower II was another student at Harvard with an interest in archaeology, although he was not destined to concentrate in that field. As he later began a career in business, however, he was able to convince his father to buy land that would be developed, with Harry's enthusiasm and contributions, into the popular reconstruction of Plymouth Plantation near the spot of the Pilgrims' landing.

My brother, E. Mott Davis, had always wanted to be an archaeologist. He was finishing his senior year at Harvard when he was invited to participate in the expedition in 1939. It was his first experience in the field, and he remembered it well. "My first job," he said, "was holding the level rod for the surveyor, Bob Jones, who, with plane table and alidade, was drawing precise, stone-by-stone, room-by-room plans" of Awatovi.

"Bob was an exacting taskmaster," he recalled. "My job was to stand the rod on the object to be mapped, with a level held against it to keep it vertical. At the same time I had to hold the end of a steel measuring tape against the rod while Bob, always with a toothpick firmly in his mouth, pulled fiercely on the other end, enjoining me severely to 'hold that rod straight!' This went on hour after hour, day after day, for some two weeks, in the sledgehammer heat. I wondered then, and still wonder, if Jo was trying me out to see how well I could stand such a job." Eventually Mott actually got to dig, under Al Lancaster's watchful eye, with the Hopi men at Site 264.

Edward "Ned" T. Hall Jr., a graduate student at the University of Arizona, came during the last two field seasons to help remove and conserve the beams being found in the ruins of both the pueblo rooms and the mission church and to study their patterns of annual growth rings, which could be keyed to calendar dates far back into precontact times. His wife, E. Boyd (as she was always known) accompanied him, which

Left: Harry Hornblower II, 1939. Right: E. Mott Davis, 1939.

turned out to be one of the serendipitous opportunities. An accomplished artist, she spent time sketching scenes around the mesa and gave the Brews a large painted view of the camp.

Like Hall and Boyd, other participants who took part in the last two field seasons of the expedition brought special skills. Another artist was Penrose "Penny" Davis, Mott's and my older sister. After graduating from Amy Sacker's School of Design in Boston in 1938, she was looking for a job as a graphic artist. Mott steered her to inquire at the Peabody. As it happened, the museum's graphic artist had resigned earlier on the day she visited, and Penny was hired on the spot. Her talents were well known by the spring of 1939, and Brew invited her to Awatovi to help Wat Smith make scale drawings of the kiva murals and add notes on the colors.[14] She always said the experience "was a high point" in her life.

Erik K. Reed, an employee of the National Park Service in Santa Fe, was a specialist in Southwestern archaeology. Like so many others, he visited Awatovi, and Brew talked him into spending his two-week vacation in 1938 cleaning and identifying the excavated human bones. Reed later recalled that he and his wife had stopped by Awatovi on their way home to Santa Fe from Flagstaff, Arizona. "As we were leaving," he said, "Jo remarked to me that he wished he could get hold of a physical anthropologist, or at least someone who had had Dr. Hooton's course—Physical Anthropology

Left: Ned Hall and E. Boyd, 1938. Right: Penny Davis at work drawing kiva murals, 1939.

number 4. I smiled shyly and said, 'Well, I had done that much,' and so I took the first of my working vacations that August."

Another specialist, Anna O. Shepard, the "ceramic technologist," was well known for her research into the intricacies of native methods of making pottery. She came to Awatovi for two weeks in 1938, accompanied by her father (Warren Shepard was a retired research chemist), to conduct experiments on local clays the Hopis had used to make pottery in precontact times. Despite the brevity of her stay, Brew listed her as one of the permanent staff, an indication of his esteem for her contribution.

Two other people whom Brew valued enough to name part of the permanent staff, although neither was an archaeologist or ever officially hired, were local residents James "Jim" O. McKenna and Wilmer "Chi" Roberts. Brew credited them both for serving as "agents." McKenna owned a secondhand furniture store in Winslow, Arizona. He and his wife, Mary, had befriended Brew in 1935, providing information about local people and the town. Over the years of the Awatovi Expedition, the McKennas visited camp often and were the source of a much-prized piano—and of the Brews' wedding bed.

Looking back years later, Brew acknowledged the McKennas' contributions this way: "Throughout our activities in Arizona, Mr. and Mrs. James O. McKenna of Winslow served as guides, counselors, and friends to the Expedition and its staff. Their

Erik Reed, 1938.

Anna Shepard and her father performing test firings of sherds and clay samples, 1938.

James and Mary McKenna.

Chi and Alma Roberts.

pleasant garden with its prolific peach trees was a welcome oasis on our trips to town, and their assistance was invaluable in the outfitting of the camp. Their many successful coups included . . . providing the best cookstove I have ever met, a piano for the pottery tent, and an Episcopalian clergyman to officiate at the marriage of the Director."[15]

Chi Roberts was the expedition's connection to the outside world. With the Babbitt Brothers of Holbrook, he was a partner in the Jeddito Trading Post, just seven or eight miles from camp, where the closest telephone was located. He dealt mostly with the Navajos of the area because the post was on the Navajo Reservation and closer to many of those families than to the Hopi villages. From the beginning, Roberts was one of Brew's main sources of knowledge about the area and its people. He and his wife, Alma, became friends who often invited the crew to their home for entertainment and refreshments.

"While the expedition was in the field and in the intervals between seasons," Brew later wrote, "one of its greatest benefactors was Mr. Wilmer C. ('Chi') Roberts, proprietor of the Jeddito Trading Post. Our gratitude to him is heartily shared by the numerous visitors to our camp, who would not have found it but for him, and by untold students and travelers familiar with the northeastern Arizona Indian country between 1919 and 1950. His activities as agent for the Expedition, his scientific and historical library of the Southwest, his Navaho orchestra, and his gracious hospitality contributed immeasurably to the success of our enterprise and to the happiness of our staff."[16]

The staff and crew that Jo Brew would lead in 1936 and subsequent years represented an extraordinary combination of experience, eagerness, good humor, and willingness to work hard. It was not coincidence that brought these particular people together at Awatovi; it was the irresistible lure of Brew's enthusiasm, a fascinating archaeological site, and, according to many, Lin Thompson's cooking. The archaeological discoveries and the comforts and cordiality of the field camp Brew set up made the Awatovi Expedition an unforgettable experience.

The frame-and-canvas housing of the expedition's camp, "New Awatovi," can be seen behind this group relaxing around the campfire in 1938.

– 4 –

New Awatovi

Knowing they would be in the field for at least three years running, Brew and his colleagues needed a semipermanent camp. In 1936 the closest town to Awatovi that had a hotel was Winslow, 70 miles away, and there was no place at all on the Hopi Reservation or in Keams Canyon that could house and provide work space for 20 to 30 people for three months of the year. Furthermore, the crew's experience with wind, storms, and sand in 1935 also called for something more substantial than canvas tents.

The second spot Brew had chosen for a camp the previous year became the expedition's "permanent" home. As Watson Smith later described it, the camp sat in a "natural shallow basin formed by the sand dunes that cover a good portion of the top of Antelope Mesa. These dunes are basically moving dunes, although in some places they have become anchored by vegetation. That was the case with the spot picked for the camp, and the dunes around us gave protection from the extremes of wind." Wat christened the camp "New Awatovi."[1]

For most archaeologists, life in camp is just as important as the digging, at least in memory. Surprisingly few accounts exist of what it is like to live in an archaeological field camp for several months on end. Most popular books about archaeological expeditions highlight the excitement of discoveries or the struggle to get from one place to another when roads are bad. Perhaps one of the most famous tellers of archaeological tales was Agatha Christie, who wrote an autobiographical account of her travels to Iraq and Syria in the early 1930s with her then-new husband, archaeologist Max Mallowan. *Come, Tell Me How You Live* (1946) is largely an account of the people she met and her experiences learning about archaeology and the culture in which the expedition lived and worked for six months at a time. Although Christie's trips were almost contemporary with the work at Awatovi, the two expeditions were vastly different. Mallowan, for example, hired 200 Kurds as his crew and had them build a seven-room adobe house for him and Christie during the first season.

In the Southwest, Sylvester Baxter provided one of the earliest and most detailed accounts of a field camp, originally published in the journal *American Architect and Building News* in 1889.[2] He was in the field in 1887 and 1888 with the Hemenway Southwestern Archaeological Expedition under the direction of Frank Cushing. In 1887, Baxter reached Tempe, Arizona, by train and was met by Frederick W. Hodge, Cushing's assistant. They drove east in a buckboard to Camp Hemenway. In its detail, Baxter's description of the camp is unequaled by anything else I have found in published reports of archaeological projects. "Mr. Cushing's tent," wrote Baxter,

occupying the centre of the camp, has a cozy, home-like appearance, with the touches of decoration and aspect of order that betray the feminine presence [of Mrs. Cushing]. . . . The rest of Camp Hemenway consisted of a tent occupied by Mr. Hodge with his desk and records, a tent adjacent occupied by Mr. C. A. Garlick, the surveyor and practical superintendent, a small tent in which Miss Magill was domiciled, commonly known as the "dog-tent" from its diminutive size and fancied resemblance to a kennel [progenitor to a "pup tent"?], a tent occupied by Dr. ten Kate, a Sibley tent [a large military pyramidal tent] for guests, a large tent for housing the collections, with a shelter of canvass, called by its Spanish name of *ramada*, . . . adjacent as an annex; a tent for the Mexican laborers, a tent for the photograph material and other stores, a shelter for the baggage, a little "dark-tent" for photographing operations, and a shelter for the harnesses.[3]

Farther on in his account, Baxter described a day's routine at Camp Hemenway:

The laborers have early gone afield to carry out the instructions that Mr. Cushing has dictated to his secretary the night before; the two doctors are out with them looking after the skeletons of the Ancients; Mr. Hodge is at his desk in his neatly-kept tent writing out his notes or busy with the accounts; Don Carlos is looking after practical affairs, turning out some needed carpentry at the bench under one of the mesquite trees, or is on the way to Phoenix for supplies, or is at work on his surveys, while Mr. Cushing is out keeping the run of the work on the excavations. . . . Another busy man is the cook, who has a difficult task in suiting the appetites of so many, some of whom have been made dyspeptic by the exigencies of desert fare.[4]

Along the yardstick of archaeological camps in the western United States, New Awatovi fell somewhere between the makeshift ones in which archaeologist Earl H. Morris and his wife, Ann Axtell Morris, roughed it in the Four Corners area in the 1920s and the comfortable house that A.V. Kidder built for his large family at Pecos around the same time. Ann Morris described one of her and her husband's camps this way:

The great overhanging canyon wall which protects the Cliff Dwellings continues up canyon for some distance, sheltering a flat strip of ground forty feet wide and several hundred feet long. . . . It was a corking campground. A tent or two was put up, but most of us preferred to eat and sleep in the open, so rooms were portioned off by running the cars nose-on against the cliff wall. Behind each car was a bedroom, and in the middle we set up the stove and dining-room table. This wide-open arrangement meant that we had to get up in the morning before too many Navajo came to look at us, and that we had to take our baths after dark, but the fresh air and abundance of landscape more than compensated.[5]

In contrast, Kidder's daughter Barbara Kidder Aldana remembered the five comfortable summers she and her family spent at Pecos:

Across the flat land dotted with prairie dog hills, down the arroyo, up the other side and there it was—our house, our dear adobe house of three rooms front and three rooms back with a double sleeping porch to one side. There were several tents with wooden floors and sides and fly roofs, and way to the back the two privies, "funnies" we called them, and the dining room–kitchen to complete the campsite in the lovely sweet-smelling red earth, juniper, piñon, and tall pine country, with the most wonderful people.[6]

Planning the expedition in the winter of 1935–1936, Brew hoped to accommodate his staff in style. He evidently wrote to Russell T. Smith, an architect in Williamsburg, Virginia, who replied with a rough sketch of a U-shaped building encompassing a kitchen, a dining room and lounge, a drafting room, a specimen room, an office, various little storage rooms, and, down one arm of the U, three "dorm" rooms. Brew even went so far as to have Smith draw up a finished blueprint of the building, with a few modifications, including putting the men's and women's dormitories on opposite sides of the building.[7]

Smith's design proved too grand for the budget. In an undated memo, handwritten on a yellow lined sheet, Brew wrote: "Seems good but fear expense too great." Attached to the blueprint is another undated, handwritten note by Brew that reads: "This one was not built. We decided to have each man in his tent with his office and/or laboratory, with a dormitory tent for the undergraduates, and a cook shack dining room." Even this plan never fully materialized: no dormitory tent was ever erected. The camp Brew ultimately did build, however—which evolved as residents added their own

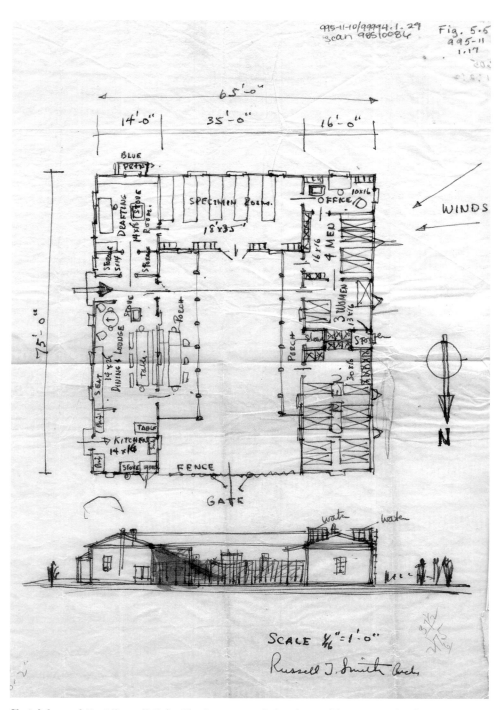

Sketch by architect Russell J. Smith of a proposed structure with quarters for the crew, for eating, and for the archaeological lab, spring 1936.

Arthur Masaytewa pours water into the cistern as Everett Harris readies another jug in the wagon, 1938.

touches — served the staff's needs admirably, drew visitors in droves, and fueled nostalgia for years afterward.

Jo Brew, Al Lancaster, Lin Thompson, and Burt and Hattie Cosgrove were in camp by August 3, 1936, at the swale in the sand dunes that was New Awatovi. Immediately they set up some "temporary" tents — regular canvas tents pegged to the ground, the same ones that had been used the previous year. But during that first week, Al, Lin, and some Hopi men began the carpentry for more permanent quarters, installing floors and half-walls and then upper frames over which they hung 10-by-12-foot canvas tents. The sides of the tents hung below the tops of the half-walls and could be either tied down against the cold or rolled up to catch the breeze.

Most of these "permanent" tents had framed doorways, but only Jo's office tent seems to have had a full door. The others had a sort of half-door on hinges, the same height as the board walls. The top half of the opening could be covered with a canvas flap when necessary. Strips of wood covered the seams between the horizontal wall boards in an attempt to keep out the ever-moving sand, but many of the staff remembered that everything inside the tents was always covered with a thin layer of sand blown from the surrounding dunes.

The area Hattie chose for the Cosgroves' tent became known as Snob Hollow. The women on the staff had their own privy over the dune southeast of Snob Hollow, and the men's latrine was over another dune to the north. A wooden shelf arrangement was

Al Lancaster and a helper building the storage cellar for food and supplies, 1936.

built for Snob Hollow and another for the men, where small basins and soap were kept for morning and evening washing up.

By August 27, the end of the third week, Brew was able to report to Donald Scott that "the building of our camp is well along, we have 7 tents floored and walled, three Hopi tents [up], a cellar, a cement lined six-barrel cistern which gives us a good supply of cold water in camp, and today the carpenter is putting the sisal paper [tarpaper] on the outside of our house [the cook shack]."

The cistern, dug into the dune behind the cook shack, had a cement bottom and sides and a small wooden superstructure that covered it and allowed a bucket to be let down and pulled up. I do not know how big the barrels were that Brew mentioned, but it was probably possible to store 40 or 50 gallons of water in each. Hopi crew member Everett Harris, usually with a helper or two, brought water by wagon and mule team two or three times a week from the spring partway down the north side of the mesa. The cellar, too, was built into the dune behind the cook shack. Lin Thompson used it to store food and supplies.

Brew purchased most of the staff's food and as many other camp necessities as he could from Halderman's Trading Post in nearby Keams Canyon or ordered them through the Jeddito Trading Post, from Babbitt Brothers in Holbrook. At both stores he established accounts that he paid monthly. The museum advanced funds to him either as cash before he left for the field or by deposit to his personal bank account in Malden, Massachusetts, from which he wrote checks to pay the bills in Arizona. When he needed equipment or supplies unavailable in Winslow or Holbrook, he asked the museum to order and ship them to him.

Brew's requests left a trail of unusual correspondence in the museum's archives, such as a letter from Madeline Crosby, the Peabody's secretary, telling Brew: "Your linen tags have been ordered as well as cloth to make your specimen bags. We are having these bags made by students here. We are borrowing a sewing machine for the purpose and will use any more we can lay our hands on for next week."[8] White cloth specimen bags like these can nowadays be purchased from geological supply companies.

As it turned out, even the relatively elaborate camp set up in 1936 was only a beginning. By the start of the 1937 field season, Brew felt a need to expand the facilities. There would be more staff in camp that year, more artifacts to take care of, and more visitors to accommodate. Fisher Motz's wonderful map of the 1937 camp and Edward Beckwith's aerial photograph, taken the same year, show the positioning of most of the tents. In his weekly letter to Scott, dated July 23, Brew summarized what was being done: "I thought best to bring a real carpenter out from Holbrook. . . . In eight days work [he] built four new tents, floors, walls, doors, wash stands, and stripping over the joints on the outside, including the new 14 x 20 pottery tent with seventy-two bins [for sherds]. In addition to the tents, he extended the cook shack ten feet, so that we now have two tables of the size of our last year's dining table."

The extension of the cook shack, Brew wrote, "was a surprisingly simple matter. We pried the front wall loose, laid it gently on the ground, added ten feet of wall and roof, and replaced the front. This was done without even removing the screen door." On the same day he wrote to Madeline Crosby: "This we feel is quite a city; one of the largest in northern Arizona, in fact."

The pottery tent Brew mentioned was to become even more a center of camp life than the cook shack. For Hattie Cosgrove, it was a much-improved work area, and she wrote Scott that "the new quarters make work so much easier for me. I am not so crowded and things seem to go faster for me. I am most proud of the fine sherd tent. It not only makes work easier . . . but it has proved the most comfortable place in camp during the hot days. I have left it so I can open it on all sides and the draft through makes me the envy of camp."

Brew had long tables (one 8 feet and the other 10) and benches built where people could sit to sort and classify pottery. One whole side of the tent, from the floor to the top of the wall frame, was occupied by bins for the storage of artifacts, mostly potsherds. The artifacts came in from the site each evening in apple boxes, and the bins were sized so that an apple box would fit right into each one, tagged and ready to be sorted.[9] Similar bins served the smaller "stone and bone" tent where Dick Wheeler and Dick Woodbury successively resided and worked.

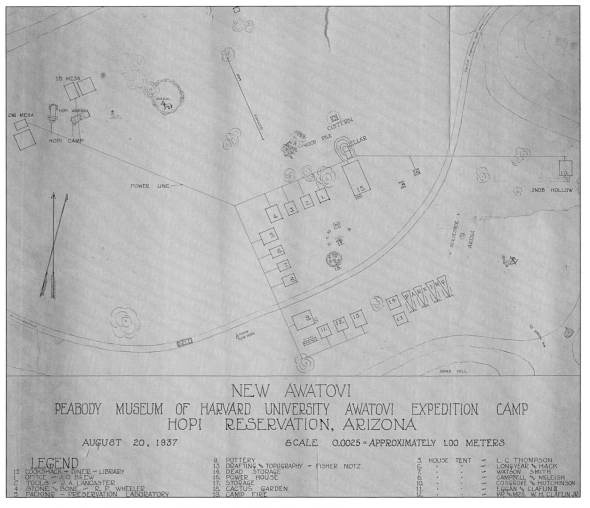

Drawing of the Awatovi field camp by Fisher Motz, 1937.

The cook shack was the only real building constructed at the camp. With front and back doors and real windows, it housed, in addition to Lin Thompson's kitchen, the dining area and the camp's library and bulletin board. The building must originally have measured about 10 by 15 feet, with another 10 feet added to its length in 1937. Lin's kitchen must have been about 5 by 10 feet, and the dining area 10 by 15. The interior was unfinished, with studs left exposed. The walls were of 1-by-10 or 1-by-12 boards, and the exterior and roof were covered with tarpaper. The tarpaper succumbed to the winter winds and had to be replaced every year. The cook shack's ragged sides can be seen in many of the pictures of camp.

Aerial view of camp, August 1937. The Hopi crew's tents are at far left.

In 1938 Hattie suggested another practical addition to the cook shack. Jo described it in his journal this way: "Steve [Alden Stevens] laid out 'Awatovi' on the eastern slope of the cook-shack roof, and Jay [Hooton] is filling in the outlines of the letters with white paint. This probably will not be very visible to aeroplanes, but it will be to automobiles driving into camp. Lin says, 'A fine sense of humor you've got.' But I think he is getting as much fun out of it as any of us, even though it is rather a liberty with his cook-shack."

At the beginning of the 1938 season the staff installed floors and walls in the storage tents, probably in an effort to keep out pack rats. Brew wrote to Scott on July 10: "We took up the floor of Mrs. Cosgrove's [pottery] tent and cleaned the underneath thoroughly. Most of the inhabitants consisted apparently of pack rats, but we found one black widow spider and her web. After cleaning the place out, we relaid the old floor and then put immediately on top of that a tight-fitting new floor of twelve-inch wide boards with a fifty per cent overlap, so that it seems to me that it will be virtually impossible for any spider to get up into the tent through the floor."

Hattie Cosgrove in the pottery tent, probably 1937.

Several new 10-by-12 tents went up in 1938. One was what Brew called an "office" tent, and it seems to have been used exclusively for that purpose. It had shelving along one of its long sides, a typewriter table at one end, a desk at the other, and two long tables. Brew reported that he had purchased them at Jim McKenna's secondhand furniture store in Winslow for $5.92. Another tent was added in Snob Hollow, to be used by Evelyn Nimmo and Haych Claflin.

Yet another welcome amenity that came with the 1938 field season was a quieter electric generator. The 1936 archives are mute about what sort of generator Brew used, although apparently the camp enjoyed electricity that year. The first one must have been noisy, because on August 4, 1937, Brew wrote to Scott that "even without a muffler, the new plant is practically noiseless in comparison with the Battle of Gettysburg we had last year." Earlier he had told Scott how he had a carpenter build "a small powerhouse to hold our Delco [generator], and Al built a concrete floor [for it] with a drain. The planks, to which the motor was bolted when it came, are set in the concrete, and the motor can be removed for winter storage and then set back on the bolts for the next season."

Several poles erected around camp carried the electrical wires. From the ridgepoles of all living and work tents, the cook shack, and each of the Hopi tents hung one elec-

Interior of the cook shack, 1937.

tric light bulb, which was allowed to be on from dark until 10 p.m. Then Al promptly shut off the generator.

In October and November every year, a wood-burning stove in each tent held off freezing temperatures at night. The stovepipe had to pierce the canvas, and Hattie Cosgrove took on the job of sewing the canvas to accommodate the pipes and then repairing the holes at the beginning of the next season.

In 1938, work in a large kiva found under the altar of one of the Franciscan churches had to continue until mid-December because the crew had uncovered well-preserved wall paintings in it that could not be left unprotected over the winter. The excavators had removed the remains of the original roof in order to uncover the kiva below. Brew had a wood stove placed in the kiva, and his journal entry for November 5, 1938, attests once again to the ability of Lancaster and the others to make necessary inventions in the field:

> The lumber for the [new] roof of Wat's kiva came out yesterday [from Winslow] on the mail [truck], and today Al, Wat, and Leland put the roof up, using the legs of our large camera tripod for the main joists. These are douglas fir, 4 x 4, 16 feet long, and should make

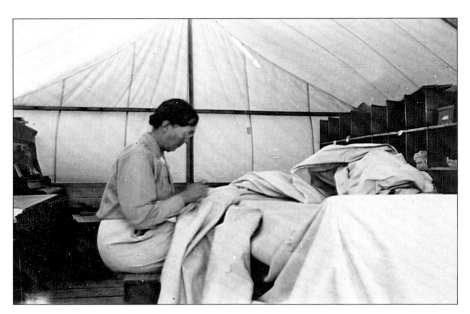
Hattie Cosgrove mending tent canvas torn during windstorms, 1939.

a good support. The three spare windows [originally intended for the cook shack, I believe] were put in for a sky-light, and provide apparently quite sufficient light, not only for working purposes but also for black and white photographs at least. Part of the roof is arranged with six inches between the 1 x 12's and a tarp is thrown over this, so that, by drawing back the tarp, more light can be admitted.

At the end of each season, the staff took down all but one of the canvas tents and stored them, probably at the Jeddito Trading Post. They left one tent up to house Alec Dennis, who was hired as a guard during the winters at a rate of $15 a month. The tent frames and the cook shack remained in place over the winters, and some supplies were stored in the cook shack; Brew mentioned "unloading" them into the plaza at the beginning of the 1938 season. At the beginning of the 1937 season, Brew told Scott: "When we arrived at Awatovi we found the tent frames to be in excellent condition. In the whole camp, two boards only had to be replaced. It was very gratifying as well to find nothing missing. Extra cedar poles and pieces of lumber piled in the open were undisturbed."

Surveying for archaeological sites on rugged Antelope Mesa was not always a job for automobiles. Sometimes, getting to remote and roadless places meant renting, at 50

Top: View of camp from the east sand dune, 1938, showing "AWATOVI" painted on the cook shack roof. Bottom: The field camp under snow, probably 1938. Note the wooden stove pipes in most of the tents.

Wat Smith on the ladder into Kiva 788, which was discovered under the altar of Church 2 and, after its original roof was dismantled, reroofed against the cold in November 1938.

The camp prepared for winter, 1937, showing the tent frame skeletons. Alec Dennis's tent is at far left, and the cook shack is the roofed wooden building in the rear.

cents a day, one or two of the mules or horses that some of the Hopi men rode to work from their villages. But Brew and his staff still needed vehicles to survey efficiently, to transport crew and equipment to sites they wanted to excavate, to haul supplies, and occasionally to get away from camp for a little fun. Like many other archaeologists before and since, they gave their cars names and imputed personalities to them, and some of the vehicles became celebrities in stories told around campfires.

Motor vehicles were simpler machines in the 1930s than they are now, but archaeologists had to know how to maneuver them over rutted tracks, how to avoid getting stuck in sand or mud, and how to make the inevitable repairs themselves. No four-wheel-drive took them confidently off-road; no quick cell-phone call to a mechanic brought a convenient tow truck to the rescue. Ann Axtell Morris summed up the challenges she and her colleagues faced in Canyon del Muerto, Arizona:

The bed of the canyon is invariably bad, worse, or worst. When the sand is not deep and dry it is deep and wet, and safety zones where a driver might land his car with a fair chance of ever starting it again are few and far between. A canyon trip is invariably one headlong rush, with momentum pitted against all the laws of gravity. . . . When the bend is rounded and the old masonry tower [near Antelope Cave] comes into sight, the procedure is somewhat as follows: (1) The driver grips the wheel tighter and steps flat on the

"Pecos," the venerable 1929 Model T Ford, 1939.

gas. (2) All hands on board devote themselves to most conscientiously holding their breaths. (3) When safely by, everyone exhales in relief.[10]

Archaeologist Neil Judd, in his 1968 autobiography, *Men Met along the Trail,* told a wonderful tale—if partly apocryphal—about Earl Morris and his Model T, "Old Black." They were "far out among the Lukachukai Mountains one day [when] the dry sand proved too much, and Old Black burned out a bearing. Morris contemplated his predicament overnight and then replaced the bearing with a square of bacon rind and so finished out the season. You don't get bacon rind like that any more!"[11]

The Ford Model T turned out to be the ideal field vehicle in the Southwest in the 1920s and 1930s. Judd had more to say about the famous vehicles: "Model T's were everywhere in the 1920s. Kidder's 'Old Blue' and Earl Morris's 'Old Black' were only two of a long and faithful lineage. Like Navaho sheep they stood well off the ground; they were designed to straddle high centers, to go where any other four-legged creature could go. From the time they got their first wagons at Fort Defiance and elsewhere after Bosque Redondo, Navaho men drove those wagons on trails which they had formerly ridden horseback. After Model T's replaced wagons, the same old horse trails were traveled by Model T's."[12]

The Awatovi Expedition had as many as three company vehicles at any one time. "Pecos" was a 1929 Model T Ford originally owned by the Claflins. (Other than its

The Cosgroves' Dodge truck fitted out with benches and with wire mesh sides for packing supplies, 1937.

name, it had nothing to do with Kidder's project at Pecos Pueblo, which had ended in 1927.) Brew had used Pecos in his fieldwork at Alkali Ridge and had driven it from Santa Fe to Antelope Mesa for the 1935 field season. He had a great fondness for Pecos and mentioned it regularly in his letters and journals. In his first letter to Donald Scott during the 1935 season, dated September 28, he said, "Pecos is much maligned in recent years. It runs better than ever and pulls through sand in second speed that the V-8s around here cannot negotiate in 1st speed. I have already been offered an even trade on a V-8, two new Chevrolets, and a Packard."

Although Pecos lasted through all five years of the expedition, it was not entirely trustworthy, and in 1936 Brew acquired a new sedan. After the Claflin family's visit to camp that summer, Brew wrote Scott: "In reply to your question about the new car, I believe it is to be a 'gift from heaven.' My understanding is that you are to purchase it with money given to the Museum for that purpose"—presumably by Claflin.[13] After using this car for two seasons, Brew sold it for $475 and applied the money to "the purchase of a 1938 model of my selection." His choice, a Plymouth sedan, though hardly the stuff of legend, became a mainstay during the final two seasons as Pecos became increasingly unreliable.

To Pecos and the sedans, the Cosgroves added a Dodge pickup truck that the museum had purchased earlier for their use in archaeological work in New Mexico.

It was eventually outfitted with wire sides and benches to carry crew and equipment. A few other staff members brought their own vehicles and made them available to the expedition. Alden Stevens arrived by car in 1935 and probably in 1938. Ned Hall, Wat Smith, and John Longyear also came in their own cars and used them to help carry crew and staff members between sites, to Keams Canyon, to the Hopi towns for visits and dances, and on sight-seeing trips. Longyear recalled in 1991 that his Oldsmobile was ill suited for the road into camp, because its clearance was too low.

In either 1937 or 1938, Brew posted on a bulletin board in the cook shack a notice headed "Instructions for Driving Staff Cars." It explained that "because of the unusual nature of the roads over which we drive, certain special regulations are necessary which are not usually essential on modern highways. Members of the staff are required to observe the following rules while driving staff cars. It is suggested that owners of private cars observe these rules also while associated with the expedition." The list offered guidelines for safe driving such as "Always slow down for stock and wagons," and it cautioned that "all staff cars should be checked before leaving camp for gas, water, shovel, and jack." It mandated a maximum speed for each company vehicle and exhorted: "Don't try to find out how fast the staff cars will go. They will all go faster than it is safe to drive on most of the roads we use." As a final safety precaution, the notice instructed: "Drivers must always blow the horn when coming into camp. The horn is relatively inexpensive, and a liberal use is suggested on blind corners and roller-coaster roads."

Besides extreme driving conditions, the staff coped with extremes of weather. Summer and fall in the Southwest are generally hot and dry, but violent summer thunderstorms can move quickly through the countryside, dropping heavy rain. On Antelope Mesa, as throughout the Southwest, one can see these storms coming from many miles away and be prepared. Dick Woodbury's letters home described the dramatic changeability of the weather at Awatovi. In July 1938 he wrote: "This has been a hot day, 102 degrees in the shade, and yesterday was the same. But last night I had a blanket over me. And now it is cloudy and raining in five or six places around the horizon." The following month he reported: "It is rather wet for working as it rained hard for a couple of hours Sunday night, as well as for a few minutes Saturday afternoon. But the thunder and lightning are beautiful and grand."

Because all the expedition's field seasons except the last ran into November or December, the staff and crew also had to tolerate cold temperatures and even snow. The biggest weather problems, though, were wind and blowing sand. The late summer and fall of 1935 had been especially plagued. On November 3 that year, Brew wrote to Scott: "Last week we rode out a two day sandstorm with a net loss of two tents—one occupied by Hopis [and the other] one a 'company tent,' the one we had on the 1931 trip. . . . The storm returned with even greater intensity Saturday. . . . Today the wind has gone and it is clear and cold. . . . We have had two brief snowstorms but have missed the big snows of the north. . . . Pecos lost her top but we have a makeshift arrangement which I believe is better than the original. The Ethiopian Campaign has nothing on this." (The Italian army had invaded the deserts of Ethiopia in early October 1935.)

Expedition members vividly remembered the wind, the blowing sand, and the beauty of storms in the distance. One story repeated in later years featured a sandstorm and dust devil that came through camp in 1937. Ken MacLeish was working on his dissertation, keeping notes on three-by-five cards. The wind took his cards—hundreds of them—and blew them all over Antelope Mesa. The staff and crew spent a good deal of time rounding them up. This episode was so dramatic that Penny Davis, who must have heard of it around the campfire, swore it happened while she was there, but it didn't—Ken was at Awatovi only in 1937 and Penny only in 1939.

Penny did have strong personal memories of the weather. In 1989 she recalled:

The first three weeks, the wind blew incessantly except at night, and I spent a lot of time mending tent flys and replacing grommets. I believe I did not know what a grommet was until then. Another problem with the wind blowing all the time was that everything was covered with sand. Every morning before we left for the site we would batten down the tents, and every night when we got back there would be sand all over the inside—a fine layer of sand over everything, even inside the foot locker. We were also well dusted with sand, particularly our hair, so that a quick washing needed to be done quite often.

But except for requiring the staff to spend time repairing wind damage to the tents, the weather seldom stopped work for long during any of the five field seasons. Sometimes the crew had to wear goggles to protect their eyes from the sand, but if wind and blowing sand were too bad, there was always something to be done in the labs.

When Ted Kidder visited on August 23, 1939, he was able to write in his journal: "It's a grand camp, the fifteen or so tents and the cook-shack arranged in neat lines around a rectangular sandy plaza, the whole in a small bowl among the dunes so that they get the benefit of a little shelter from the winds that lash this open mesa top." By the end of the Awatovi Expedition, New Awatovi had become a comfortable home to many staff and crew members, whether for a single season or for year-after-year returns.

High spirits at New Awatovi. Left to right: John Hack,
Evelyn Nimmo, Haych Claflin, Carlos García-Robiou, 1938.

Life in Camp

Life in an archaeological camp can be a wonderful memory—or a lingering nightmare. The outcome depends mostly on food, basic comforts, and the quality of the social life, although it also helps to have good weather and an interesting site to dig. People will grumble if they don't like the food or have no chance to bathe now and then. If the beds are uncomfortable, people can't sleep and work is affected. If cliques form or there is a troublemaker on the crew, discontent undermines morale. So does boredom, if there is nothing to do after hours and on weekends.

When the food is good, the research interesting, and the weather fine, when the accommodations are adequate, the people compatible, and the diversions enjoyable, then living in an archaeological camp is an experience worth treasuring. And so it was at Awatovi. "Jo has accumulated an efficient and smoothly running staff of evidently happy people," wrote A.V. Kidder in his journal on August 20, 1939. "I've never seen a nicer feeling, nor a more 'pull-together' camp." H. Warren Shepard, when he visited camp with his daughter Anna Shepard in 1938, noted in his diary: "A sign by the road as we came over the sage-brush covered sand dunes that surround the camp, says 'Slow Densely Settled.' This sign is indicative of the spirit of the camp. They do not work too hard and there is laughter mingled with conversation when they are not actually at work. I do not mean there was lack of seriousness. The spirit I mention simply contributed to contentment and congenial cooperation."

In one sense there is little routine on an archaeological project. Every day may bring a surprising find or a new revelation in understanding the site. Yet there can be a sameness to the ordinary chores of both camp life and archaeology—recall Mott Davis's experience in "holding the level rod" day in and day out for two weeks. Washing pieces of broken pottery, keeping meticulous records, and writing tiny numbers on artifacts may be incredibly tedious to some. But at Awatovi, at least in memory, no one was ever bored, and there were plenty of diversions. That the Awatovi staff and crew had

Cooling off in the cattle tank at the Tallahogan Spring, 1939. Left to right: Mott Davis, Haych Claflin, John Hack.

electricity, great food and plenty of it, and things to do in good company after hours was no accident. Jo Brew especially enjoyed the social life of archaeological camps and saw to it that his colleagues stayed happy and entertained.

Although New Awatovi boasted no dorm rooms or running water, the staff were not exactly roughing it. To some of them the camp seemed almost plush. John Longyear, just arrived from fieldwork in Utah, wrote to his future wife in early August 1937: "I am sitting here in my luxurious tent, on a real chair and writing [on a typewriter] at a fine table. I can see right now that I am going to be living a life of indolent leisure here."

Longyear was the only staff member who mentioned in his letters taking a shower. He told his fiancée: "We all took a shower. While bathing, we can watch the sunset on the Hopi buttes, which are scattered all over the desert about ten or fifteen miles away. It must be the most beautiful shower-bath in the world." Apparently this wasn't literally a shower; it probably involved buckets and a trough down the side of the canyon, where drinking water was also gathered from a pipe inserted into the spring. The drinking water—also used for cooking, brushing teeth, and so on—was kept in the cistern near the cook shack. On his way to Awatovi in July 1936, Brew had visited Frank H. H. Roberts's field camp at the Lindenmeir site in Colorado and admired the showers there. "He has a splendid shower bath at camp, which I shall copy with improvements for our more rigorous climate," he wrote to Scott on July 26.

Left: Jo Brew having his morning shave, 1938. Right: Evelyn Nimmo washing a few clothes with part of her weekly ration of water, as Haych Claflin looks on, 1938.

But in fact no showers were ever built for the Awatovi camp, and nothing in the documents indicates why. Later Longyear wrote: "I got good and dirty, and last evening I took a bath in the wash tub. There are so many horses drinking out of our shower bath reservoir that there is no water left to take showers." Because no one remembers showers in the sense we think of them now, I believe John might have been referring to pouring a bucket of water over his head.

The trough attached to the spring from which the camp drinking water came seems to have been where people bathed and cooled off. Mott and Penny Davis both remembered that in 1939 each person received a five-gallon can of water for use in camp and had to make it last for brushing teeth, cleaning hands, and shaving for the remainder of the week. Work clothes were taken to Keams Canyon weekly to be washed, but staff members washed their personal clothing by hand at camp with the remains of their five gallons. Penny recalled: "The trick was to use as little [water] as possible for everything, including having water do double-duty sometimes, i.e., pour water into the basin, about 2 inches worth, rinse the hair, letting the water go back into the basin; use this water for the initial washing of the 'shirt-of-the-day'; hang the shirt outside the tent while the rest of the ablutions take place, and by the time you finish them, the shirt is dry. I remember that in the beginning we all ran out of water before the new ration came, but after a few weeks we had water left over. You only need half a cup of water for brushing your teeth, for instance. It was not a particular hardship, just an adjustment."

　✛

Few women made archaeology their profession in the 1930s, but women certainly took an interest in archaeology, and projects other than Awatovi had women as participants. The University of New Mexico field school at Chaco Canyon in the 1930s, for instance, was directed by Florence Hawley (Ellis) and boasted several women on the crew each year. Jo Brew was never averse to having women on field projects. Still, as the first woman at Awatovi, Hattie Cosgrove felt some trepidation that her presence might upset what she called a "normal" field camp. Within a week of her and Burt's arrival in 1936, she wrote to Donald Scott:

> Being the lone woman in camp I seem to be a sort of privileged one, for my house [tent] was the first to be erected after the temporary quarters were set up. The first two nights Burt and I slept in our truck bed. . . . I chose the site for my house for I thought that after they had had a man's camp for the past years [presumably both at Alkali Ridge and on Antelope Mesa in 1935] they might find it inconvenient to have a woman in their midst. I thought it best all way around for our tent to be slightly apart from the general row of quarters and am glad we did so, for it has worked out splendidly.

Hattie tried to maintain some standards of propriety in camp, but she was as pragmatic as the next person. In the spring of 1938, when she learned that Evelyn Nimmo was going to join the expedition that summer, she sent the young woman many words of advice. This was Evelyn's first trip away from New England, not to mention her first dig, and Hattie explained: "There is one big thing to remember—no one wears decent looking clothes. We all are awful looking. It is a great place to wear out old underwear, shoes, etc. I am trying to make up my mind to wear skirts this year instead of the old pants I usually wear, but when I think of it I just don't see how it will be possible."[1]

Certainly the Awatovi archives hold no pictures of women in shorts and halter tops or men in cutoffs, as one would see on a dig in the Southwest today. Blue jeans were not the ubiquitous garment they are now, but pants were the order of the day. Even Hattie, in her sixties, often wore pants tucked into knee-high, lace-up boots. But she wore dresses when she could, particularly when going to Winslow, Keams Canyon, or Hopi dances, and sometimes even at the site. Her biographer, Carolyn Davis, tells a wonderful story of one occasion when a Japanese photographer from *Life* magazine was visiting. Everyone was getting ready to go to the Hopi mesas for a dance, and Hattie had changed into her more "formal" attire. "Mr. Natori looked blankly for a moment at Hattie, then bowed and apologized. In his accented English he then explained that he hadn't recognized Mrs. Cosgrove 'without her pants on.'"[2]

Left: Hattie Cosgrove in boots and riding pants, holding Everett Harris's baby sister, Harriet, who was named for her, 1938. Right: Hattie dressed in her going-to-town clothes.

Hattie's casual Western practicality contrasts with the formality archaeologist Alden Hayes described for A.V. Kidder's camp at Pecos only 10 or 15 years earlier. The "elitist East" approach of Kidder's camp undoubtedly reflected his somewhat Brahmin life in Massachusetts, and it sounds more like the camps of the late nineteenth century in the world of Classical archaeology: "The amenities were preserved in the camps of the past, and Kidder ran his like a New England preparatory school. . . . Ladies wore skirts, and the men shaved with regularity. Neckties were worn, partly from habit, but also as an unobtrusive symbol of status—workmen expected their supervisors to look the part."[3]

Although the lifestyle may have been more relaxed at Awatovi than at Pecos, the group residing in camp still faced certain requirements. Posted on the bulletin board in the cook shack, together with the rules for driving cars, was another sheet about what people had to do if they were in camp during a storm:

CAMP DUTY

In case of storm – RAIN or SAND

1. See that all tents are closed.
2. Close ventilators in powerhouse.
3. Close flap of dead-storage tents.
4. Close windows of truck and Ford sedan.
5. Place all canvas chairs under cover.
6. Remove letters from mailbox (rain only).
7. Be sure tarp is covering lumber pile.
8. Keep top of cistern closed at all times.

ELECTRIC LIGHTS

THE ELECTRIC LIGHT PLANT

WILL BE SHUT OFF AT 10 PM.

The bulletin board also carried newspaper clippings about the Awatovi work and other finds in the Southwest and cartoons appropriate to archaeology or to group relationships. Some of these, taken from the bulletin board at the end of the 1939 season, survive. The cartoons obviously originated in *Esquire* magazine, which seems to have been a favorite.

For camp residents' comfort in their tents, Brew abandoned the canvas cots he provided in 1935 for folding iron cots with mattresses and a table or converted box to be used beside the bed. People usually kept their clothing in a small trunk or footlocker at the foot of the bed. All tents had at least one chair, either a straight wooden one or the folding canvas variety. Campers brought their chairs with them out to the campfire in the evening. The only photographs of the interior of one of the living tents are some that Carlos García-Robiou took of his own tent. It is impossible to tell, of course, whether the creaseless bed and neatness of the room were for the benefit of the photograph or reflected his normal habits.

The living and working tents surrounded three sides of a "plaza" where the evening campfire glowed and where Hattie started a cactus garden in 1936. The campfire itself was an informal spot with a few rocks to delimit where the fire should be. A neat row of rocks encircled the garden, which might well have begun as a spot where cacti grew naturally. In 1937, Leland Dennis built a miniature adobe pueblo to adorn the garden.

The only permanent fixture near the campfire was an old, stuffed leather chair, which slowly disintegrated over the years. Warren Shepard, in his diary of his 1938 visit, recalled this feature: "When I think of Awatovi, the outstanding figure is Joe [*sic*] Brew in his soiled and out of shape 10 gallon hat, and then the great upholstered

Harvard Reveals Golden Age of Hopi Indians

Early inhabitants of Arizona region found to have known use of coal as fuel — Friendliness developed with first Europeans to come—Records of art excavated.

Courtesy Peabody Museum

Digging Out Desert Civilization

Upper—Excavations in Western Mound at Awatovi. Lower Left—Sitkyatki Ware, Last Historic Period, Highest Point in Pue Ceramics. Lower Right—Bone Implements, Tubular Bone Beads and Whistle

Discovery that coal was used as a fuel by Hopi Indians in America several centuries before the continent was found by Columbus was announced today by Harvard University.

Ashes, clinkers and coal dust found in ruins of the pueblo village of Awatovi, northern Arizona, indicated the fuel was used for both heating and cooking, possibly as early as 1100 or 1200 A. D.

It was the earliest use of coal in the United States, John O. Brew, of Harvard's Peabody Museum, director of two expeditions to the village, declared, antedating the Spanish conquest of the southwest by two to four hundred years.

Although coal was known in ancient China and Greece and has been used in Great Britain since the Middle Ages, it was not discovered by the descendants of the American settlers until about 150 years ago. Extensive use did not develop in the United States until the nineteenth century.

Mr. Brew and his corps of eight to 10 white men and 15 Indian helpers found fireplaces in the ruins of Awatovi filled with coal clinkers last fall. They hope to add to their knowledge on this point on a third expedition, commencing in about a week.

Two hearths were found in each room at Awatovi, Mr. Brew said, one containing ashes of wood and the other of coal. Why the Indians thus used both fuels has not yet been learned, the archeologist stated. Those at Awatovi apparently were the only Indians to use coal.

In 1540, Coronado's men marched through the southwest. Awatovi was the first Hopi village they encountered. Throughout the ensuing century and a half of Spanish domination, this town had the closest relations of all the Hopi with the whites.

Whether the Spaniards learned to use coal, Mr. Brew did not know. The fuel, a lignite of many grades, mostly poor, often crops out of the surface of the ground in the southwest, visible to the naked eye. It is extensively mined today.

Besides the use of coal, the two Harvard expeditions have learned many other details of the social, religious, mechanical and artistic life of this group of Hopis who resided in the Jeddito Valley from about 1100 until the town was destroyed and its people massacred by neighboring tribes in 1700.

Coming of the Spanish

The Awatovi community had joined with the other pueblos in a revolt against the Spanish in 1680,

two seasons at Awatovi, beginning a long-term program of excavation of hundreds of Hopi ruins scattered along the windswept mesa rim of the Jeddito Valley. Located in the approximate center of the once vast spread of the pueblos, the Jeddito Valley is part of the area in which this peaceful agricultural race gradually concentrated, as savage nomad hunters and recurrent droughts forced the abandonment of outlying small towns during the early centuries of the Christian era.

Thus, this region forms part of the oldest continuously inhabited area in the United States, containing an archeological record of the rise and fall of a great people.

Harvard workers at Jeddito have discovered remains showing that some of the sites were inhabited by

How to Pronounce Names Indicated

Here is the way John O. Brew of the Peabody Museum of Harvard University pronounces the principal Indian names connected with his excavations:

Hopi—Hope'-ee.
Awatovi—A-wot'-o-vee.

the basket makers, pioneer Indian farmers of the southwest before the development of the characteristic pueblo civilization. From this first occupation, probably roughly about 300 A. D. until the present, there is a steady record of human habitation

in the Jeddito Valley, the Har test diggings have disclosed. area is still an important cent Hopi life.

Mr. Brew's excavations reveal Awatovi was founded in the "[pueblo period," perhaps about A. D., and that the debris in buried rooms contain a contin record of human habitation for six centuries.

Although some archeologists assumed that the western moun Awatovi covered the remains huge prehistoric "apartment ho the Harvard tests show that thi not the case. Beginning as a s house of a few rooms only, addit rooms were added from time to t but all the rooms were not occu at the same time, since older re were filled with debris and the ones were built on or beside ther

This article about the expedition, believed to have been clipped from the *Christian Science Monitor* of June 16, 1937, was posted on the cook shack bulletin board.

Luke Kawanusea and his wife, Vivian Tewanyinima, enjoying
cartoons in *Esquire* magazine, 1938.

rocking chair at the camp fire. It was once leather covered. Too cumbersome to move,
it has remained there through sunshine and shower. The end of one rocker is burned
off. Bulging springs, though, proclaim that all is not lost. 'Old age hath yet his honor
and his toil.'"

The chair was known affectionately as "the Throne," and it came, like so many
other things in camp, from McKenna's store in Winslow. Dick Woodbury nostalgically
remembered the fate of this renowned chair:

> By the end of the 1939 season it was risky to sit down on—many springs threatened to
> come through the dilapidated covering and cause bodily harm. It was probably near the
> end of the summer that Jo decided it should be burned—ceremoniously, of course. I
> don't recall details, but I did announce that "If anyone finds a silver dollar in the ashes,
> it's mine!" It was assumed that I'd lost one, but actually it just seemed a good idea in
> case one turned up. A few coins did appear, nickels or dimes and quarters, I think. The
> wooden frame was pretty well consumed and the springs carted off, leaving a charred
> ashy spot where The Throne had been.

Like the Throne, the camp cars and the staff's adventures driving them over
unpaved reservation roads fostered long-remembered tales and more than one

Hattie's cactus garden with Leland Dennis's miniature adobe house,
1937. The pottery tent is the large one behind it on the right.

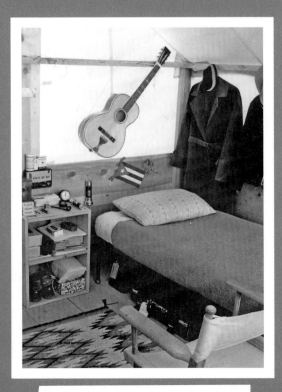

Carlos García-Robiou's neat tent, 1938.

The decomposing Throne, 1939.

Searching through the ashes of the incinerated Throne, 1939. Left to right: Dick Woodbury, Wat Smith, Penny Davis, Evelyn Brew, Happy Foote. They found $1.75 in spare change.

Jo Brew stuck in the mud near Awatovi, 1939.

nickname. A turn in the "Cactus Highway"—a track through the dunes that led from camp to the gravel road connecting Holbrook with Keams Canyon—became known in late 1938 and 1939 as "Charlie's Corner." "Charlie" was a nickname that Lin Thompson bestowed on Evelyn Nimmo, and she told me how this spot in the road got its name:

> During my first year at Awatovi, a group of us started off in Pecos. At one point . . . I asked to be allowed to drive. My driving experience was minimal, my experience with Pecos even more so, and the two-rut road was dry and full of loose sand. While simultaneously negotiating a hill and a curve, I lost control of the car and hit a tree. It was a very small tree (and also the only tree anywhere around), so that it bent over under the weight of Pecos and its contents, and then sprang up again underneath. We could go neither forward nor backward, and had left camp without any helpful tools [much against the rules]. Fortunately, some guests happened along just then and rescued us. Since there was no damage either to car or to passengers, we went on with the excursion. Afterwards the place was known as Charlie's Corner in honor of the only person who had succeeded in getting a car up a tree.

Cars, especially those of visitors, were always getting stuck on the sandy road leading into camp from the highway. Guests would appear walking into camp, and several people would go back down the road to dig and push them out. It was fortunate that some of the staff were handy with auto repairs as well. Both Wat Smith and Penny Davis remembered one occasion when knowledge of the workings of a combustion engine came in handy. Smith's version of the story goes like this:

> Our supply of gasoline, held in a 50-gallon drum within the plaza area, was inevitably contaminated by water condensing out of the ambient air. When a car's tank was filled from a nearly empty drum, some water would be carried along with it. One morning, en route to Kawaika-a with Carlos as a passenger, our engine stopped. Investigation indicated water droplets in the carburetor and probably the fuel lines all the way back to the tank. There followed several long moments of silent cogitation. Suddenly, Carlos was galvanized into frenzied action. He jumped up on the rear bumper and rocked the car up and down, shouting, "Make an emulsion! Make an emulsion!" as we looked on, bemused. It took a moment for the rest of us to apprehend what was going on. But, of course! If you shook the car with sufficient violence, the water would be temporarily emulsified in the gasoline, which could then be ignited in the engine. We joined in with vigor, the car bucked and bounced, an emulsion was created, and the engine roared. A salutary lesson for any motorist on the long, long trail.[4]

Jo Brew was not one who could have been called knowledgeable about auto mechanics, but he was inventive. Years later, Evelyn Brew recalled a trip she and Jo took soon after he purchased the expedition's brand new 1938 Plymouth:

> On our first trip to Walpi to attend a dance, Jo could not get enough power to get the car up the very steep hill [to the top of First Mesa]. In those days one was not supposed to drive a new car above a moderate speed, and to secure compliance, governors were placed in the cars to prevent faster speeds. Jo got out, opened the hood, and removed three things, one of which he was pretty sure must be the governor. The car responded positively and we made it to the top of the mesa. On his next trip to town, Jo handed the three items to the garage mechanic and asked him to put back the two that weren't the governor.

⛌

Al Lancaster went out to the site every day to supervise the Hopi men who were digging, and Brew usually accompanied him first thing in the morning to discuss progress and plans for the day. Hattie Cosgrove tackled the sherds that had been brought in the previous evening and assigned work to her helpers, just as Dick Wheeler and later Dick Woodbury did for the stone and bone. Wat Smith continuously refined his techniques for exposing and recording the kiva murals, and a cadre of people helped him scrape the plaster carefully off the designs.

In mid-July 1938, soon after that year's field season had started, Dick Woodbury, on his first archaeological expedition, described this routine to his family back in Washington, D.C.: "Things are really under way now. About 15 Hopis on the dig; Mrs. Cosgrove sorting sherds and cataloguing good types; Helen Claflin and I drawing and cataloguing the bone and stone objects; Harold [Winchester] helping the foreman (Al Lancaster) tag things as they are found with room, level, and material; Evelyn Nimmo typing records in the office tent; Jo Brew keeping an eye on everything; and Lin Thompson turning out three superb meals a day."

The day always started with Lin stepping out the front door of the cook shack and shouting a loud yo-ho to wake everyone at 6:00 a.m. He served breakfast at 6:30, and everyone was ready for his or her assigned work by 7:30. At noon, staff and crew took a two-hour break for lunch and rest in the heat of the day. Chores resumed from 2:00 to 5:30, followed by supper at 6:00 p.m. This was the schedule for five and sometimes five and a half days a week.

Everyone remembered that after supper, people usually sat around the campfire and talked. A few might play horseshoes or go sliding on a favorite sand dune until dark. Jo

Crew and staff heading out to work in the morning, 1939. Penny has her drawing board under her arm.

often mentioned in his journal the scores from games of pinochle and occasionally crib-bage. The Hopi men sometimes played cards in the cook shack or looked at scholarly publications about their people. Dick Woodbury remembered that one of the Hopi eld-ers asked Brew to remove some of the anthropological books from the library because the younger men should not see the descriptions of Hopi ceremonies and katsinas. Al Lancaster's field notebook for 1938 corroborates Woodbury's memory: "Sylvan [Nash] says that Dr. Fewks [*sic*] describes the initiation dance so accurately that Gibson [Namoki] would not let George [Dewakuku] and Luke [Hovelo] read about it. Because these boys could not be initiated [yet] and should not know about the ceremony."

When the food is good at an archaeological camp, mealtimes are everyone's favorite part of the daily routine. Jeff Reid and Stephanie Whittlesey, in their history of the University of Arizona's field school at Grasshopper Pueblo, observed that "cooks are very near the top of the camp hierarchy, often more important than the director. . . . [A] field school runs on its belly, and the cook can make or break the field season."[5] Julian Hayden, writing of his experiences in camp with his father at Kiet Siel, Arizona, in 1933, described with loving memory the food prepared by their cowboy cook:

> Josh Allen was a wonderful cook and we ate like kings, or like cowboys on the roundup.
> Always a five-gallon bucket of pinto beans buried simmering in the fire pit . . . Dutch
> oven biscuits like thistledown, steaks and roasts and stews and fresh liver from Navajo
> beef which was driven in regularly, stood overnight, and butchered the next morning. It

Climbing back up a large sand dune after sliding down, 1939. Left to right: Al Lancaster, Dick Woodbury, Penny Davis, Bob Jones.

was so cold in April that our favorite breakfast, with pancakes, bacon, and eggs, was a large enamelware bowl containing a biscuit drowned in half-and-half bacon grease and Karo [syrup].[6]

Lin Thompson was a cook of the Josh Allen school, and his fame is a matter of legend as well as fact. In 1935 Katharine Bartlett, of the Museum of Northern Arizona, visited Brew's camp on Antelope Mesa and reported that "he has the finest cook extant in archaeological camps."[7] John Longyear, Evelyn Nimmo, and Dick Woodbury all wrote home about memorable meals Lin served. On August 5, 1937, for example, Longyear wrote: "For supper tonight we had steak, chile, lima beans, potatoes, beets, two kinds of salad, cherry-ade, coffee, tea, pineapples, coffee meringue pie, cake, biscuits, and cookies." On July 11 the following year, Nimmo told how "for breakfast this morning we had prunes, cereal, coffee, hot cakes with syrup, hash, and fried eggs." The next month, Woodbury wrote home describing a "sample menu for this noon: roast beef, canned asparagus, canned whole tomatoes (cold), coffee, fresh rolls, mashed potatoes and gravy, coconut bread pudding. Lin makes cake about twice a week. He makes all our bread, and rolls or muffins nearly every day; pancakes every morning as well as hash; cookies twice a week or so, and cinnamon rolls of the most scrumptious sort every few days."

Some of the crew in the cook shack on an evening in 1939. Larry Gallegos is third from left.

Everyone remembered Lin's cinnamon rolls and pancakes. Indeed, by the time he again worked for Jo in the field after World War II (starting in 1949 with the Upper Gila Expedition in New Mexico), his fame had spread. Having been part of that expedition near Quemado, New Mexico, during the summers of 1950 and 1951 (when we mailed to Penny the batch of cinnamon rolls that inspired her "Ode" on p. vi),[8] I can testify to the intoxicating smell of Lin's chocolate doughnuts frying while I worked in the lab tent. Evelyn Nimmo Brew suffered the temptations of Lin's baking at Awatovi. "Since I did most of my work in camp," she told me, "I was in double jeopardy—I got little exercise and was within yards of the kitchen where Lin was concocting his miracles. The most dangerous of these were cinnamon rolls, which were ready for consumption, warm, in the middle of the morning. I put on ten pounds my first summer there."

The bulk food Lin needed was ordered by Jo by telephone from Jeddito Trading Post to the Babbitt Brothers store in Holbrook. Babbitt delivered the goods to Jeddito, and one of the staff picked them up a couple of times a week. Brew's journal tells us that he sometimes fretted over the effect the cost of food was having on his budget. In his entry for July 19, 1938, he noted: "Pinto beans at 7 cents a pound seem rather high, but then we are used to figuring the farmers' price on these, which at present is 4.7

Left: Lin Thompson making his mouth-watering cinnamon rolls, 1938. Right: Lin butchering meat for supper.

cents a pound. Klim [powdered whole milk] costs around 70 cents a can and Lin uses one can every three days for the cereal cream. This is too high, and it will be eliminated after we finish the present case." He probably had Lin substitute condensed milk.

Some fresh food, particularly vegetables and meat, was purchased from Halderman's Trading Post in Keams Canyon. "Got a dozen very good melons for 50 cents and two dozen cucumbers for 20 cents," Jo recorded in his journal on July 16, 1938. "In general, though they do not run as good as this, prices are lower this year. Halderman's beef is still at 12 cents a pound."

Al Lancaster often brought vegetables from home after visiting his family in Colorado, as well as large quantities of eggs—30 dozen one time, according to a note in the journal in November 1938. Evelyn Brew remembered going to Halderman's with Jo one time when he purchased a live ewe: "Jo and I went off in the Plymouth and brought back a sheep that bleated all the way back to camp. Lin butchered it while we were at dinner. I don't remember what he made of it except a stew that I was completely unable to eat, having made its acquaintance at a happier time."

Fresh meat, butter, eggs, and other perishable items that had to be kept cold in the absence of an ice box, much less a refrigerator, were, as Evelyn recalled, placed in a wire mesh box that was covered with wet burlap and hung from the piñon tree behind the cook shack. Anyone who has traveled in the dry Southwest knows this method of keeping water cool. The low humidity and breeze would have evaporated the water, keeping butter hard and meat fresh for several days.

Dick Woodbury remembered another occasion when fresh meat appeared in camp:

> Someone Jo knew (and they were legion) arrived in camp one day with a huge side of buffalo in the back seat. It had been donated for the use of the Indians at the Gallup Ceremonial and was from a herd (perhaps in Wyoming or Montana, I'm not sure) that had been culled. The problem was that [the man] had been on the road a good many days and didn't think the meat would last till he got to Gallup. But this was no problem for Lin. He said it looked great, washed it down with vinegar, butchered it, and served us steaks for dinner that night.

Dick also said that some of the meat went to the Hopi men in their camp. The Hopis prepared their own meals, and Jo's journals hint that the First and Second Mesa men ate around separate campfires. Now and then the journals list canned food for the Hopis among the groceries to be ordered, and as I mentioned earlier, they sometimes shot jackrabbits for supper.

Lin Thompson seldom ate with the others, being busy in the kitchen, and any woman who offered to help with the dishes was summarily dismissed. Evelyn remembered approaching the kitchen one day when she smelled cinnamon rolls, and Lin, who didn't like interruptions while he worked, said, "Well, Charlie, what the hell kind of chocolate meringue pie do you want for lunch?" Despite his brusqueness, Lin could listen and did sometimes contribute to conversations. He had a wonderful wit, told good stories, and loved puns. Mott Davis recalled: "I think I established my status with Lin when, at a meal, we were talking about the various mesa affiliations of the Hopis and I said that I was from Mesa-chusetts. After appropriate groans around the table, the conversation continued, but for some time Lin could be heard back in his area of the kitchen, chuckling and muttering 'Mesachusetts.'"

Evelyn Brew, after mentioning that she had gained 10 pounds because of Lin's meals, went on: "One evening at the pinochle game, I was sitting between Lin and Al. One of the players remarked to Hattie, 'We have a round robin (kings and queens of all suits) between us, Hattie.' Lin's instant comment was, 'We have a round robin between *us*, haven't we, Al?'"

The only one of Lin's stories known to have been recorded appears in Warren Shepard's diary: "Lin could tell a story as well as cook. There was a question at breakfast table one morning about pack rats leaving something in place of what they carry off. Lin said that was because they always had something in their mouths, and had to drop it before anything else could be taken, and then he told of a camp where silverware was gradually disappearing. One night, they were up later than usual over a game of cards, when they saw a pack rat come in. Assured that here was the thief, one of them picked up his gun and fired. The rat was not killed, but badly scared, for the next morning the missing silver had been returned."

Lin created decorated birthday cakes for the staff and in 1939 turned out a magnificent layered wedding cake for Jo and Evelyn's wedding. But the staple he obviously felt was necessary for getting the crew ready for a day's work was pancakes. Warren Shepard had this to say in his journal: "I well remember Lin's cooking, and the two long tables and the light and tender pancakes every morning. A choice of syrup, honey, peach jam, or jelly for them, was evidence of Joe's liberal providing." Wat Smith described the delicacy this way:

> The single product . . . that transcended all else in his conception of culinary art and in the pride he took in its production was griddle cakes. Every morning at Awatovi we were greeted with stacks and stacks of delicious griddle cakes. There was rarely a complaint on the part of the personnel because the griddlecakes were ambrosial and we anticipated them each morning with joy. Some visitors, however, felt that half a dozen griddle cakes was four or five too many, and occasionally quiet complaints were made to Jo, who, however, would never listen to them. Lindsay was the cook. Lindsay made the best griddle cakes in the world, and you were going to eat those griddle cakes or else.[9]

Lin would be immensely amused to know that the griddle upon which he cooked all those ambrosial cakes is now a catalogued item in the collections of the Museum of Northern Arizona—a fitting tribute to a great camp cook.[10]

One notable difference between the Awatovi camp and those of today, except perhaps for those few on Indian reservations, was the absence of liquor and beer. Jo was known to have a small supply of liquor in his tent, but no one else seems to have had any. It was illegal on the Hopi Reservation, and the Peabody adhered to the law. But no one I interviewed thought to mention this lack—it was accepted at the time and therefore unmemorable. When A.V. Kidder visited in August 1939, he mentioned having a scotch with Jo in Jo's tent, but only twice in the Peabody documents is any liquor alluded to, once in the account of the Brews' wedding (see chapter 6) and again when Dick Woodbury wrote home on a hot August day in 1938: "Another sizzler. . . . Today no breeze, no shade, no ice, no beer, no lake, no clouds, no moisture."

Mott Davis recalled one potential calamity involving liquor. It took place in the summer of 1939 when Frederick W. Hodge, venerable director of the Southwest

Hattie cutting her birthday cake, made by Lin, 1938.

Museum in Los Angeles, visited Awatovi. Hodge was in his late seventies at the time. After supper he went into the pottery tent carrying a black suitcase, put it on a table, and opened it with a grand gesture. It contained essentially a full bar. After some behind-the-scenes consultation, Mott and Dick Woodbury were sent out to wait on the path to the Hopi tents and report immediately if any of the Hopi men wanted to come over for the evening to socialize. As it turned out, none did, and crisis was averted.

✢

Jo Brew thoroughly enjoyed the social side of fieldwork and saw to it that his staff had opportunities to do the same. Although the Awatovi Expedition had scientific goals to be met each season, Brew and his colleagues faced no contract deadlines as many archaeologists know them today, nor was this an academic field school that had to instruct students. The flexibility in the camp's schedules and daily routines allowed participants time to have fun. Some of their diversions may seem almost childish to us now, but Jo's journals and letters and people's memories attest that the staff entered enthusiastically into card games, cat's-cradle competitions, horseshoe pitching, physical stunts and shows of prowess, magic tricks, and sand-dune sliding. Jo himself seems often to have been the instigator. Everyone particularly remembered the four- or six-handed pinochle games in the cook shack, which became something of a tradition on Peabody Museum projects. Wat Smith wrote in his autobiography: "Pinochle became a very important factor in the intramural life of New Awatovi. . . . It added immeasurably to the social life of the community."[11]

One possibility for weekend diversion was a trip to Keams Canyon for a movie or for supper with some of the Indian Agency staff. Evelyn Brew recalled an occasion when the superintendent of the Indian Service at Keams Canyon invited everyone to supper and then a movie. But much to everyone's surprise, he expected his guests to pay for the movie. No one had any money on hand except Jo, who promptly paid up. Penny remembered being advised to sit on the aisle of the movie theater "because there was more fresh air." Mott recalled another occasion: "This night the picture happened to be a murder mystery. After ten minutes or so, a corpse was discovered crammed into the rumble seat of a car. With that, a whole Navajo family, who had been sitting down in front, got up and fled the theater. I should think the folks at Keams would have been smarter than to show a murder movie in a place where the audience might include people with a strong fear of the dead."

As the staff grew from one field season to the next, so did the entertainment. Best remembered is the appearance in the pottery tent in 1938 of an old, secondhand upright

Carlos García-Robiou playing the piano in the pottery tent.

piano, thanks to the addition to the crew of Carlos García-Robiou. Smith provided this account: "After Carlos came to camp, he joined us on one of those Saturday night occasions [at Chi and Alma Roberts's house], and after Alma had played the piano for a little while and had left to prepare a repast, Carlos very modestly sat down and began to play. It turned out that he could play almost anything: dance music, popular songs, classical music, and, as we subsequently learned, works of his own composition.

"This was a challenge to Jo Brew, always sensitive as he was to the social amenities of an archaeological camp. . . . It evidently fermented in his active mind that here was an asset that had to be exploited, but how to do so was less clear. It was all very well for Carlos to be a pianist, but it was not feasible to go the seven miles down to Jeddito every evening or so."[12]

Jo decided that if he couldn't take the pianist to the piano, he would bring a piano to New Awatovi. His journal entry for September 15, 1938, continues the story: "Carlos and I spent the afternoon [of September 10] largely in an effort to run down a piano with the very great help of Mrs. McKenna, who seemed to know every piano in Winslow. For a long time we had no luck. People either did not wish to sell or wanted very fancy prices, but finally we heard of one in a warehouse belonging to Bill Crozier, who now runs the bus waiting room." Crozier gave Jo the keys to the warehouse so that he and Carlos could go look at the piano. They found it, and "Carlos played a little on it. It sounded very well indeed and surprisingly enough seemed to be perfectly in tune."

Jo and Evelyn Brew dancing to Carlos's music, 1939.

Returning to Crozier's place, they began to bargain. Crozier wanted $25 for the instrument, having sold one for that price the year before. "Although half expecting to get him mad," Brew recounted, "I told him that we came from the East, where pianos were a drug on the market and we had come into town expecting to pick one up for ten bucks. He said, 'Give me fifteen and she's yours.' This deal was closed immediately."

To everyone's delight, Jim McKenna brought the piano to camp in his pickup the next day. It was installed in the pottery tent, and the musical evenings began. Both Penny and Mott remember the singing because it was something of a tradition in the Davis family as well. Mott had a good voice and had brought along his recorder, which he played from time to time. Carlos had bought a guitar for $6 on that trip to Winslow for the piano, and young Bill Claflin sometimes played it during gatherings at the Roberts's home. Penny's ability to remember words to many favorite songs and her enjoyment of singing added to what was often rousing entertainment. "Some evenings we had sing-alongs," she remembered. "'Lonesome, That's All,' 'I Dreamt I Dwelt in Marble Halls,' 'On Top of Old Smokey,' 'Strawberry Roan,' and 'The Brooklyn The-a-ter Is Burning' were some of our favorites, all sung with great feeling."

Mott told me years later: "There were several able pianists in camp at various times, the two I remember being Carlos and Elvira [Mrs. Ross] Montgomery. She knew a number of popular songs of the early 1920s, when she had been a girl, and our favorite was 'Lonesome, That's All,' which we sang with special gusto. When she was a teenager she and her friends would play a record in which Reinold Werrenrath sang [this favorite], and at one line—'And I'd give the whole world for just one caress'—they would all swoon on the one. So we gave the one a special emphasis that rang over the northern Arizona desert."

The evening parties at the Robertses's, where Carlos's talents were first revealed, seem to have taken place about every two or three weeks during the last two years at Awatovi. Presumably they were as much fun for the Robertses as for the crew. They certainly were occasions to get a little dressed up. Chi Roberts had a set of kettle drums, which he played well, and Alma or Carlos played the piano. Jo mentioned that one evening "Bill [Claflin] played the banjo and Happy [Foote] the guitar." The living room was cleared for dancing, particularly to some of Carlos's Cuban renditions but also to such traditional favorites as the Virginia reel. One highlight of these parties, according to Dick Woodbury, was cold lemonade and cookies.

Sometimes some of the Hopi workers came to the pottery tent or to the campfire to listen to the music. They also contributed their own songs and entertainment from time to time. On July 15, 1938, Jo recorded in his journal: "After darkness . . . the [Hopi] boys put on a sing for us and soon began to dance. Everett [Harris] and Hoppy [Dennis] gave us the concluding number of the home dance, and then the

An evening of music at Chi and Alma Roberts's house, 1939. Left to right, front row: Bob Jones, Penny Davis, Mott Davis, Wat Smith; middle row: Alma Roberts, Haych Claflin, Chi's niece; back row: Jo Brew, Mrs. Edgar (Chi's sister), Hattie Cosgrove, Chi Roberts, Chi's niece, Dick Woodbury, Evelyn Brew.

whole crowd put on the Corn Maiden Dance. Emory [Dennis] did the grinding, using one of our metates, and Hoppy was the narrator. This was one of the most impressive Indian dances I have ever seen, the six boys standing in the firelight, and Emory kneeling before them grinding, his green silk handkerchief around his head, and Hoppy squatted beside him telling the story."

Some evenings, as the archaeologists sat around the campfire talking shop with guests, they could hear the Hopis singing at their own campfire by their tents. The clear dark sky, the firelight, good friends and colleagues nearby, and the soft atonal songs as background proved to be lifelong memories. One can imagine what it felt like to be camped at Site 264, about a mile east of New Awatovi, on a summer's night, as Mott, Dick Woodbury, and five or six Hopi men were in 1939. "The workers often practiced dances at night by our campfire," Mott remembered, and they sang as they danced. "When we bedded down and things were quiet, one could sometimes hear the distant voice of a Navajo singing. A far cry from New England."

Mott and Dick Woodbury both retained vivid memories of some spontaneous singing by the Hopi crew. "One Wednesday morning in late August," Mott told me, "we all left [Site 264] for the Snake Dance at Shipaulovi. Dick drove the Dodge truck;

the Hopi men sat on the benches and sang at the top of their lungs the whole way, a drive of an hour or so. On the road up the end of Second Mesa, the rocks echoed and re-echoed the roar of the exhaust and the rousing chorus of eight or ten lusty male voices raised in Hopi songs. . . . When we came up over the lip of the mesa into the parking area at Mishongnovi, the whole town was out to see what the uproar was about."

Dick recalled a similar story. "One of my pleasures was to drive the fine Dodge truck. It would hold six or eight workmen, their tools, and the day's specimens quite well. One day, coming back on a Friday, the huge towering clouds that had been growing all afternoon suddenly erupted into a thunderstorm and downpour. Spontaneously, a chorus of powerful men's voices started a Hopi song, with thumping on the floor of the truck for a drum. They were overwhelmed with joy at the rain— and it being a Friday, with the workday ending early, they could head home, hoping that their fields had been lucky. Their joy was contagious, even though I had no crops to worry about, and we all enjoyed the wonderful, special smell created by rain on parched ground."

When their villages scheduled dances, the Hopis always left camp to take care of their responsibilities at home, and Jo understood this as a necessity. These were rituals vital to their daily lives and to the growth and survival of their crops. Sometimes the archaeological work could go on because only First Mesa men were gone; sometimes it was just those from Second Mesa. At other times, particularly at the end of August, dances were held in several villages at once, and everyone, Hopis and archaeologists alike, took off for the Hopi towns. The Gallup Inter-Tribal Indian Ceremonial also took place at the end of August, before the end of the tourist season, not far over the state line in New Mexico. The Museum of Northern Arizona in Flagstaff sponsored some craft shows around this time as well. Work at Awatovi might cease for three or four days at a stretch as Jo saw to it that the staff and crew had an opportunity to see the dances, the craft shows, and the rodeo in Gallup. For several of the staff from the Northeast, it was their first exposure to these Western traditions.

Jo's first letter to Donald Scott of the 1937 field season, written on July 23, offers a view of his attitude toward the importance of these dances to his crew:

We have been very fortunate to arrive in time to see the Home Katchina dances. Previously we have always got here after the Katchinas had left and our season has always closed before their return. Further good luck permits us to see on Monday next a revival of the Hopi Shalako. This will take place in the afternoon following the Home Katchina dance at Shimopovi. According to our information only a few of the older inhabitants have ever seen this dance. None of my boys [the Hopi crew] have, and I shall not open the dig until Tuesday next week in order to permit them to attend.

Hopi houses on First Mesa, 1938.

The staff attended dances on First and Second Mesas, including katsina dances and Snake dances. Visits to the Hopi towns were also opportunities for the families of the Hopi crew to invite staff members into their homes and serve them food before the dances. Everyone remembered the hospitality of the Hopi women. On August 19, 1937, John Longyear wrote home describing such a visit before a dance at Mishongnovi: "Jo and I went over to old George Harris' house and had a meal there and a good one, too. After that we visited various friends in the village, and Chester [Dennis] took me over to his house where we visited with his wife and little baby." In 1991, Haych Claflin wrote to Evelyn Brew that "attending the Snake dance was thrilling and especially the night that Pa was loaned Luke [Kawanusea's] house during the ceremony. We spent the night on the roof right above the kiva and we could hear distinctly the chanting inside." The Awatovi staff felt privileged to be able to sit on the first-story roof of a building on the plaza to witness the ceremonies.

Dick Woodbury, in a letter dated June 3, 1939, described a dance he witnessed at Shipaulovi: "The wind was terrible, so that the air was full of dust and whatnot. But it was a nice dance, with about 25 men in kilts and with black velvet shirts decorated with red, yellow, and green silk ribbons. Their masks were blue with large bunches of black feathers in back and the tops covered with fine white downy feathers. And of course, they wore all the silver and turquoise necklaces they owned. They had the usual tortoise-shell rattles tied to the left knee, and carried bows. There were also five clowns in G-strings and covered with mud, who furnished general hilarity by pantomime and wisecracks. There were two other clowns dressed as mosquitoes (long stingers on the masks and fluttering arms) who kept stinging the other clowns and finally drove them off. That referred to the legend that Shipaulovi was founded by people who were driven out of a town in the Little Colorado River because the mosquitoes were so bad."

Time off work to witness Hopi ceremonies was only part of Jo's largess toward staff members new to the Southwest. In 1938 he drove Evelyn and Carlos to see the Grand Canyon, and in 1939, over the Fourth of July weekend, Wat Smith escorted Dick, Penny, and Carlos on a four-day tour of archaeological sites, national parks, and Las Vegas. Penny remembered that Wat put a nickel in a slot machine, won nothing, and the group went on its merry way. Dick Woodbury remembered it differently: "Wat stopped at a small building labeled 'Roulette,' and we went in. He bet a silver dollar, the wheel spun, and he won 10 dollars, which he picked up, said 'thank you,' and we left."

Putting up the welcoming sign on the Cactus Highway, 1939.
"You are entering Awatovi. Elevation: 6,425. Population: 34±"
Left to right: John Hack, Haych Claflin, Carlos García-Robiou.

– 6 –

Mobs of Visitors

Scarcely a day went by at New Awatovi without visitors showing up. Most of them were unexpected, but all of them were welcomed, first by signs on the Cactus Highway just ahead of the last dune before camp. Most of the visitors got fed, and often Brew gave them a place to bed down for the night.

"The group in camp today is probably the most interesting and most fantastic combination we have ever had," Jo wrote in his journal on August 15, 1938.

> The staff itself would probably make good biographical reading, and in addition, [there] are the following: Patrick Tracy Lowell Putnam of the Belgian Congo, authority on Bantu linguistics and Congo pygmies;[1] his Spanish-American wife from Santa Fe, whom he is taking back to the Congo in a few weeks; Ross Montgomery, ecclesiastical architect, who, almost certainly, has designed and built more churches than any man going at present in this country; Eric Thompson, Middle American archaeologist of the Carnegie Institution, with his wife, who comes from County Kent, and her sister, Miss Keens, who is on her first trip to the States; Peter Blos, a portrait painter from Berkeley, California, seven years in this country from the Bavarian Alps; and the usual background of Hopi boys. Under these circumstances, the campfire was naturally entertaining, the high spot probably being Pat's description of a pygmy elephant hunt.

Jo usually mentioned guests in his journal, and Hattie kept a list of visitors in 1937, 1938, and 1939, along with notes about where they were from, how long they stayed (she used the codes "SV" for short visits and "OV" for overnight), and sometimes how many meals they were served. The flow increased over the years as word about the excavation of the mission ruins and the kiva murals spread. Although few of the murals could be left exposed at the site, by late 1936 scale drawings of them, colored with colored pencils, were available for guests to look at. Word of Lin Thompson's cooking only added to the camp's allure.

Jo Brew painting a sign for the curve in the entry road to the camp, 1937.

Occasionally the guests arrived in hordes. On August 25, 1938, Jo wrote in his journal:

In the late morning Carl Guthe [director of the Museum of Anthropology at the University of Michigan] and his wife and two sons, Jim and Ted, arrived. . . . After the snake dance great mobs rolled in from Second Mesa and we had thirteen extra under canvas, twelve of them on cots, and one on an air mattress. Rene d'Harnoncourt [director of the Indian Arts and Crafts Board] and Miguel Covarrubias [a well-known Mexican artist] in Al's tent, Mr. and Mrs. [Kenneth] Disher [with the Navaho Arts and Crafts Council] in Tent 6, a friend of [Ted] Pitman's named Mrs. Collins in the brown tent, five men in the pottery tent, and Mrs. Guthe and Gwynneth Harrington [also on the Arts and Crafts Board] in Mrs. Cosgrove's tent. Ted Pitman slept on an air mattress on the floor of the shipping tent.

Hopi dances were particular occasions that drew visitors to New Awatovi. Dick Woodbury described another such event in a letter home on August 29, 1939: "This has been a busy past week. We haven't gotten much work in because the combination of visitors and dances was too much. Monday we went to Mishongnovi for the Flute Dance. . . . Tuesday and Wednesday the camp was full of people; some of them archeologists who were invited and got most of the attention, and others were tourists who got less. There were 42 arrivals Wednesday."

7/22   Gordon McGregor.
{ Dr. Roberts — Government Dentist   Lunch — 1
{ Mrs. Hare   Keams   SV
{ Miss Brown   Keams   "

Phillip Johnston - Los Angeles   "
Dick y. Morthen - Pueblo Motor Inn - Flagstaff

7/23   3 Hopi men   overnight — 2
                                " — 1
     Siestewa
     Delbert
     Hopi boy   S.V

7/23   ~~Pill~~ Phil Phillips   supper   1
       De Forrest   "   1
                              "   1

7/24   Mr. Mrs. Roberts   3 nights
7/25   Harry Chopin   "   7
     Mr. Chandlee   Hollywood   7
     Miss Mildred Smith   "   dinner   2
     Miss Scott   2 nights   5
     Miss Blank   dinner   1
                               "   1

7/27   Man & wife } teacher at Stanford University   SV
     2 children } graduate of Yale   SV

7/28   2 men - sheep inspectors
     Father Winifred   Keams   S. V
     " Connely   Tucson.   SV
     "   ~~Cincinnati~~   SV
     "   St Michael   SV
     " child   Tucson   SV
     5 adults — Holbrook   SV
     (1 an architect)   SV

7/29   Mr. & Mrs. Honey   SV
     4 women   SV
       Field

SV-5

33

Hattie Cosgrove's guest list for July 22–28, 1938.

George Dewakuku and family, visitors to the Awatovi camp in 1939.

Both Woodbury and Mott Davis remarked in their remembrances that Jo must have invited everyone he knew to come visit. Friends of friends, sometimes complete strangers, were welcomed and accommodated, and friends and relatives of the staff appeared as well. Families of the Hopi men were constant visitors. Groups of Hopi schoolchildren also visited, including one group that included Fred Kabotie, who taught school at Hopi and was to become a well-known artist. Staff members from the Indian Service office and hospital in Keams Canyon dropped by frequently.

Jo especially enjoyed guests who could talk shop with him and give him information or ideas about what was being uncovered at Awatovi. These visitors read like a Who's Who in archaeology and anthropology. In one of his weekly letters to Donald Scott in 1936—written on August 27, during the Hopi dance season—he mentioned again that "great mobs arrived." Florence Hawley brought her University of New Mexico field school; Gila Pueblo's Allentown field school with Emil Haury visited; and so did "Frederica de Laguna and party, and a number of ethnologists and sociologists; a party of Franciscan padres, etc., and Paul Martin."

One particularly descriptive journal entry gives a sense of Jo's excitement. He wrote it on August 26, 1938, the day after the visit of one of the great mobs:

> I had one of the pleasantest mornings I have ever had on the site, showing the excavations to d'Harnoncourt, Covarrubias, and Guthe. They were all very much interested in the general picture and in the church. Covarrubias expressed great glee at hearing the church situation discussed from a detached archaeological point of view. Watson very

Top: Evans Poleahla (center) and family during a camp visit, 1938. Left to right: Louise Adams-Nahsonhoya and daughter Phyllis, Nash Nahsonhoya with daughter Charlene, Evans Poleahla holding daughter Angelita, Deborah Nahsonhoya-Poleahla (Evans's wife; daughter of Louise and Nash) and daughter Delphina, and Rose Qöyamö Poleahla (Evans's mother). Bottom: Hopi schoolchildren visiting camp, 1938. Fred Kabotie is at far left.

Jo Brew (in hat) gives a tour of Awatovi to special guests, 1938. Left to right, standing: René d'Harnoncourt, Brew, Carl Guthe; seated in rear: Gwyneth Harrington, Mrs. Guthe, and Miguel Covarrubias. The two seated youths are Guthe's sons, Jim and Ted.

kindly came out to the site and showed them a small fragment of painted wall before he left for Gallup. He had left a few samples of the upper paintings on the Kiva C-D fragment so that they could see a number of different layers and how they were scraped down.

After viewing the site, we came into camp and looked first at photographs, and then spent about two hours on the drawings of the kiva paintings. They were, of course, very much interested in these and from them I picked up a lot of ideas as to the theory of design, etc. . . . While we were looking at these in the pottery tent, Hosteen John Wetherill walked in, looked at the paintings for awhile, said he didn't realize we were doing any such work as this around here, and proceeded to get all excited about everything. He stayed for lunch and I took him around the site after the d'Harnoncourt party had left.

Jo probably was excited, too, because John Wetherill was a legendary figure in the Southwest. One of the first Euro-Americans to settle in the Four Corners area, he was the first white man to see, describe, and take others to the great stone arch now known as Rainbow Bridge. He led most of the early archaeologists to sites no one else had visited. One of them said of him that "he could shoe a mule without swearing, and he could lead a pack train where a pack train had never gone before."[2] Wetherill's Navajo friends gave him the honorific title *hosteen.* Jo would have been honored to have him come by and show enthusiasm for the kiva murals.

Archaeologists and anthropologists were probably the most frequent visitors to New Awatovi. Emil Haury remembered taking his University of Arizona field school students from their Forestdale camp:

> The visit to Jo's camp was always a highly anticipated pleasure, [and I remember] that he took care of us well in every respect. And I know from a recent conversation I had with one of the students who made one of those trips that the visit to Awatovi was one of the highlights of the summer.
>
> One evening I recall the general conversation and behavior of the group transformed itself from the serious to the jocular. My contribution, as I remember, consisted of doing several string tricks. . . . In addition to cat's cradles, I particularly liked one stunt that involved taking a single piece of string, tying the two ends firmly together, doubling the loop, and having somebody then cut the string, producing four ends. The gimmick was, of course, to demonstrate the gluey nature of your saliva by putting two of the ends in your mouth and magically chewing the string together again, popping it out of your mouth as a single piece. This was good for lots of ohs and ahs. And then there was another trick I think I did which entailed removing a man's shirt without taking off his coat. This took a little surreptitious prior preparation but it never ceased to amaze the unsuspecting audience.[3]

Another visitor who lent his unique talents to the evening entertainment was Warren Shepard, Anna Shepard's father. Dick Woodbury recalled that Shepard "performed an after-supper stunt one evening: sitting in a straight chair, he took hold of one ankle and lifted the foot behind his neck and then did the same with the other foot. He was lean and wiry, obviously." Wat Smith remembered Shepard "as an accomplished gymnast who entertained the Awatovi camp by wrapping himself horizontally around the legs of a chair at the level of the rungs, and with no contact with the earth, he circled the chair neatly and quickly and without unbalancing its stance."[4]

For the staff at Awatovi, these visits were occasions for socializing and comparing information. Woodbury wrote home on July 17, 1939: "The chief event of the weekend was a visit by Emil Haury, head of the department of anthropology at the University of Arizona, with ten of his summer school student archeologists, including three girls. They are digging a series of pit houses near Showlow, south of Holbrook, and we compared camps enthusiastically, concluding that they had the edge because of being in a large pine forest and having abundant water and a shower bath. But we have electric lights and Lin."

Emil Haury, sitting on the Throne, with a group of field school students from the University of Arizona, probably 1938.

The two most prominent Southwestern archaeologists of the time, Earl Morris and Ted Kidder, each came to camp several times during the five years of the Awatovi Expedition. In 1939 Morris brought his two young daughters with their nanny for a week's stay. Liz Morris, who became a professional archaeologist herself, was five at the time, and both she and her sister retained clear memories of the trip. She told me in 1990 that she remembered "the staff sitting in folding camp chairs in a circle around a huge bonfire at night after dark. And on one memorable night we all stood away from the fire to see northern lights on a rare appearance that far from the North Pole. It was one of the few times I have ever seen them, and that was the first time."

At the end of August 1939, Kidder came for a week of rest and relaxation. He was a faithful diarist, and his journal records his enjoyment of the camp, the people, and visits to the sites where the fieldwork was being done. On Wednesday, August 23, he wrote that at 3:30 in the afternoon he was sitting "in the corner of the little ruined church that the priests built in the wreck of the convento when they returned after the

Earl Morris (left) and Ted Kidder relaxing in front of the pottery tent at Awatovi, late August, 1939.

[Pueblo] Revolt. Cool gray afternoon. Everybody gone to Mishongnovi for the Snake Dance except Lin, the cook, and Jo and Evelyn Brew. . . . I walked over here and cruised about the ruins, marveling, as we always do at these Hopi sites, at the vast amount of beautiful yellow and orange sherds [Sikyatki Polychrome]. Hopi buttes very dark under the lowering sky."

The next day he had a chat with staff member Charlie Amsden and Peabody director Donald Scott, who also happened to be at the site, about the Great Depression–related troubles of the Laboratory of Anthropology in Santa Fe, "which we all feel can no longer be kept going as a research institution and which we think should become frankly a museum of Indian art supported by local investors." (The Laboratory survived the Depression and thrives today.) Despite the professional talk, it was "a lazy afternoon, and a pleasant one. Camp fire after supper of big cedar logs; later in the sherd tent where Carlos García Roubiou [*sic*] played the piano and [visiting archaeologist Frank] Hibben sang cowboy songs."

On Friday Kidder spent the afternoon "under the same juniper" and drew a cartoon for the cookshack bulletin board depicting "his journey to Awatovi as it was recounted to his grandchildren and as it actually took place." The cartoon was one of two he made during this last visit to Awatovi; the other shows a D-shaped kiva and, poking fun at Jo Brew's girth, the expedition's matching director.[5] That Friday was the day "Earl Morris drove in in the old big-wheeled '26 Packard—flat-brimmed felt hat, khaki shirt and breeches and leather putties—the same fine old Earl—no better man ever lived."

Cartoon drawn by Ted Kidder for Jo Brew,
describing Kidder's visit to Awatovi in August 1939.

Kidder's cartoon of Site 111's D-shaped kiva, August 1939.

While the expedition members worked at Awatovi, a throng of anthropologists studied the Hopis elsewhere on the mesas and worked in northern Arizona in other capacities. Most of them dropped in at Awatovi at one time or another. Solon Kimball, who worked with the Soil Conservation Service, and Gordon McGregor, who was conducting a study for the Indian Service, visited often, usually staying for a meal. Others were just passing through, among them Conrad Arensberg, John Province, Al Whiting, and John Gillen. Fellow archaeologists were constant visitors. Ted Sayles from Gila Pueblo and Dr. and Mrs. Harold Colton and Katherine Bartlett from the Museum of Northern Arizona came every year on their way to the Hopi dances. Other anthropologists and archaeologists who appear in Hattie's lists include

Guests and staff relaxing in the shade, 1939. Left to right: Conrad Arensberg, Johnny Hack, Dick Woodbury, Kirk Bryant, Solon Kimball, Mott Davis, and Al Lancaster.

Clyde Kluckhohn, John McGregor, George Murdock, Alexander Spoehr, Mischa Titiev, Fay Cooper-Cole, Phil Phillips, Harry Mera, Isabel Kelly, John Rinaldo, Ralph Beals, and Louis Caywood.

Other visitors were more nationally prominent or even famous. On July 22, 1939, Jo wrote: "Earl Morris arrived in the evening with Dr. Vannevar Bush, president of Carnegie Institution, along with ex-Senator [Frederic C.] Walcott of Norfolk, Connecticut, a trustee of the Institution. . . . We had a very pleasant hour and a half in the cook shack. Bush and Walcott are both very interesting men and extremely affable." Others would become famous, including "a man named [Barry] Goldwater in a new Ford beachwagon. He seems a very pleasant fellow and also very capable. He is a designer, apparently the son of the owner of the Goldwater department store in Phoenix."[6]

Hattie recorded the last dignitaries to visit camp on September 3, 1939: "Cavalcade of agriculturists (30 cars and 80 people) headed by Under Secretary [of Agriculture] M. L. Wilson of Washington, D.C. The trip was made to study the relationship of man to nature in the Southwest." Jo had been in Winslow most of the day, but his journal for that day says:

When we arrived in camp we found that the Department of Agriculture traveling S.C.S. [Soil Conservation Service] conference had been at Awatovi. . . . They apparently had a very good time. Volney [Jones] and Johnny [Hack] described their work which, of course,

Top: Some 30 government cars in camp, in what Hattie called a "cavalcade of agriculturists," September 3, 1939. The cars brought the men of the Soil Conservation Service for the tour. Bottom: Members of the Soil Conservation Service touring the Awatovi site, 1939. Jesse Nusbaum is pointing; New Awatovi is on the horizon.

Father Victor Stoner and his dachshund, Gus, 1938.

was the closest to the business of the conference. They also drove through the sand dunes and viewed Tallahogan Canyon, taking pictures at the Nelson wickiup on the rim, where Mrs. Nelson [a Navajo woman] reaped a harvest of fifteen cents a [photographic] shot.

In his journal entry for August 24, 1939, after remarking on "a stream of visitors all day long, a number estimated . . . as somewhere between 40 and 50," Jo commented that "just before supper Father Stoner and Gus arrived." Victor Rose Stoner had been a regular visitor since 1937, when he was an army chaplain visiting Civilian Conservation Corps camps in southern Arizona to say mass. He had just completed an M.A. degree in archaeology at the University of Arizona, where he wrote a thesis on the Spanish missions of the southern part of the state. He was co-founder and first editor of *The Kiva*, the journal of the Arizona Archaeological and Historical Society, and later served as president of the society. He had read of the excavations at Awatovi in a Tucson newspaper in June 1937 and wrote to Jo that he would like to visit. Interestingly, Jo never mentioned Stoner's visits in his 1937 letters to Scott. Instead, information about the priest comes largely from Watson Smith's *One Man's Archaeology* and an obituary that Wat wrote for Stoner.[7]

Father Stoner saying mass at the altar of Church 2, September 1937.

Wat's memories and Jo's journal imply that Father Stoner's visits to the Awatovi camp may have been more enjoyable to him than they were to others. Wat wrote: "I think Father Stoner was motivated in part (though it may be egregious to say so) by the opportunity for a square meal at our very excellent cuisine and also for the opportunity of conversing with those of us who were there."[8] If so, Stoner was hardly alone.

Gus was Father Stoner's dachshund, who always accompanied him. Jo had a rule against dogs in camp, and Lin objected to them, too. Wat says Lin liked to grumble about people who showed up just in time to eat, particularly if they were not archaeologists contributing to the expedition. He considered Kirk Bryan, John Hack's professor, to be in this class of non-archaeologists. When Gus took a disliking to Bryan and either bit him or threatened to (Wat says Hack denies the story), the dog earned a place forever in Lin's good graces.

Stoner was behind a memorable incident for those who were at Awatovi in September 1937. The Church of San Bernardo de Aguatubi had been uncovered by this time, with its altar area intact. Father Stoner, as an itinerant priest, carried an altar stone and his vestments with him. He conceived the idea of saying mass at the old altar. The ceremony took place on September 5, celebrating the "first and only Mass at that spot since mid-August 1680."[9] Photographs of the occasion show six people witnessing the ceremony. John Longyear, who had a movie camera, took both still and moving pictures of the event.[10] Wat remembered it as "an event of serious historic significance [that] should not be forgotten."[11]

Thanks again to Stoner, this seemingly happy event also had some political fallout. Apparently he later complained to Arizona's Senator Carl Hayden that the altar at which he had said mass had been "destroyed." Indeed, as happens continually in excavations, the archaeologists had removed it in order to dig deeper under the church. In defense of the Peabody staff, Jesse Nusbaum wrote to John Collier, the U.S. commissioner of Indian Affairs, explaining that the altar sat above a kiva with "kiva-wall embellishment [murals] more significant than any other found to this time in the Southwest I firmly believe. In final analysis, the remarkable archaeological findings of primitive Arizona civilization below the mission altar, must be weighted against the removal of the remains of a plinth of masonry that constituted an altar base of later and foreign introduction."

But it was in regard to another matter that, according to Evelyn Brew, Father Stoner eventually became a thorn in Jo's side. In the spring of 1938 Stoner learned that a burial found under the altar of Church 2 was considered to be that of a Caucasian—probably one of the Franciscans. He wrote to Jo asking what steps would be necessary to have the bones sent to Tucson for burial beneath the cathedral. His letter, now in the Peabody archives, continues: "A movement is on foot to have the martyrs of the Pueblo Revolt of 1680 declared saints. . . . There is every reason to believe that eventually all these numerous martyrs, soldiers, colonists, and friars, will be declared saints. Surely Harvard would be willing to let us have the body when Harvard's interest is purely anthropological while that of the Church reaches far deeper."

In mid-July Jo replied diplomatically that "Harvard will be willing to cooperate with the Church in making the best disposal of any European skeletons we find." By fall Stoner seems to have decided that the burial was that of either Father Porras, the founder of the mission, or Father Figueroa, another of the early priests. Earnest Hooton, the prominent physical anthropologist at Harvard, had determined, however, that the skeleton in question was that of a "chap in his early twenty's," according to Jo's journal on November 21, 1938. Porras was known to have been in his sixties when he died at Awatovi in 1633, and Figueroa, as an experienced priest, must also have been older than his early twenties. The bones could not have belonged to either of them.

Stoner, unsatisfied with Jo's response, wrote to Senator Hayden again, asking for his help in acquiring the remains for reburial in Tucson. Hayden drew the Department of the Interior into the matter, and through it the Indian Service superintendent at Keams Canyon, Seth Wilson. He in turn referred the question to Jesse Nusbaum, the department's consulting archaeologist. Jo wrote a long letter to Superintendent Wilson explaining the identification of the burial, but he was concerned enough over the political situation to visit Nusbaum personally at Mesa Verde, where Nusbaum was park superintendent at the time. There the two men arrived at the brilliant decision to return any bones of "European physical type" to the Franciscan Order—of which Father Stoner was not a member—because the Awatovi mission in the seventeenth century had been Franciscan.

Jo's journal for November 29, 1938, tells that he visited that day with the priest at the Keams Canyon mission, "who promised to give me the name of a father at St. Michaels, the headquarters of the Franciscan mission for the area, to whom the bones could be sent." In later years, Wat Smith followed up on the whereabouts of the bones and discovered that although they had arrived at St. Michaels and stayed there for "a good many years," they had at some unknown date been removed—for what reason, by what means, and for what destination he could not determine. "It thus appears that a mystery has been compounded upon a mystery," he concluded, "and one may only hope that those uneasy bones have somewhere found a resting place. Sic transit gloria."[12]

Visits from interesting or at least colorful people were always diversions for the staff, but they were good at generating their own special events, too. One was an evening during the 1939 season when Carlos García-Robiou and Mott Davis showed slides without a proper slide projector. Photographic color slides were new at the time, and few of them were taken during the five years of the project. Certainly, no one brought a projector out from Cambridge to show them. Carlos and Mott, both being mechanically clever, rigged up a contraption to do the job. In his journal on July 25, 1939, Jo reported that "Carlos and Mott Davis have made a machine for projecting Kodachrome slides. It is rigged up with an automobile light bulb shining through a Voightlander camera. The current is taken off our 32-volt system with a nail in a basin of salt water providing the resistance. Carlos also has an extension arm rigged up for a table lamp." The staff's reception of the slide show went unremarked. Mott later remembered only that the projector worked.

Mott and Carlos also devised a communication system that summer, when Mott and Dick Woodbury were working for several days at a time at Site 264, which lay east of Awatovi on a small peninsula. They had a clear line of sight from there to the horizon near the Awatovi camp, and with flashlights they could send messages in Morse code back and forth reasonably successfully. On the night of August 11, a Friday, Mott recalled, "we had finished one of the attempts to signal back to camp from 264 and were going to bed when we saw that the northern sky was all aflame. At first we

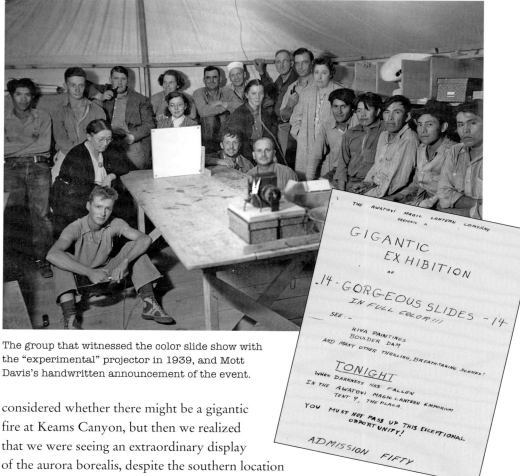

The group that witnessed the color slide show with the "experimental" projector in 1939, and Mott Davis's handwritten announcement of the event.

THE AWATOVI MAGIC LANTERN COMPANY
PRESENTS A

GIGANTIC EXHIBITION

OF

-14- GORGEOUS SLIDES -14-

IN FULL COLOR!!!

SEE:-

KIVA PAINTINGS
BOULDER DAM
AND MANY OTHER THRILLING, BREATH-TAKING SCENES!

TONIGHT

WHEN DARKNESS HAS FALLEN
IN THE AWATOVI MAGIC LANTERN EMPORIUM
TENT 9, THE PLAZA

YOU MUST NOT PASS UP THIS EXCEPTIONAL OPPORTUNITY!

ADMISSION FIFTY

considered whether there might be a gigantic fire at Keams Canyon, but then we realized that we were seeing an extraordinary display of the aurora borealis, despite the southern location and the summer season. Wild flashing on the southwestern skyline indicated they were seeing the spectacle in camp and Carlos hoped to draw it to our attention, albeit silently and incoherently. I signaled back, *We see it."*

Penny, too, remembered this occasion well. It happened as everyone in camp was going to bed. All of a sudden, Penny said, she heard Carlos yelling, although she couldn't figure out what he was saying. Thinking something terrible had happened, she stuck her head out of the tent and saw him jumping up and down and flailing his arms about. Shouting in a combination of English and Spanish, he was pointing to the sky and the spectacular northern lights. (This was the same event Liz Morris remembered when we spoke in 1990.)

Mott remembered having a conversation a few days later with Chester Dennis, one of his special friends among the Hopi crew, in which they compared notes about the cause of the aurora: "I said it had to do with electricity in the sky; he said the Hopis felt it had to do with the kachinas. Each of us was interested in what the other had to say, and we acknowledged the difference of view, and it rested at that."

The long 1938 season provided an opportunity for a well-planned Halloween party in the pottery tent, to which Chi and Alma Roberts were invited. Evelyn wrote the invitations in verse—the first of many poems she wrote for her own and her friends' enjoyment over the years:

> Although Friday night may very well seem
> A bit premature for Hallowe'en,
> We issued a plea to the powers of Night
> That they on us mortals bestow the right
> To hasten the coming of All Saints' Day
> Because of our guests who are going away.
> Witches and wizards, goulies and cats,
> Ghosts and goblins and claw-winged bats
> Held a séance on the top of the moon
> And signed with black blood to decree this boon.
> So hie yourselves at seven o'clock
> To the tent where the ivory minstrels talk
> In costume as funny as can be.
> (Those who forget must pay a fee.)
> So come in a sheet, or come in a shawl,
> Or come as you please, but come, one and all.

Jo made a special trip to Winslow for jack-o'-lanterns, paper hats, and candy. In his journal entry for Friday, October 28, he judged the party "a complete success," the costumes showing "considerable thought and ingenuity. The outstanding performance by general acclaim was Charlie Amsden as a boulevardier. He looked every inch the dapper French aristocrat, with a magnificent neck-cloth, the ribbon of the Legion of Honor, a powder puff in his lapel, and the Order of the Lucky Strike hanging around his neck. His hair was powdered to an iron gray and the ensemble was completed with Bill Claflin's cane and a pair of bright yellow gloves. He also had a monocle attached to a string and a good French accent."

Hattie, Jo remarked, "was made up extremely well as a Chinaman, with the typical long mustachios and a magnificent queue made from a black silk stocking." Among the other memorable costumes (he described every one in detail) were Alma Roberts's fortune teller "in a sheet and a Queen-of-Sheva mask with long black eye-lashes. This was so incongruous with her real character that it was most effective." Madeleine

Halloween party in the pottery tent, October 1938. Left to right, standing in back: Wat Smith, Jo Brew, Alden Stevens, Madeleine Amsden, Charlie Amsden; seated: Donald Scott, Al Lancaster (?), Leland Dennis, Hattie Cosgrove, Marian Stevens, Alma Roberts; on floor: Carlos García-Robiou, Evelyn Nimmo, Louise Scott. Chi Roberts was at the party but is not in the picture, so perhaps he was the photographer.

Amsden dressed as a witch, but "her original intention, apparently, was to come as The Boss, expanded to the proper dimensions by a couple of pillows. Unfortunately, she was talked out of this through fear of injuring my feelings." Al Lancaster came dressed "in a harlequin costume made from remnants of coloured cloth left over from Johnny Hack's surveying flags and a hooded mask of the same material. Watson, in one of the most successful costumes, came as Dick Wheeler, immediately recognized by all. Wat arranged his hat in the shape of Dick's black hat and covered it with a focusing cloth. Dick's tremendous black beard he duplicated with cotton stuffing from an old mattress, dyed with India ink."

Evelyn and Hattie had gone all out decorating the cook shack for the party. Jo wrote: "There was a lighted Jack O'Lantern at each place and place cards which consisted of a little box full of Hallowe'en candies. The walls were decorated with friezes of paper cats and pumpkins. Dinner was very pleasant, with long conversations in extremely polite French between Mr. Scott and Chevalier Amsden."

Thanksgiving in 1938 was celebrated with an appropriate meal and another poem by Evelyn. Jo reported in his journal that "Lin put on an excellent dinner for us, with one of the most delicious clam chowders I have ever had, an excellent salad, and a well-cooked and stuffed turkey with sweet potatoes stuffed with sausage meat, etc., and pumpkin pie with whipped cream. In the evening we had a fruit pudding with lemon sauce." At the table, Wat read Evelyn's poem, "Thanksgiving Day, Oh, Thanksgiving Day":

It is only fit and proper as we reach Thanksgiving Day
To count up all our blessings in our very humble way.
We have much to make us thankful as the winter days roll by,
Though we shiver in November as we sweltered in July.
We are thankful for our Jo, who brought the turkey for our feast,
Though I prophesy by supper there'll be naught left of the beast.
I think it only proper for our Lindsay to give thanks,
Though his biscuits are like manos and his pies resemble planks.
Still we had to have a turkey in the very worstest way.
If only he could cook, he'd be the champion of the day.
We are thankful for Don Carlos, who plays with stone and bone
And disappears your nickels until his pockets groan.
In playing pinochle he has one sole and saving grace.
Whenever you're against him he always has the ace.
And then there's Mrs. Cosgrove, who virtues make a heap.
She lights the fire mornings while I pretend to sleep.
Without her gentle influence bad manners then would soar.
There'd be elbows on the table and no feet on the floor.
For Watson we are thankful. Without his kiva wall
We'd have left in mid-October, and there'd be no feast at all.
And then there's Father Al, the master of the pun,
Who acts as pastor of our flock and bosses everyone.
We make a nice community, and so with truth I say
How awfully, awfully glad we are to have us here today.
I've thought of all superlatives and words there cannot be
To give the proper emphasis in giving thanks for me.

Innumerable and varied human relationships have been launched during archaeological fieldwork, but so far as I know, only one wedding has been performed in an archaeological camp. It was celebrated at Awatovi on June 11, 1939, and outshone every other social event of the expedition's five years.

In February 1939, in Cambridge, Jo Brew and Evelyn Nimmo became engaged, and they decided to hold their wedding at Awatovi soon after the start of the 1939 field season. Evelyn remembered years later that Donald and Louise Scott thought it improper for an engaged couple to be in a field camp situation and not be married.

Wat Smith wrote two detailed accounts of the momentous occasion, one of them in the expedition's daily journal, which he kept in Jo's stead during the days surrounding the wedding and Evelyn's and Jo's honeymoon (see photo on page viii). The other he included in his autobiography. Written more than 40 years later, that version differs in some respects from the one in the journal. Undoubtedly Wat was aware that the journal was to reside in the official records of the expedition at the Peabody and so needed to reflect a certain decorum. For his personal retelling, he felt no such restrictions.

In the autobiography, Wat heralded the wedding by saying: "Perhaps the most colorful single event that characterized the five years in the field at Awatovi, and very likely the most piquant performance ever to enliven any field expedition in the history of Southwestern archaeology, occurred on the 11th of June, 1939." The field journal described, in Wat's mock-formal style, the "nuptial preparations" the preceding morning, when "the entire personnel of the camp, including the culinary department, turned from their regulation duties to the systematic disruption of the camp morale."

He continued:

Under the direction of Hattie, steps were taken to transform the pottery tent into a wedding chapel. In order to accomplish this end, chatelaine Cosgrove, with miscellaneous minions, denuded the pottery tent of all scientific impedimenta, except the sherd board. Meanwhile, Dick and Penny, pooling their joint artistic abilities, created four black-on-pine direction markers for the confusion of unexpected guests. These were subsequently installed at strategic points between the main highway and camp.

Upon the return of the signpost expedition, who had garnered a generous supply of aromatic *Juniperus utahensis,* Hattie's crew masked the pottery bins with juniper bows [boughs], creating an entrancing bowery effect. At the same time other matrimonial symbolism was installed by the hanging of wedding chimes [which Penny recalled had been purchased in Cambridge and brought in by train for the occasion]. Festoons of rare crepe paper in chaste white were disposed by Dick with the aid and advice of Penny, Hattie, and Wat. Several fine Navajo rugs (courtesy Chi Roberts) covered the parquet floor. On the completion of the chapel decoration, Señor Carlos of the photographic department was called in to immortalize the decorative scheme.

Concerning Lin Thompson's preparations, Wat joked, "the senior member of the culinary department occupied himself with shaving, in order to prepare sufficient lather for the icing of the wedding cake." Not only that, but "*Al took a bath.*" Wat continued:

Mention of the bride and groom has heretofore been omitted for the reason that their activities during the day were not susceptible to intelligible analysis. In the late afternoon, however, the Director so far recovered his customary aplomb as to retrieve Pecos from Keams Canyon, where it had been undergoing spring repairs. Pecos' stamina proved to be just sufficient to get it to its stall before the audible collapse of several of its members.

The Last Supper was undistinguished by special circumstances, but the early evening was rendered harrowing to certain hysterical members of the camp by what we shall call the Latin Legerdemain of Carlos, who progressed rapidly from the relatively innocent divertissement of Cats-Cradles to coin disappearance, to the more diabolical prestidigitation of the Quartros Regis. Despite the incisively intelligent attentions of his audiences, he ingeniously succeeded in bemusing them by distracting their attention from the intricacies of his manual dexterity by explaining his deceptions in the clarity of his own mother tongue, which he maintains to be Spanish, generously interlarded with his adopted language, Hopi. After the tenth repetition of this performance, Penny, the last survivor, gave up and abandoned herself to insomniac incubus.

The morning of the wedding, a Sunday, brought anxiety. "Throughout the morning," Wat wrote in the journal, "the McKennas continued not to arrive, to the increasing consternation of the whole community, especially since they had contracted to bring with them pink ice cream and the bride's bouquet, not to mention one extra special [double] bedstead."

"Two vacant chairs," the journal notes, "were ruefully regarded during the lunch hour, but eventually all fears were allayed by a rapidly approaching dust storm from the heart of which issued the Halls, hotly pursued by the McKennas." *One Man's Archaeology* picks up the story:

Suddenly, there burst over the summit a totally unexpected open sports car containing Ned Hall, his wife E. Boyd, and their little white poodle, driving like Jehu, if I knew how fast Jehu traveled, and over a road that didn't invite rapid motion. They were obviously in a state of panic. They drove into the center of the camp in a trail of dust and sand, and were immediately followed, also at a tremendously high rate of speed, by the McKenna pickup. Both the Halls and the McKennas stopped abruptly in the middle of the plaza.

The pottery tent, decorated.

Penny Davis and Carlos García-Robiou
hanging decorations for the wedding
in the pottery tent, June 11, 1939.

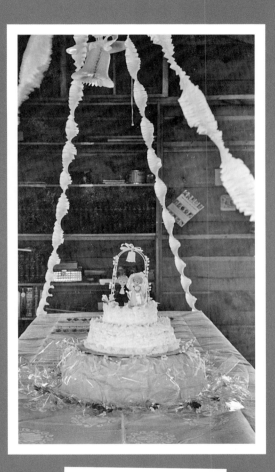

The wedding cake, made
by Lin Thompson.

Mr. and Mrs. J. O. Brew, ready for their honeymoon,
June 11, 1939.

The Halls at first were a little shaken, but it developed . . . that they, having planned to attend the wedding, were peacefully moving along the road a few miles from camp when they were aroused by the frantic blowing of a motor horn behind them. Looking back they had seen the pickup truck approaching with Jim McKenna wild-eyed at the wheel, blowing the horn as hard as he could and apparently gesticulating out the window. Not being able to get off the road because it consisted only of wheel tracks in the sand, the Halls found it impossible to get out of the way. Their only recourse to keep from being run over by the pickup truck was to drive on as rapidly as possible, and hope to stay ahead. They had barely managed to do so before arrival.

Well, that was the situation, but the explanation of it is a little more intricate. It was told by Jim McKenna, who hailed from backwoods Mississippi and talked in a character-istically slow deep-south drawl with a great deal of picturesque profanity, which I will not try to reproduce. But the substance of the tale was this. It seems that as Jim and Mary were coming up the highway somewhere north of Indian Wells, he had put the car into low gear in order to go through a rough spot, and when he shifted back into high, the gears stuck, so that at the next rough spot they were unable to get it out of high. The only thing to do, or the only thing that Jim felt they could do, was to go just as fast as possible regardless of everything, in order not to stall the motor, and in order not to stop, because if they stopped they couldn't have started again in high gear. Jim followed this procedure until he got to the point of catching up with the slower-moving Halls. Realizing then that he couldn't stop or even slow down, and that he would run over the Halls if they didn't get the hell out of the way, he did everything he could to make plain to them the situation. Fortunately, they understood, if dimly.

Both parties having arrived safely, if shaken, the next job was to unload the wed-ding bed. "But when the pickup was investigated," Wat remembered, "it was discov-ered that the footboard and the spring were there but the headboard was missing. . . . Jim and Mary surmised that at one point or another as they bounced along the road in high gear, it had fallen out." Search parties went out looking for it, but without suc-cess. About a week later it "turned up in the Keams Canyon garage, where it had been brought by a Navajo who said he had been driving along the road near Indian Wells and had seen it lying beside the road. Not knowing what it was or whose it was, but feeling that it should be saved, he had picked it up and brought it to Keams Canyon for reclamation, thus resolving not only a mystery but a crisis." By then, Jo and Evelyn had already returned from their week's honeymoon, and in the meantime Happy Foote had made a "very effective wooden substitute," according to the journal on June 19, when Jo again took over the recording.

During the search for the headboard, Wat drove out to the main road from Holbrook to wait for the minister—the Reverend David Jones, an Episcopal minister from Winslow—and any other guests who might miss the turn onto the camp road. Wat wrote in his autobiography:

> I took my stance at the top of the southern escarpment of Antelope Mesa above Jeddito, where I could see several miles along the road from Holbrook as it crossed the Jeddito Valley and rose up the escarpment of Antelope Mesa. As I watched I descried a little plume of dust rising several miles away and moving toward me. I supposed this to be generated by one of our expected guests, who turned out to be Clarence Halderman, his wife, Peggy, and Mrs. McKim, Peggy's mother.
>
> It was illegal to have liquor on the reservation and although in our camp we had observed that rule scrupulously, on the occasion of the wedding the regulation was relaxed and for understandable reasons. Clarence, however, and his wife and particularly Mrs. McKim, who were all competent with the bottle, didn't observe the law quite so scrupulously. As [they] drew up beside me, Clarence, at the wheel, greeted me vociferously and held out a bottle. "Have some ice water," he said. Clearly, Clarence was in no condition to be refused and, although I was reluctant to drink his euphemious "ice water" at that particular time, I had to take it. My reluctance was based not simply upon my law abiding instincts, but on the fact that the next person I expected to see was the clergyman, Davy Jones. I need not have been so scrupulous, but I felt at the time that it would be indiscreet for me to be in a position to greet the minister with a tainted breath.

As the afternoon wore on, many other guests arrived at camp. According to the autobiography: "Not only was the camp personnel, that is the staff, to be involved in this event, but also all the Hopi personnel and their friends and relations from First and Second Mesas. In addition, the Hopi superintendent, Mr. Seth Wilson, from Keams Canyon, the Navajo superintendent, Mr. Fryer, the Franciscan Fathers from Keams Canyon, and other people from the neighborhood." In the camp journal, Wat listed the Hopis present as "Siestewa, Delbert, Willard[?], Emory, and Leland," the last two being Dennis brothers.

While the guests arrived, the journal recounts, "the dining room was prepared under the aegis of Hattie to harmonize with the decorative motif which had been previously carried out in the wedding chapel. Resplendent in the center of the refectory board rose a many storied wedding cake glistening in the glory of Thompson pulcriture and surmounted by a miniature bride and groom, strongly suggestive of Charlie McCarthy and Gracie Allen. . . . Above this piece de resistance hung three wedding bells. . . . The whole works was tastefully garnished with carefully crinkled cellophane."

The autobiography adds a detail about the last-minute preparations that the journal omits. The bridegroom, Wat recalled, got dressed up all right, and then he and I set out to find the other functionaries, namely Al Lancaster, who was to give away the bride, and Davy, who was to conduct the ceremony. They were not immediately apparent; they were not evident anywhere. We finally discovered them in one of the tents, none of them the worse for wear. Al Lancaster was, of course, totally abstemious. He was absolutely a nondrinker. On entering the tent, however, we were confronted by Davy and Clarence [Halderman], Clarence well supplied with "ice water," which he had been generous in sharing with Davy. Davy by this time was feeling no pain, and I recall my impression of him as I saw him at that moment. He was standing facing the door of the tent, the flap of the tent being closed, with Clarence on one side of him holding the bottle of [so-called] ice water. Davy was rocking gently backward and forward from heel to toe but, nevertheless, with ineffable grace and without danger of collapse. As I viewed the scene I confess to harboring misgivings. I was a man of little faith, and I wondered in my own mind just exactly how Davy was going to get through the duty which he was about to undertake. I need not have worried.

The journal picks up the official version of the story:

Breathless expectancy brooded over the entire throng as the bridegroom, immaculate in white flannel trousers, mouse-colored waist-coat and blue coat, approached the altar with studied nonchalance, closely followed by his best man [Wat himself] arrayed in his ice-cream suit and deftly concealing the wedding ring on the little finger of his right hand.

    The bride, flanked by her captivating bridesmaid [Penny] and her Chesterfieldian giver-awayer [Al], drew nigh. The bridal gown, cunningly contrived for the occasion of shimmering chiffon of blue and white commas, effectively [reflected] the ethereal beauty of its wearer. She carried the bouquet, which had survived its stormy passage in the McKenna truck. The bridesmaid's dress of raspberry crepe was especially fetching and contrasted pleasingly with the more sober hue of the bride's garb. The bridesmaid carried a bouquet of sweet peas.

As the wedding party walked from the door of the tent, Carlos played the wedding march on the piano. Once they had taken their places before the minister, he "spoke graciously of his early youth and his acquaintance on the USS *Brooklyn* with the bride's father, Hugh Nimmo [during World War I], and expressed his pleasurable surprise at the coincidence which destiny had provided in selecting him to tie the knot. Following the benediction, all present abandoned themselves to the usual period of promiscuous osculation."

In *One Man's Archaeology*, Wat remembered what came next: "Following the cere-mony, the [bridal] party issued forth into the plaza where they were greeted by all the guests and where the wedding certificate [actually the marriage license] was produced and the witnesses were invited to sign it. That precipitated an almost riotous scramble. Some of the elderly Hopi who were present were unable to sign, but they had thumbs, so that wedding certificate is probably unmatched in the records of Arizona, having more signatures and more thumb prints than any similar document that I can imagine." (Evelyn showed me this document in 2003. There were but two thumbprints on it and nowhere near 50 signatures, the number of people Wat estimated were present.)

Everyone then filed into the cook shack, where, the journal recounts,

a delectable collation had been thrown upon the table by the culinary department. The guests were staggered by the sumptuosity of the spread, but soon recovered themselves and laid-to with gusto. The hors doeuvres prepared by the chef had been cleverly squoze onto saltines . . . and were ingeniously contrived to mystify the eater as to the formula of their contents. For those of a more delicate constitution, potato chips were provided, accompa-nied by cold sliced meat and over-fed olives, together with chicken salad and pickles. Steaming on the stove stood generous samovars of coffee, accompanied by one (1) quart of cow's cream. The gastronomic and sybaritic climax of the repast was reached with the cut-ting of the wedding cake by the bride and its distribution with slices of relaxed Neapolitan ice cream." Wat added that "those who received symbolic mementos from the innards of the cake were Mrs. McKenna—the dime, Happy—the ring, [and] Willard—the button.

Jo and Evelyn, "amid a shower of rice," then left for a honeymoon visiting national parks and some of Jo's old haunts from his earlier fieldwork in Utah and southern Colorado. They spent the first night at La Posada in Winslow, where the owners had offered a free night as a wedding present. "A large party was formed for a visitation at San Bernardino de Awatovi, officially guided by the assistant to the director, Mr. Lancaster, assisted by Mr. Woodbury, Mr. Smith, and Senor Garcia-Robiou," wrote Wat. The rest of the guests began to depart, but it took some effort to get the McKennas' stalled pickup on the road again. "A rescue party headed by Old-Sober-Sides-With-the-Women Lancaster in the Dodge truck, with the assistance of Dick, Penny, Everett, Carlos, Clarence, Wat, Lin, Happy, and Leland, at last succeeded in pushing the McKenna car onto safe ground. When last seen, Mr. McKenna was approximately on the road, at ninety miles an hour." After some singing around the piano, the last few guests "depart-ed into the night, leaving the camp in darkness and to us."

Hoppy Dennis loads a cookstove and bed springs on a wagon
during the breakup of camp, September 1939.

– 7 –

End of the Expedition

No one at the Peabody Museum intended for the Awatovi Expedition to end in 1939. By the time the 1938 season was drawing to a close, Brew felt he needed at least one more year of work beyond August 26, 1939. He mentioned his plan to Superintendent Wilson of the Indian Service in Keams Canyon and discussed it informally with some of the Hopi clan leaders he knew.

By this time the Hopis had organized an administrative system in accordance with the Indian Reorganization Act, and its officers were to oversee tribal affairs and relationships with the Indian Service and bodies such as the Peabody Museum. Brew soon found that the Hopi Council did not want to act on a request for further excavation until it was clear which clan had jurisdiction over the work at Awatovi—that is, which clan was most directly descended from the previous inhabitants of that town. At least two clans laid claim, and by the end of the 1938 field season the Hopis had reached no final agreement about who had the stronger claim.

Both the Indian Service and the Department of the Interior told Brew that it was important to seek the approval of the Hopis for any continued work, but the situation with the Hopi Council, though not unfriendly, remained ambiguous. Brew was uncertain who among the Hopis might ultimately be acceptable to the tribe, the superintendent, and the department as having the authority to grant permission. Despite these unresolved concerns, on February 3, 1939, Donald Scott wrote an official request for renewal of the museum's excavation permit for one more year, to run until August 26, 1940.

The request stalled. In April 1939, a Hopi delegation traveled to Washington, D.C., and asked the Indian Service and the Department of the Interior not to approve the extension beyond August 26 of that year, when the current permit ended. We know this only through an undated article in an unidentified, but presumably Washington, newspaper in the Peabody archives. The final paragraph sounds familiar to archaeologists today: "'What good does it do to dig there? the villages want to know,' protested

[Byron] Adams [a member of the Hopi delegation]. 'If it were on some other mesa, where no one was living, we might feel differently. But we are still alive. Our civilization is not dead. They are digging up our ancestors and they are touching things we have said shall not be touched.'"

Brew was nervous over the uncertainty of being able to work beyond August 26, 1939. As a precaution, he and his colleagues elected to start the 1939 field season in May—a wise move, as it turned out. On May 30, after the crew had gathered and begun fieldwork, the Department of the Interior responded to the renewal request, turning it down with these words: "The Office of Indian Affairs has advised that your application was considered by the Indians of the Hopi jurisdiction who have control over the lands upon which you propose to conduct this work and that these Indians would not renew this permit to conduct any archaeological work on their lands."

Scott notified Brew of the letter, and the two wrote back and forth about how to respond. Brew argued that he was going to get signed permission from Luke Kawanusea, an elder of the clan that most Hopis at the time agreed had the closest relationship to Awatovi. Superintendent Wilson had told Brew that this written permission was necessary in order for Wilson to agree to forward a request for reconsideration of the permit application. Luke Kawanusea and Vivian Tewanyinima both signed the letter—undoubtedly written by Brew—on June 20, and Brew immediately took a copy of it to Wilson at Keams Canyon.

According to Brew's journal entry of July 22, 1939, Wilson came to camp that day, two days after Jo had gotten the permission letter signed by Luke, and told Brew that he must get "approval of First Mesa as well as Luke Kawanusea for the renewal of [the] permit." Brew had just sent Scott a telegram with the news that Luke had signed the letter, so this setback was frustrating. Wilson had, however, arranged a meeting with some of the elders at First Mesa for the next day, and in fact there followed two days of meetings, resulting in what Brew felt was encouraging agreement.

In the end it went nowhere. One of the elders from First Mesa had told Brew privately that he condoned the continuance of work on the mesa, but he had not expressed this sentiment during the meeting itself, and Wilson wanted to hear it from the man directly. At this point the record goes silent. Brew said nothing more in his journal about further negotiations or conversations, and the museum never submitted a request for reconsideration to the Department of the Interior. It was definite: Work at all sites on Antelope Mesa would have to be completed by the end of the workday on August 26, 1939.

The remainder of the 1939 field season was hectic as the staff threw themselves into completing all research. They had to finish recording the kiva murals at both Awatovi and Kawaika-a. Only that season had someone noticed, in an eroding

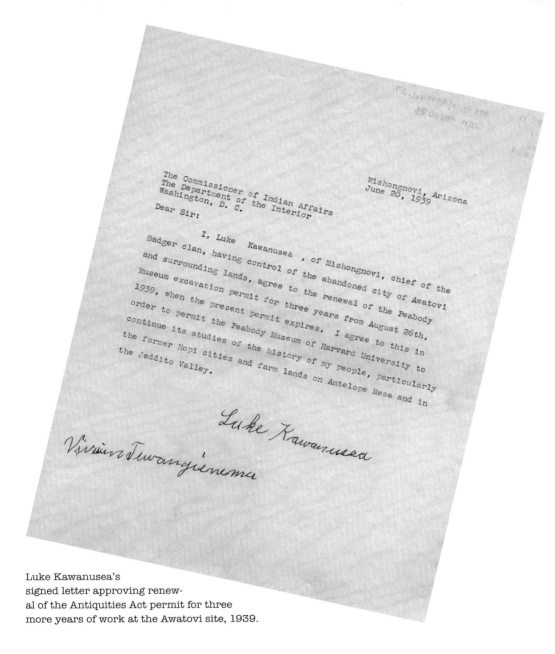

The Commissioner of Indian Affairs
The Department of the Interior
Washington, D. C.

Mishongnovi, Arizona
June 20, 1939

Dear Sir:

     I, Luke Kawanusea , of Mishongnovi, chief of the Badger clan, having control of the abandoned city of Awatovi and surrounding lands, agree to the renewal of the Peabody Museum excavation permit for three years from August 26th, 1939, when the present permit expires. I agree to this in order to permit the Peabody Museum of Harvard University to continue its studies of the history of my people, particularly the former Hopi cities and farm lands on Antelope Mesa and in the Jeddito Valley.

Luke Kawanusea

Vivian Tewangiemma

Luke Kawanusea's
signed letter approving renew-
al of the Antiquities Act permit for three
more years of work at the Awatovi site, 1939.

part of Kawaika-a, painted plaster in several of the rooms. Wat Smith launched a crash program to investigate these mural decorations, and 15 kivas "in varying states of preservation were excavated."[1] In addition, the staff and crew had to finish test-excavating and mapping the small sites on the mesa and then refill the excavation pits so that cattle and sheep would not fall into them. Despite constant diversions—not least the Brews' wedding—and the usual mobs of guests, by mid-August plans were being made to dispose of the camp equipment, and wooden boxes were being constructed for shipping huge quantities of artifacts and equipment back to Cambridge.

Although Brew seldom mentioned affairs of the world in his journal, news of the situation in Europe did reach Awatovi as staff members and guests brought newspapers from the Jeddito Trading Post, Holbrook, and Winslow. A.V. Kidder, in his journal of his week's stay at Awatovi, mentioned on August 26: "The papers that came in last night indicate that Europe's on the verge of war—it seems to mean very little out here." On September 1, the day Germany invaded Poland, Brew remarked that "the war news from Europe is very serious. It appears that Poland and Germany are actually fighting."

Although fieldwork stopped on August 26, it took nearly another month to finish up maps, notes, and packing. What does one do with a camp like New Awatovi when the expedition comes to an end? As staff members left, those who remained took down the tents and stacked the lumber from them by size. Brew gave one canvas tent and its lumber to one of the Hopi men and sold most of the rest, undoubtedly for small amounts, to various other Hopis. His journal of September 10 reported: "In the afternoon King and Archie Naha came over and bought the cook-shack for $85.00. They will use it in situ and get the cellar, cistern, one privy, and the powerhouse, which they will use as a granary, thrown in. It is very pleasant to think of the outfit continuing to be used."

Negotiations about the sale and other items the Nahas wanted continued over the next several days. A formal document on Peabody Museum letterhead, notarized on September 14 by Chi Roberts, who was a notary public in Navajo County, Arizona, made it official:

> To whom it may concern:
>
> For one hundred dollars, cash received, I today have sold to Archie Naha the cookshack at Awatovi with tables and shelving included, the vegetable cellar, the cistern, the small house which formerly held the electric motor, and one two-hole privy.
>
> Also included are three steel-spring cots with mattresses, one cream can, and four five-gallon oil cans, and also the cook stove which has been in the Second Mesa Hopi tent with enough joints of stove-pipe for the stove and a heater in the other end of the shack.
>
> It is also understood that all small scrap lumber left at Awatovi when we are through breaking camp is included in this, and whatever cedar posts are left.
>
> It is also understood that I shall be permitted to occupy these buildings until we are finished breaking camp, which will be sometime during the week of September 18.
>
> J. O. Brew, Director
> Awatovi Expedition of the Peabody Museum

A letter from Brew to Emil Haury during this packing-up time reveals that Haury purchased a dozen "trench picks," various kitchen utensils, and "1 Delco electric light plant with wires and fixtures for approximately 22 tents," all for a total of $113.70. The equipment continued to serve archaeology as part of the University of Arizona field school at Forestdale and perhaps beyond.

What happened to some of the other equipment and to the piano is also known. Brew's journal for September 9 says: "During the course of the morning Al, after measuring the truck and the piano, decided that he could carry the piano on the back of our Dodge truck and so it will go up to Ackmen [Colorado] for the use of his children. It was loaded in the afternoon. The tail gate of the truck was taken off and a solid bed of 2 x 4s made which projected out approximately two feet beyond the back of the truck. A load of tools, chairs, etc., for Al and Lin was put in the body of the truck and the piano was put on the newly-constructed platform in the rear."

In 2005, Bill Lancaster, one of Al's sons, told me what became of both the piano and the Dodge truck: "The folks kept that old piano as long as they lived on their farm. I was the only one that ever played it. My youngest sister, Sarah, decided she wanted to take music lessons, so Mom let her take it to Tucson. When Sarah and her husband were transferred, they . . . could only move so many pounds, and that piano must weigh three-quarters of a ton. I drove from Pecos, Texas, to Tucson and picked up the piano. I kept it for years and then my daughter took it. She still plays it. She is the only one of Al and Alice's offspring that can play. It is still in very good shape."

As for the truck, Bill Lancaster said: "I learned to drive in it, as did several of my siblings. My dad finally sold it to a neighbor. I had always wondered what had happened to it. I recently went to the abandoned place where the old man lived that bought it from my dad. I found the wheels and the fenders and running boards. Someone had torn it all apart. What a beautiful flashback in time it gave me to just see the parts."

With New Awatovi a memory, the staff and crew scattered. The war diverted nearly everyone's lives for the next few years, but some of the staff returned to Cambridge and stayed involved in writing reports about the project or in working for Harvard or the Peabody Museum. Some went on to careers otherwise devoted to archaeology; others said farewell to a summer's adventure and turned to the world of business after 1939. Bill Claflin, for example, continued as treasurer of Harvard through the war years but resigned in 1948 to return to the investment business. He was appointed

The Dodge truck, sold to Al Lancaster, packed to the gills and with the piano hanging out the back, ready for the trip to Al's home in Colorado, September 1939. Al and Happy Foote are ready to go.

to many directorships, including that of the United Fruit Company, and continued to manage his Soledad Sugar Company in Cuba until 1960, when it was confiscated by the Castro government.[2] He died in 1982 at the age of 88.

Donald Scott remained director of the Peabody Museum until 1948, when he turned the reins over to Jo Brew. He remained busy in publishing and in 1955 established a fund for the Harvard University Press Faculty Prize, an annual award of $2,000. In 1967, shortly after several weeks of trail riding in Arizona, he died suddenly at his ranch cottage near Santa Barbara, California, at the age of 82.

Jo and Evelyn Brew returned to Cambridge, where Jo, in addition to teaching at Harvard, completed his dissertation—not about Awatovi but about his earlier findings at Alkali Ridge. The museum published it in 1946. He wrote some journal articles about Awatovi and contributed chapters to *Franciscan Awatovi*, the book on the mission ruins published by the Peabody Museum in 1949—although the bulk of the data analysis and writing for the book fell to Ross Montgomery.

Evelyn meanwhile spent the war years working as an assistant to the editor of the American Chemical Society in Cambridge. Afterward she took up her secretarial job at the Peabody again for several years. In 1941, the same year the Peabody appointed Jo assistant curator of Southwestern archaeology, Evelyn gave birth to their first son.

They named him Alan, after Al Lancaster, and when a second son was born in 1944, they called him Lindsay, after Lin Thompson.

Jo's promotion to curator proved to be only the next step in a long, distinguished, and productive career in archaeology, museum administration, and—on the national and international scene—historic preservation. He became curator of North American archaeology at the Peabody in 1945 and director of the museum in 1948, a position he held until 1967. He was appointed a member of the Committee for the Recovery of Archaeological Remains (CRAR), a small, independent group of archaeologists created in 1945, and soon was elected chair. The purpose of CRAR was to convince Congress to fund the excavation of sites to be affected by the building of federally funded reservoirs, particularly in the Missouri River Basin. Jo was named to the National Park Service's Advisory Board and, in the international realm, for many years chaired UNESCO's International Committee on Monuments and Sites.

After retiring as museum director, Brew continued teaching at Harvard until 1974 and even after that remained active on many committees. In 1984 he wrote to friends that he had retired from "all my commitments save 3: (1) The Advisory Council of the National Park Service; (2) A committee which, annually, selects a scholar to work for a year in the Rome Center for Historic Preservation, and (3) A board of 3 which advises the Tennessee Valley Authority on archaeological matters."[3] Jo Brew died in 1988 at the age of 81. Evelyn Brew, always active politically on the local and state levels, moved from Massachusetts to Minneapolis in 2007 to be near son Alan and his family. At the time she described herself as "a liberal, a quilter, and a backsliding Unitarian."

Hattie Cosgrove, too, returned to the Peabody after the end of the expedition and stayed for another 10 years, primarily studying the Awatovi pottery collections. She reached retirement age in 1942 but was asked to stay on through the war because of personnel shortages at the museum. She then worked as a volunteer until 1949, when she retired to Albuquerque, New Mexico, where her son lived. She died there at the age of 92, in 1970.

Watson Smith devoted his time to studying the Awatovi collections at the Peabody until 1942, when he was commissioned a captain in U.S. Army Air Force Intelligence. He served in New Caledonia and Guadalcanal in 1942 and 1943. In 1943 he married Lucy Cranwell, staff botanist for the Auckland Museum in New Zealand. While the couple lived in Cambridge from 1948 to 1954, Wat held Brew's old title of curator of Southwestern archaeology at the Peabody.

Lucy and Wat had a son, Ben, and in 1954 the family moved to Tucson, Arizona, where Wat established what he called the "Peabody Museum West of the Pecos" at his home. From that outpost he continued to work steadfastly on analyzing data and writing and publishing reports about the Awatovi excavations as well as other, later

Peabody projects in which he participated.[4] He served as a trustee of Brown University, his alma mater, and as a trustee of the Museum of Northern Arizona in Flagstaff from 1956 to 1979. He died at home in Tucson in 1993 at the age of 96. According to one obituary, "he was a man of protean gifts—a philosopher, a digger in the soil of history, a prolific and graceful writer, a conservationist, and a human being of rare warmth, humor, and intuition."[5]

John Hack, the geologist, returned to Harvard in 1939 and, spurred by the need to finish his doctorate, became the Awatovi Expedition member who produced written reports the fastest. He wrote a dissertation on the physical environment of Antelope Mesa and received his Ph.D. in 1940. The Peabody published it in 1942 as "Reports of the Awatovi Expedition 1," alongside Report 2, Hack's *Prehistoric Coal Mining in the Jeddito Valley, Arizona.* Hack spent most of the remainder of his career as a geomorphologist with the U.S. Geological Survey. He received a Distinguished Service Award from the Department of the Interior in 1972 and in 1988 won the Binghamton Geomorphology Symposium Award "for his extraordinary contributions in the field of geomorphology."[6] He died in 1991.

Like Hack, Dick Woodbury continued his studies at Harvard, receiving an M.A. in anthropology in 1942. After serving in the Air Force as a weather observer in the South Pacific, he returned to Harvard, wrote a dissertation on the stone tools from Awatovi, which became Report 6 in the Awatovi series, and earned his Ph.D. in 1949. In 1950 he began his teaching career at the University of Kentucky. After stints at Columbia University, the University of Arizona's Interdisciplinary Arid Lands Program, and the U.S. National Museum, he taught and held administrative positions from 1969 to 1981 at the University of Massachusetts, Amherst. Woodbury retired in 1982 to Shutesbury, Massachusetts, with his wife, Nathalie. Both Dick and Nathalie received the Distinguished Service Award from the Society for American Archaeology in 1988. In 2007 the two were involving themselves in the plight of stray dogs and cats and in the history of their town, writing obituaries and book reviews, and contributing to and critiquing many versions of the manuscript for this book.

Penny Davis returned to work briefly at the Peabody, reproducing scale drawings of kiva murals with Wat Smith through the fall of 1941. She married Eugene Worman, a graduate student in anthropology at Harvard, in February 1942, and both immediately went to work for the navy in Washington, D.C., as civilians. Penny made silhouette drawings of U.S. Navy ships, as well as some British and German ones, for training and identification booklets. After the war she continued her career as an illustrator, working for archaeologists at the Carnegie Institution, among other organizations. She and Gene had two sons and eventually moved to Amherst, Massachusetts, in 1973. They lived there until 1996, when Gene suffered a stroke, after which they moved first to Arkansas for six years and then to an assisted living facility in Chesapeake, Virginia, where their elder son lived. Gene died in 2006 at the age of 92. Penny celebrated her ninetieth birthday in September 2007, and she died two months later.

Mott Davis, all the more determined after his Awatovi experience to become a professional archaeologist, returned to Harvard and spent 1940–1941 doing graduate work. In 1942 he married Beth Ogden, a Radcliffe anthropology graduate. Following time out during World War II to work as a civilian for the Air Transport Command in Washington, D.C., and then to manage the family farm after the death of our father in 1943, he accepted a teaching position in 1948 at the University of Nebraska. One son was born to Beth and Mott on the family farm, and another in Lincoln, Nebraska. He completed his dissertation and received his Ph.D. from Harvard in 1954. Two years later he joined the faculty at the University of Texas, where he taught for the rest of his career, receiving many teaching awards. Mott died in December 1998, a month after his eightieth birthday.

Not everyone, of course, went east. Al Lancaster returned home to Ackmen, Colorado, after helping to close up camp, but he never strayed from archaeology. He spent most of his long career after Awatovi working for the National Park Service in the Southwest, where he developed extraordinary skills in stabilizing and restoring Puebloan ruins. Between 1940 and 1962 he was assigned to work at Aztec Ruin, Chaco Canyon, Hovenweep, El Morro, and—his longest assignment—Mesa Verde National Park. In 1962 the Department of the Interior awarded Lancaster its highest tribute, the Distinguished Service Award, the first of many such honors he would receive over the years.

Perhaps the most heart-warming recognition came in 1959, when Lancaster was presented with a special plaque at the annual Pecos Conference, signed by 84 colleagues and inscribed: "Loyal friend and valued colleague; discoverer, excavator, preserver. Your example has inspired us. We have benefited by your assistance and advice. Mesa Verde, Alkali Ridge, Awatovi, Hovenweep, Tumacacori, and Chaco Canyon bear witness to your skills. The archaeologists of the Southwest salute you."[7] In 1964 Al and his wife, Alice, retired to Durango, Colorado, where he died in 1992 at the age of 98.

Still other Awatovi staff members embarked on or returned to distinguished careers in anthropology and other academic fields after the expedition's end. Ned Hall, for example, received a Ph.D. from Columbia University in 1942 in cultural anthropology. That year he wrote a report of his findings about the Awatovi tree-ring samples he had studied; it was published in the journal *Tree-Ring Bulletin* in 1951. He and E. Boyd divorced sometime during World War II, and she returned to Santa Fe to become "probably the leading authority on Spanish Colonial arts and crafts."[8] Hall later taught anthropology at Northwestern University and became well known for his books about nonverbal communication.

Dick Wheeler, the "stone and bone" man in 1936 and 1937, was able to return to archaeology after the war, obtaining his master's degree at Harvard. By 1950 he was in Lincoln, Nebraska, directing the excavation of sites to be inundated by reservoirs being built on the main channel and tributaries of the Missouri River. In the mid-1960s he worked at Mesa Verde National Park, where he managed at last to return to the Awatovi collections and write the report "Bone and Antler Artifacts"—although it was not published until 1978, in the last volume (to date) of the Awatovi report series. Wheeler later joined the National Park Service's main office in Washington, D.C., editing archaeological publications. He died in 1997 in Chapel Hill, North Carolina.

The list of Awatovi staff members whose names are still known in anthropology is a long one. Anna Shepard continued her experiments on ceramic technology, working through the Carnegie Institution under A.V. Kidder and, when that archaeology program was closed down, for the U.S. Geological Survey in Denver until her retirement in 1970. George Brainerd became a professor at the University of California, Los Angeles, and Bob Burgh held a variety of positions in archaeology and ethnography over the years. Erik Reed worked as an archaeologist with the Southwest Region of the National Park Service in Santa Fe from 1939 until his retirement in 1970. Volney Jones spent his career at the University of Michigan in Ann Arbor and became known as one of the founders of "paleoethnobotany," the study of archaeological plant remains.

Tom Campbell, a member of the 1937 staff and another to receive a Harvard Ph.D., went on to enjoy a long teaching career in archaeology and ethnohistory at the University of Texas, Austin. John Longyear, whose letters home so colorfully described camp life at Awatovi, also taught anthropology, in his case for 30 years at Colgate University. He developed a teaching museum of anthropology there that now bears his name. Charlie Amsden returned to the Southwest Museum in 1939, but the tuberculosis from which he suffered while working at Awatovi took his life in 1941, at the age of 42. His book *Navaho Weaving*, published posthumously, became an enduring Southwestern classic.

Carlos García-Robiou, the life of the party, continued his career as a professor of anthropology and archaeology at the University of Havana. He married in 1940 and had a son and a daughter, Vivian, who was living in Maryland when I made contact with her in 2005. In the summer of 1941 Carlos collaborated with Irving Rouse, of Yale University, in a joint project in the Maniabon Hills of Cuba. He was listed in 1953 in the *International Directory of Anthropological Institutions* as a professor and as curator at the Museo Montane at the University of Havana. He died of cancer in 1961. Vivian remembered that the Claflins visited her family in Havana during one of their trips to their sugar plantation, and she recalled her father telling of his happy days at Awatovi.

At least six of the Hopi men who worked at Awatovi were drafted or enlisted in the army in World War II—Leland, Emory, and Alec Dennis, Kenneth Polacca, Sylvan Nash, and Eric Lalo. Alec Dennis served overseas, in Germany, but none of the others did, as far as I could find out. All six returned safely to the reservation. Most of the Hopis worked in later years for the Indian Service (eventually the Bureau of Indian Affairs), the Forest Service, or some other state or federal agency, either on or off the reservation. Some of the men moved away to other towns in Arizona, usually because they married non-Hopi women. But even those working off-reservation seem to have maintained close ties with their homes and families and to have participated in ceremonies and fulfilled their clan obligations.

Sadly, two of the Hopi crew died early, accidental deaths. Sometime in the early to mid-1950s, Leland Dennis, Jake Poleviyuma, his son Jake Jr., and perhaps two or three other Hopis flew to southern California to help fight a forest fire. According to Jake Jr., at one point the fire got away from them, and they were told to turn back. Leland jumped into a small ravine, presumably thinking the blaze would jump over it. But the ravine was full of dry brush, which caught fire, and Leland was killed. He was the only one to die in that fire, and his family believes the Forest Service erected a monument acknowledging his sacrifice. His remains were brought back to his family for the appropriate ceremonies and burial.

The other man died by fire as well. Sometime probably in the mid- to late 1960s, Randolph David went into a kiva with a lantern and some gasoline to prepare the kiva for an upcoming ceremony. His friends assumed the gasoline somehow ignited, because he was burned to death. "All that was left was his silver belt buckle," said Jim Tawayesva, Luke Hovelo's son, in 2001.

It is unfortunate for this story that Jo Brew, Wat Smith, and Donald Scott saved so few of the letters they received from their Hopi friends. Smith mentioned in his autobiography that he and the Scotts stayed in close touch with some of the crew: "Mr. and Mrs. Scott always made efforts to keep the channels open, and for years they wrote letters and sent gifts to many Hopi friends. . . . Leland [Dennis] . . . was a demon correspondent, and I still have a file of letters [not among his files at the Arizona State Museum] that he wrote to me during the 1940s and 1950s telling of his house-building, his corn-planting, his cattle, and of course, his children. . . . Evans Poleahla from First Mesa later worked for the agency at Keams Canyon and developed a serious interest in the history and evolution of Hopi ceremonialism. We exchanged letters and I sent him books on the subject."[9]

Jo Brew corresponded with Hopi friends too. One poignant letter from Hoppy Dennis, written to Jo on November 14, 1947, reveals the homesickness of a young man living and working far from home:

Hotel Lincoln, R[oom]. 30
3129 Block Ave
East Chicago, Ind.

Dear Sir:

I've just awfully wondered if you still remember me. As for me, I still remembered you, so tonite, while I'm not doing anything on hand, I just thought of you. So, I'm going to drop you a few lines and also to tell you that I'm way out here in Indiana, working for Inland Steel Co. I came out here October 5. This is my first trip out here to east. Well, I'm just doing fine with my job here, but the only thing I don't like is this cold weather that they have around here. So now I feel like going back home to good ol sunny Arizona. So, I guess you'll remember me now when you hear Arizona. I'm just one of those Dennis boys that used to work for you out in the Hopi country.

Well, Joe, how are you getting along over there. I hope you are just fine. By the way is Mrs. Cosgrove still around there some where. If she is still there just tell her I said hello to her. Well Joe, I've left my home. Since March 28th in 1942, and I've never gone back to see my folks. So I really don't know how all my brothers and sisters are getting along. But I still hope that they are all in a good health. Joe, when are you going back to the Hopi country again and work on the ruins.

Boy, I sure wished I could go back there now, as I really missed the old gang. Like Al Lancaster, Watson Smith, and all the others. Ha. How is your wife Evelyn. I guess both of you are fine too. I'm not so sure if this letter will find you as its been a long time since we all left each other back home in Arizona. But at the same time I'm sure you'll be glad to hear from me. So if you do, I would like for you to answer my letter back maybe. I'd probably go that way [to Cambridge?] or come over there to see you all. I don't think I will stay around here very long [on] account of the cold weather. Beside, I left my wife and kids back in Phoenix.

Oh yes, I want to tell you that I've got a [P]ima wife. She's a different tribe than I am. Their reservation is located on south of Phoenix. I've been with her for almost six years now. She is very nice and I've got two little girls now. Well, Joe there is nothing much I can say now until I hear from you. . . .

I'm just one of your Hopi friends. Good by and so long, I'm your friend, Elwood L. Dennis (Hoppy along)—remember that name?

Clearly, the camaraderie of the Awatovi experience forged lasting ties among all whom it touched. Yet the Peabody's era of expeditions to the American Southwest was drawing to a close. In 1949, after Brew had been named director of the museum, he inaugurated a project called the Upper Gila Expedition to study the precontact cultural sequence along the Gila River in west-central New Mexico.[10] It lasted for three summers, and then the Peabody withdrew from the Southwest as its archaeologists turned their research interests to other areas, largely the lower Mississippi Valley and Central and South America.

Only once, to my knowledge, did anyone express serious interest in excavating further at Awatovi after 1939. In the Peabody archives is an exchange of correspondence labeled "CONFIDENTIAL," between René d'Harnoncourt, general manager of the Department of the Interior's Indian Arts and Crafts Board, and Jo Brew, dated June 2 and June 26, 1941. D'Harnoncourt wrote that the department had "received from the Southwest Museum [in Los Angeles] a request for permit to conduct archaeological excavations in the western refuse slide of Awatovi." He asked whether the Peabody intended to "reopen its activities there."

Brew, in a long letter, said that scientifically the museum had no objection, but there was no "western refuse slide," only the rooms of the pueblo, which the Peabody had extensively excavated. Moreover, analysis of the museum's data from the Western Mound and elsewhere at the site was still in progress, with the results to be published over the next four years. "During the course of the preparation of the reports we may find it necessary to return to Awatovi to check certain details. Consequently it seems to me that it might be inadvisable to disturb the site before our reports are well along toward completion. . . . Of course, after our reports are out and the results of our work are available, there could be no possible objection to some one going in to Awatovi, then, to carry on further or to check our results."

John Collier, commissioner of Indian Affairs, replied to this comment saying that "for the present, at least, no new agency should work at Awatovi." And indeed, no one has.

Excavations in the Western Mound, 1936.

– 8 –

A Scientific Legacy

Side by side with the lasting memories and friendships formed by the Awatovi staff and crew stand the expedition's enduring scientific accomplishments. In many ways the expedition members adhered to standard archaeological practices of the time, some of which, such as systematically surveying an area for ruins and artifacts, are still fundamental today. In other ways Jo Brew and his colleagues proved to be innovative thinkers who inaugurated practices that would become new standards in fieldwork. They were, for example, among the first archaeologists in the Southwest to collect all the animal bones they found, and they were pioneers in the study of archaeological plant remains. The Awatovi Expedition won fame for its most spectacular finds—kiva murals and the remains of the three Franciscan churches—but for archaeologists its published reports on topics such as pottery and stone tools, now classics, were equally important.

Several of the Awatovi staff deserve credit, too, for publishing their findings relatively quickly, especially given the disruptions of the war in the years immediately following the fieldwork. Timely publication was far from standard in Brew's time, and indeed for many years afterward, but without this part of archaeological research a project can have no legacy at all. As director, Brew set an example by publishing preliminary reports after every field season except 1938 (which he combined with 1939). They appeared in either *American Antiquity*, a quarterly publication of the Society for American Archaeology, or *Plateau*, a journal published by the Museum of Northern Arizona in Flagstaff.

Brew tallied the expedition's achievements in his final preliminary report, published in 1941. Over the course of five field seasons, he said, the staff and crew had located and mapped 296 archaeological sites on Antelope Mesa. In fact it had been John Hack and young Bill Claflin who, traversing the mesa by vehicle or on horseback, visited most of these sites. They collected potsherds and other artifacts from the surface and

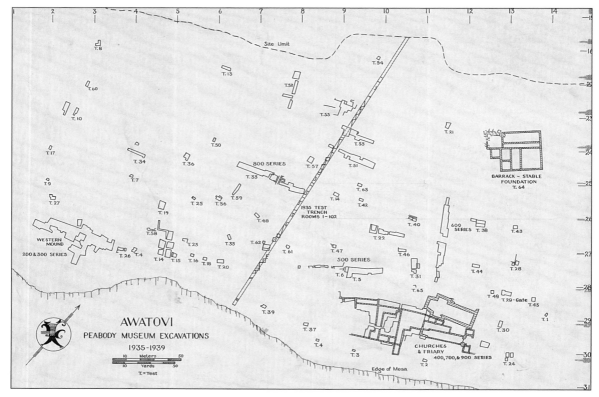

Locations of excavations completed at Awatovi in all five seasons.

for each site drew a rough map showing any surface signs of rooms. Back at camp, Hattie Cosgrove and the others could use the potsherds to roughly date the times when people had lived at each site, information that helped Brew and Lancaster select sites to excavate.

The final count of sites excavated partly or entirely came to 21. Most of the digging took place at Awatovi itself, where Brew reported that 1,300 rooms had been excavated, among them 25 kivas. Besides the long north-south trench dug in 1935, the crew excavated another 65 small test pits in parts of the site away from the Western Mound and the mission area, which saw the most concentrated excavation. The test pits allowed the staff to define the limits of the site and to collect artifacts revealing the approximate dates when different parts of the village were occupied.

The crew dug another 200 rooms at other sites, mostly along the south rim of Antelope Mesa, overlooking the Jeddito Valley. Kawaika-a, as I mentioned earlier, received some last-minute attention when it was found to have murals in several kivas. Otherwise, most of the attention outside of Awatovi went to relatively small sites that appeared to have housed ancestral Hopis for particularly long spans of time.

Excavation of a kiva mural at Kawaika-a, 1939.

One of these was Site 4, near the Jeddito Trading Post—the site that had so excited Brew during the 1935 field season. Another, designated Site 4A, was a nearby "complex of Basket Maker III or Pueblo I pit houses," together with "a single row of at least ten masonry surface rooms."[1] Its aboveground rooms and pottery revealed that it had been used into Pueblo II and III times. Near one of the stone masonry rooms in the long row was a subterranean D-shaped kiva, one of the few of its kind found on the mesa.[2] Because Charlie Amsden took a particular interest in these two sites, Brew had him supervise their excavation, largely during the last two field seasons. Amsden no doubt would have written a report on them had he not died in 1941.

A third small site, Site 264, was, according to Brew, "one of the two most important of the early sites excavated by [the] Awatovi Expedition."[3] (The other was probably Sites 4 and 4A together.) It also turned out to be the only small site studied during the expedition that became the subject of a published report. After the war, a young man named Hiroshi Daifuku arrived at Harvard from Hawaii for graduate study, and Brew offered him the large collection from Site 264 to write up for his dissertation. The Peabody Museum published his study, *Jeddito 264*, in 1961, with the subtitle *A Report on the Excavation of a Basket Maker III–Pueblo I Site in Northeastern Arizona with a Review of Some Current Theories in Southwestern Archaeology*. Daifuku was interested

View of rooms during excavation at the medium-sized site called Pink Arrow, 1939.

in the way architecture had changed as the ancestral Pueblo people of the Southwest moved from pit houses to aboveground pueblos as their dwellings. Site 264 spanned just the right years for Daifuku to observe this shift.

Although Brew originally planned several publications about the small sites of Antelope Mesa, they slipped through the cracks after the war and were never written. In his 1941 preliminary report, Brew summarized in only a sentence or two the work done at 15 small sites besides those just described. Site 102, for example, was "a small P II unit . . . two rooms and two outside fire-pits." Site 169 got a slightly longer description: "An early P II site near Site 108: two pit houses; important because of striking resemblance in the masonry to the P II pit houses in the San Francisco Mountain region." Dick Woodbury, in his dissertation on the stone tools from all the excavated sites, briefly reviewed their dates and the amount of work done at each.[4] But except for information about the kivas described by Watson Smith in his *Kiva Mural Decorations at Awatovi and Kawaika-a*, no other information about the small sites has yet seen publication.

One important thing Brew and his staff did at all the sites was to take hundreds of photographs. It seems likely that Brew himself took many of the field pictures when he visited the excavations each morning, but his dig supervisors also had access to museum cameras. Certainly the staff doing the testing at remote sites had a camera available for use.

Ingenuity sometimes came into play when a photographer wanted to take a long view or needed to get high enough to see the overall plan of an excavated area. One photograph shows a tripod ladder that served the purpose. During the 1938 field season Alden Stevens experimented by building a box kite in which he affixed a camera. Apparently it was not a success. Chi Roberts, who enjoyed kite flying, had warned Stevens that air pockets were a big problem and had "dashed to the ground" some of Chi's kites. That might be what happened to Stevens's experiment, for it was mentioned only once in the expedition's journals.

Besides crisscrossing Antelope Mesa looking for sites, Johnny Hack took notes on the geology, landforms, plant life, and water sources of Antelope Mesa, Tallahogan Canyon, the Jeddito Valley, and other parts of the reservation. Perhaps most importantly, he studied the ingenious ways in which contemporary Hopi farmers grew crops in this semiarid landscape, taking advantage of every drop of rainfall, much as their ancestors must have done. Hack concluded that "the Hopi apparently have an excellent practical knowledge of the action of physiographic processes, for the position of their fields is closely related to the concentration of surface runoff and the flow of ground water."[5] He identified fields on the low flood terraces of large arroyos, fields in the bottoms of arroyos, fields watered by slope wash, sand dune agriculture, fields watered by rainfall only, seepage fields, and irrigation as techniques used by Hopi farmers to make the most of the water in their dry climate.

Hack's environmental study, published in 1942, fulfilled one of the first goals Brew had expressed in his memos to Donald Scott in 1935 during the planning of the expedition—that of linking precontact lifeways with those of historic and living Hopis. In the preface to Hack's report, Brew wrote: "We have endeavored to avoid the error charged, unfortunately often with justice, against archaeology in the past, of ignoring the wealth of information available in the numerous ethnological, historical, physiographical, and sociological studies of the Southwest, information of inestimable value for imparting life and meaning to the dust and debris of archaeology."

Hack made some unusual finds along the south-facing rim of the mesa—places where the ancestral Hopis had mined outcrops of coal. J. W. Fewkes had discovered coal ash during his excavations at Awatovi, residues of coal the Hopis had evidently used to heat their homes from the thirteenth century to the seventeenth.[6] The Spanish

The tripod photography ladder on the Western Mound, 1936.

colonists seem to have used only wood, and the Hopis abandoned coal as a heating source during the postcontact period.

Hopi potters also used coal to fire their pottery, as Frederick W. Hodge had noted at the turn of the twentieth century.[7] The results of using coal in firing pottery can be distinguished from the results achieved with other fuels, such as dung, which was introduced when Spaniards brought sheep into the area.[8] Hack discovered slag heaps with broken pottery close to a coal mine and excavated in two of them, carrying out the first detailed study of Hopi coal mining. In his report he offered an interesting twist on Hopi "ingenuity and industry": "The Hopi apparently discovered the value of coal at about the same time as the English. Coal was known in England at least as early as the ninth century A.D., but it was not generally used in London until the thirteenth century."[9]

Achieving another of Brew's goals, Volney Jones, the ethnobotanist from the University of Michigan, spent at least a month in each of the 1936, 1938, and 1939 field seasons collecting samples of plant remains from the excavations. He and Brew were particularly keen to determine which plant species the precontact Hopis had exploited and which species the Spaniards had introduced. Among other methods, Jones examined adobe bricks, largely from the church ruins. "The bricks were slaked in water and the contents removed by flotation and screening," wrote Donald Scott.[10] Many other items besides seeds and bits of plants floated out of the crumbled bricks, including

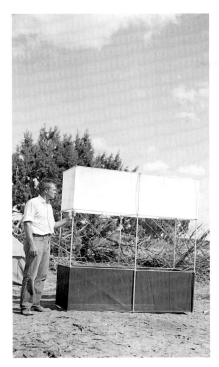

Alden Stevens standing by his camera kite, and the camera kite in flight, 1938.

"coal fragments, insects (whole and fragmentary), potsherds, fibres, twisted cordage, [and] chipped flint and obsidian."[11] Jones also collected samples from burned or charred areas as they were uncovered during the excavations in the Western Mound and in other pueblo rooms. A "preliminary list" of plants identified during the 1938 field season named corn, cotton, chili peppers, pumpkins, and gourds among the plants cultivated by the Hopis before European contact. Later, Spaniards had brought with them wheat, peaches, plums or apricots, watermelons, and cantaloupes.[12]

Hard seeds and pieces of charred plants are easy to find in archaeological sites if one knows—or invents—techniques for finding them. Much rarer are remnants of things that normally rot away quickly, such as baskets, cloth, and unburned wood. Brew reported discovering a "surprising amount of perishable material" at Awatovi, including even "pieces of carved wood from the ecclesiastical buildings." Except for the last, most of these finds came from graves in the floor of Church 2, the church used prior to the Pueblo Revolt, although some came from burials in the Western Mound and in the postcontact Hopi village.

Methods for preserving these kinds of materials were primitive in the late 1930s in comparison with current techniques and procedures, but the Peabody carefully curated the collection. Soon after the end of the expedition, a young woman named

Marcelotte Leake studied the perishables while working at Harvard on a Ph.D. in ethnobotany and anthropology. Her manuscript was never published and was missing from the Peabody archives in 1993 when Laurie Webster, then a graduate student at the University of Arizona, studied the textile collections from Awatovi for her doctoral dissertation.[13] Webster described fibers, textiles, cordage, and similar materials. She noted that after the arrival of the Spaniards and their sheep, Hopi weavers used sheep's wool more than their native cotton. The cotton seeds that were recovered from the excavations, she pointed out, came mostly from fired areas, and cotton fibers did not preserve as well as wool. Before the Pueblo Revolt in 1680, the mission controlled both sheep and wool. After the revolt, when Hopis had control of their own sheep, wool spun into yarn became a staple at Awatovi.

The bones of some of those sheep eventually found their way into the Awatovi Expedition's collections. That Brew had his workers systematically save the bits and pieces of animal bones scattered throughout the dirt fill of rooms and test pits was unusual for his time. Years later, the zooarchaeologist Stanley J. Olsen, of the University of Arizona, assessed the practice this way: "Up until about [the 1960s], it was a rare exception when an archaeological project included the collection and preservation of all nonhuman faunal material. . . . Notable among these early exceptions was the foresight of Dr. J. O. Brew, Director of the Awatovi Expedition . . . to save and catalogue by provenience all of the bones encountered."[14]

Sometime soon after the end of the expedition, Brew sent the bone collection, consisting of "hundreds of thousands of individual items," to the Mammal Department at the Museum of Comparative Zoology at Harvard.[15] There, Grover Allen began the arduous chore of identifying the species. After his death, Barbara Lawrence took up the study and wrote a short report listing the identified mammals and comparing bones of the genus Canis—which could have been dogs, wolves, or coyotes—to those known from other late Pueblo sites.[16]

By the 1970s, specialists in zooarchaeology were working closely with archaeologists to identify animal bones, provide information on the local habitats in which the animals lived, estimate the amount of meat each species provided in the diet, and reconstruct the natural environment and subsistence practices of the community. Stanley Olsen was one such specialist working on collections from Southwestern sites. In 1974 he inquired of the Peabody whether the animal bones collected at Awatovi might be available for him to study. Stephen Williams, then director of the museum, gladly sent him the whole collection—34,000 pieces. Before long Olsen reported in a short article that he had identified the remains of the first Spanish greyhound found in the Southwest.[17]

Among the bones from the pre-Hispanic parts of Awatovi, Olsen recognized coyote, black bear, mountain lion, mule deer, pronghorn antelope, two sizes of

Dog effigy carved on the handle of a bone awl from Site 111, early Pueblo II.

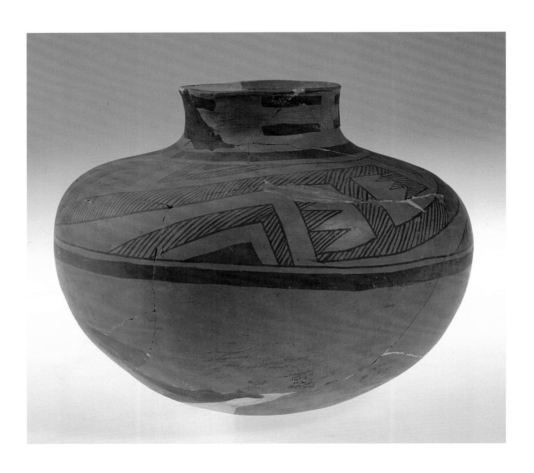

A Jeddito Black-on-orange pottery jar from Awatovi,
pieced together from fragments.

Two Sikyatki Polychrome vessels from Awatovi.
This pottery type was made between about A.D. 1400 and 1700.

Kiva mural from Kawaika-a, Test 4, Room 4.
Serigraph by Louie Ewing from a drawing by Penrose Davis.

Kiva mural from Awatovi, Room 529.
Serigraph by Louie Ewing from a drawing by Penrose Davis.

Ross Montgomery's sketch of a priest at the altar of Church 2.

A view of Awatovi before excavation in 1935 (top),
and the same view of the ruins photographed by the author in 1991.

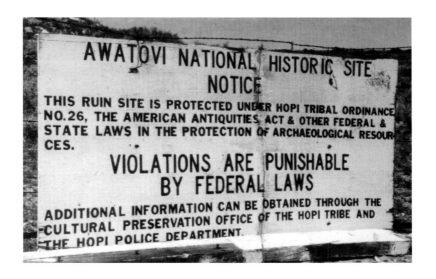

Penny Davis Worman and Mott Davis at the site of the Awatovi field camp
in August 1991 (top). Penny has her foot on the cement steps of the cook shack.
At the time of their visit, this large sign was attached to the fence
that surrounds the Awatovi site.

domestic dogs, and many species of rabbits. He found a few pieces of painted turtle carapace but no other reptiles. Several species of birds from wetland habitats, including white pelican, great blue heron, Canada goose, blue-winded teal, and cinnamon teal, had probably been hunted in the valley south of the mesa and their feathers used in ceremonies. Olsen found no fish or amphibians but plenty of the expected bones from Spanish domesticated animals—horses, burros, cows, goats, and sheep. "Nowhere, to my knowledge," he wrote in his full report, "has a collection approaching that from Awatovi been amassed which represents the domestic animals that were utilized by colonial Spaniards in the Southwest." Not all the animals were raised for food or means of transportation. Besides the greyhound, Olsen identified in one of the rooms of the mission complex a domestic cat, whose bones he believed were "the earliest domestic cat remains recovered in the Southwest."[18]

Collecting items such as seeds and animal bones was still fairly unusual in Southwestern archaeology in the 1930s. Amassing huge quantities of common, relatively indestructible artifacts such as potsherds and stone tools, on the other hand, had long been standard practice. Altogether the Awatovi staff and crew excavated, washed, classified, and recorded more than half a million potsherds. On top of those were another 8,500 "restorable specimens, special zoomorphic sherds, etc., and a collection of pottery types taken from each level to serve as a check during future analysis."[19]

While Hattie Cosgrove and her helpers processed the pottery, Anna Shepard experimented to discover precisely how the Hopis had made it.[20] She gathered red and gray clays from their natural sources at the edge of Antelope Mesa and fired them with both wood and coal in a pit similar to those used by contemporary Pueblo potters. This was not her first such experiment—she had done the same for Kidder with Pecos pottery—or her last, but it was still highly innovative at the time.

At Awatovi, Shepard learned that Hopi potters had achieved a sophisticated grasp of their technology (see pp. 170, 171). They could carefully control the amount of air reaching the pots as they fired in order to make the clay turn a desired color in a range from gray through red and orange to yellow. "Sorting of large collections of sherds leaves no doubt that these colors were the objectives and were generally attained," she wrote. Summing up the manufacture of pottery at Awatovi, she surmised that "each new development . . . must have been accompanied by experimentation on the part of venturesome potters, and also by some lag on the part of conservative potters in adopting unfamiliar material and new techniques."[21]

Of her work at Awatovi, Shepard later had this to say: "The summer of 1938 was a fortunate time to be a guest at the Awatovi Camp. Dr. Brew had an enthusiastic interest in technological studies and constantly alerted the excavators to pertinent objects they might find. . . . The establishment of satisfactory communication between archaeologist and specialist may well be the principal value of field association. Questions and discussions follow immediately as problems arise, and the informality of camp life frees them from restraint."[22]

Wat Smith took it upon himself to analyze the decorated pottery from the Western Mound, and his report became volume 8 in the Awatovi publication series. Pots with painted designs—usually serving bowls and storage jars rather than everyday cooking vessels—are useful to archaeologists because design styles varied from group to group and changed over time. When linked to dates determined from tree rings, painted potsherds can help analysts define the chronology of a site, in addition to revealing who was trading with whom. Smith found that painted sherds from the Western Mound dated from around A.D. 1200 (the Pueblo III period) to about 1450 (Pueblo IV).

Smith refused to offer much in the way of speculation about what the pottery might mean. "Both the scope and the purposes of this monograph have been limited," he wrote of his 1971 report, "and the conclusions presented must be concomitantly restricted. An analytical study of pottery alone, however detailed or comprehensive, does not provide an adequate base for far-ranging conclusions or imaginative hypotheses." He had intended to conduct "an exhaustive comparative study of the pottery indigenous to the regions surrounding the Jeddito area," but this proved to be "another optimistic plan that has not been realized."[23] Nevertheless, his exhaustive description of the painted pottery types became an invaluable reference for later archaeologists in the region.

Smith's study was not the only publication on pottery to come out of the expedition, however belatedly. Bob Burgh served as Wat's chief assistant and produced a statistical study of the vessel rim profiles, which was published in *American Antiquity* in 1959. From rim profiles it is possible, if enough of the rim is left on a potsherd, to tell the size and shape of the whole vessel from which the sherd came.

While Smith and Burgh were studying the Western Mound ceramics, they spent some "enjoyable time" discussing them with a graduate student at the University of Arizona named James Gifford. Later, pursuing a doctorate at Harvard, Gifford, with Smith's help and encouragement, studied the collection of the most common utilitarian pottery found during the excavations—a ware called "gray corrugated" because potters pinched the overlapping clay coils on the outside of the vessel so that the surface had a texture much like that of corrugated cardboard. Unfortunately, Gifford died of heart trouble in 1973, having completed only an analysis of the technology by which the pots were made. Smith later added some historic background on previous studies and published the report as a coauthored work, Report 10 of the Awatovi Expedition, in 1978.

Besides pottery, Brew reported that by the end of the expedition, participants had excavated and catalogued 11,700 artifacts of stone and bone. Dick Wheeler began the work of cataloguing and identifying them in 1936 and 1937, and Dick Woodbury, aided at times by Haych Claflin, Mott Davis, and others, carried on in 1938 and 1939. Woodbury then analyzed the majority of the stone artifacts as the basis for his Ph.D. dissertation, which the Peabody published in 1954.

At the time he was writing, few detailed studies of stone tools of the Southwest existed. Indeed, his report was the first full-scale study of such pieces since A.V. Kidder's 1932 *The Artifacts of Pecos*. Woodbury not only described categories of tools such as knives and arrowheads—the standard for reporting in his day—but also discerned patterns in the ways artifacts varied through time and across space in related Hopi sites and among other regional cultures such as those of the Hohokam and Mogollon. His report and Smith's on decorated pottery from the Western Mound remain models for technical detail.

It took somewhat longer for the bone artifacts to be studied, but Dick Wheeler had not forgotten them. In the mid-1960s he was again working in the Southwest, on the Wetherill Mesa Project at Mesa Verde National Park, and he asked Brew if he could complete his obligation to the Awatovi Expedition by researching and reporting on these objects. Brew was delighted. The collection consisted of 1,011 artifacts made of animal bone—awls, spatulas, bodkins, punches, needles, pins, and beads—and 103 pieces made of antler, including handles, flakers, and wedges.[24] With one exception these were the usual assortment of tools and ornaments that archaeologists typically find in Puebloan sites.

The exception, a carved awl found by Gibson Namoki at Site 111 (see p. 169), was exciting enough that Woodbury wrote home about it on July 23, 1939: "Friday morning while I was at [Site] 111, Gibby found a unique sort of bone awl, made (like many others) of a deer metatarsul (?), but with the head of the bone carefully carved into a dog, with head at one end of the top of the bone and tail at the other. The nicest thing about it was that eyes were made by insetting turquoises. All told, it is the finest piece of carving, bone or stone, that we have found here; the work is neat, and the dog is really lifelike, with the legs standing free and about a quarter of an inch long. It's a wonder it wasn't broken or decayed from lying in the ground since Pueblo II times, around the 11th or 12th century."

Years later, Dick Wheeler could find references to only two other effigy bone tools from Puebloan sites in the Southwest. He speculated that the plainness of both bone and stone objects from Antelope Mesa might have resulted from the precontact Hopis having put all their artistic energy into murals and painted pottery.[25]

In the 1930s, archaeologists were just beginning to use tree rings to help establish the dates of Southwestern sites. In 1929, at the second Pecos Conference, astronomer A. E. Douglass had presented to the profession his stunning discovery that counting

A sample of clay and stone objects collected from Awatovi in 1935.
Top row: pottery pipes; second row: pottery imitations of shells; third row: pendants
and beads probably made of stone, along with six small arrow points; bottom row:
two tools probably used as knives (left) and four drills.

the growth rings of certain species of trees and comparing them with a master chronology could reveal the actual year when the tree was cut. Starting in 1937, Brew had his crew save pieces of roof beams from excavated Hopi rooms on Antelope Mesa and wood from the Franciscan churches at Awatovi. That year George Brainerd prepared the samples for study at the Laboratory of Tree Ring Research at the University of Arizona. During the 1938 and 1939 seasons, Ned Hall, who was trained in the techniques of dendrochronology, continued collecting samples.

Brew wrote in his 1941 preliminary report that 2,000 tree-ring specimens had been collected, although far fewer than that were actually dated. In 1942 Hall wrote an initial report, published in 1951, on 758 specimens from 11 sites. The range of dates confirmed the staff's overall understanding of the sequence of occupation at Awatovi and on Antelope Mesa as a whole. In 1967 Bryant Bannister and some colleagues at the Laboratory of Tree Ring Research analyzed the Awatovi Expedition tree-ring samples and were able to date 474 of them.[26] They concluded their published list of dates for Awatovi by saying that "the range of dates . . . , while not allowing detailed statements on specific construction, are in good agreement with the accepted period of occupation from A.D. 1300 to 1700."[27]

Sixty-six tree-ring samples, reported Bannister, came from a single room at Awatovi, Room 724. It was "a friary room which was converted to use as a church during the brief return of the missionaries after the Pueblo Revolt. The late date of 1699 from this structure suggests that it was reroofed or substantially repaired for the reoccupation."[28]

Bannister and his colleagues also offered some insight into the value certain kinds of trees held for the ancestral Hopi builders: "The species used in construction at Awatovi are basically juniper, pinyon pine, ponderosa pine, and Douglas-fir. The latter two species do not grow nearby at the present time and it is improbable that they did so even in the 13th century. Thus it would seem that many straight-boled pine and Douglas-fir trees were transported some distance to Awatovi."

Since Douglass announced his discovery in 1929, analyzing tree-ring samples has become a standard and invaluable tool for archaeologists everywhere. Tree-ring chronologies now exist for other parts of the United States besides the Southwest, as was documented in a 2007 PBS film honoring the four-hundredth anniversary of the founding of Jamestown, Virginia. There, tree rings were used to date the building of the colonists' log cabins. Before 1930, a great deal of potential information about the dates of sites in the Southwest was lost because archaeologists and looters alike used beams from pre-Hispanic pueblos for their campfires.

Potsherds, stone and bone tools, and tree-ring samples are the main course of Southwestern archaeology. For the Awatovi Expedition, dessert came as a profusion of murals painted on the walls of precontact and historic kivas at Awatovi and Kawaika-a.

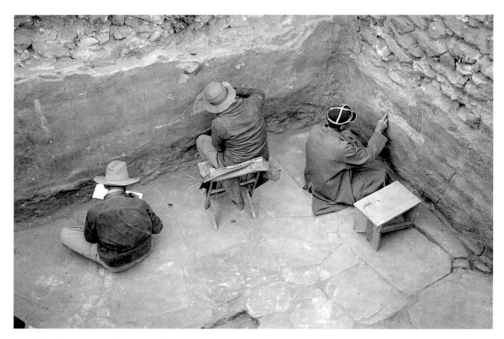

Wat Smith, Louise Scott, and Charlie Amsden scraping plaster to reveal a mural in a kiva at Awatovi, 1938.

The expedition became justly famous for them, and Wat Smith's tour de force in documenting, preserving, exhaustively studying, and thoroughly reporting them earned him well-deserved renown. He essentially spent all his time in the field at this work, from his arrival in 1936 until the end of the expedition.

The murals had originally been painted as integral parts of many Hopi ceremonies that required symbolic depictions on the walls of kivas, on pottery, or both. At the end of each ceremony, or at least before the next one was held in the kiva, people obliterated the painting with a thin layer of plaster, which might later serve as the canvas for another painting for a different ceremony. If that layer went unused for some time, then it was replenished to provide a new, clean surface for the next painting. As a result, many layers of plaster, some painted and others not, built up on the kiva walls over the years. One kiva at Awatovi had as many as 100 layers, 27 of which featured murals.

Smith and his helpers recorded 240 wall paintings at Awatovi and Kawaika-a (see pp. 172, 173). No one, including Smith, had any previous experience dealing with such finds. Improvising and learning on the job quickly, they developed a system in which they first made a scale drawing of the symbols and motifs in the outermost mural, using colored pencils to match the paint colors as closely as possible. Then they carefully scraped that painting off, with its underlying plaster, leaving the painting behind it undamaged. Haych Claflin remembered using a penknife to painstakingly scrape

A serigraph of a kiva mural from Awatovi, Room 788 (top), and Wat Smith preparing to remove the mural from a wall at the site.

Wat Smith applies plastic coating to the surface of the mural (top) and then mounts muslin to it while the plastic remains sticky.

away the plaster and then brushing off the dust with a watercolor paintbrush. A day's work, she said, removed an area of about 10 square inches.[29]

Layer by layer the staff drew, scraped, and revealed the next mural. None was complete, because the tops of the paintings were often near the ground surface and had eroded away. The paintings in the kiva under the church altar were better preserved than the others.

By the final season, adapting practices used at European Classical sites, Smith had also devised a method for stabilizing murals with cheesecloth and glue in such a way that the painting and its plaster base could be peeled right off the wall and preserved in its original form.[30] Brew wrote later that "the best of these murals" were removed this way. Several of the preserved sections are curated today at the Museum of Northern Arizona in Flagstaff, and others are at the Peabody.

Recent research by Hopi elders, contemporary Hopi artists, and scholars at the Museum of Northern Arizona and the University of Northern Arizona has involved identifying the specific imagery found at Awatovi and Kawaika-a. According to some of these researchers, "the painted murals on the walls of Hopi kivas contain images— visual metaphors—informing people of the proper way to live a full, good life."[31]

Just as the kiva murals offered glimpses into the religious lives of the precontact residents of Awatovi, the expedition's work in the ruins of the Franciscan mission revealed much about their descendants' lives under the Spaniards. At the outset of the expedition, these ruins were as unfamiliar to Brew and his colleagues as kiva paintings were. He held off tackling them until 1937, meanwhile consulting colleagues in Cambridge about what he might expect to find in the church ruins and reading up on the early Spanish incursion into the Southwest and its general missionary efforts.

Brew's decision to wait a year before beginning the mission excavations turned out to be as lucky as it was wise. At the start of the 1937 season, Charlie Amsden mentioned that he knew an ecclesiastical architect in Los Angeles. Perhaps Jo would like to contact him for advice? Indeed he would, and in September 1937, after a portion of the mission site had been uncovered, Ross G. Montgomery made his first visit to Awatovi. Brew wrote to Scott on September 11 that Montgomery "was on the site for three days and prepared a map based on Motz's ground plan, with a full description of various parts of the church, and also on this same map shows diagrammatically his conception of the alterations and the probable reasons for them in relation to the Franciscan liturgy. He also dictated a considerable amount of valuable information on church and altar construction in general, which throws further light on the reasons for many of the benches, shelves, and niches [we are finding] in the church."

Montgomery visited during each of the next two summers and over the following 10 years made invaluable contributions by rendering conjectural drawings of both the exterior and the interior of the mission church (see p. 174) and by writing major portions of the final report, *Franciscan Awatovi*.

What Montgomery was able to tell the Awatovi team in 1937 was that the huge foundations they were uncovering in Church 1—the walls were six and a half feet wide—had never had a building erected on them. Presumably Father Porras began this ambitious, cruciform building but saw only the foundation completed, either because the building proved too large to be spanned by beams hewn from native trees or because of Porras's death in 1633. In any event, his successors oversaw the building of what the archaeologists labeled Church 2, just south of the abandoned foundation. This building anchored the Franciscan mission until mid-August 1680, when it was destroyed and the priests killed during the Pueblo Revolt.

Attached to Church 2 were church offices and instruction rooms and a friary, a series of rooms forming a rectangle with a garth, or sacred garden, in the middle. Its complex history of use and reuse made its ruins difficult to excavate and interpret. Some 45 years after the expedition, Brew described its convoluted story. Whereas the church had been destroyed during the Pueblo Revolt, he wrote, "the friary had not. The decision [not to burn it] was apparently made on functional grounds. The church structure was too big to fit into any Hopi architectural concept. The friary was not, and the Hopis moved in. The friary rooms were, however, still too big, so they divided each one into two or four Hopi rooms. They also affixed their own type of room to the outside of the friary. Similarly they built rooms on all four sides of the sacred garden. . . . In effect, the friary was transformed into a pueblo."[32]

What the excavators called Church 3 complicated this arrangement of rooms even more. When the friars returned to Awatovi after the Spanish reconquest, probably in 1699, they needed a place to hold services. Of this third church Brew later wrote: "We found that the eastern row of friary rooms had been converted into a makeshift church by the elimination of both the post-rebellion Hopi partitioning walls and also the walls delineating the original friary rooms. An altar on a dais had been erected at the south (cliff) end and a baptismal font at the entrance at the north end. Also, the Hopi occupation had been cleared out of the office building–schoolhouse and it is there that the friars presumably intended to live while the Church [3] was being rebuilt or a new one erected."[33]

Without Ross Montgomery's assistance and knowledge, it seems unlikely that the full story could have been untangled. "He told us where we should find the baptistry," Brew said, "and there we found it, complete with font. He explained the 'friars' choir,' a small room with a window giving a view of the main altar. . . . He explained the doctrine of superposition. In order to demonstrate to one and all the superiority of the new religion, some physical manifestation of the new, preferably the altar, had to be

Ross Montgomery's reconstruction of Church 2.

erected directly on top of an important element of the old. . . . He predicted a kiva [would be] under the main altar [of Church 2]. . . . And under the altar we found a kiva, intact, including the roof with hatchway entrance and filled with clean sand."[34]

The mission ruins were not the only traces the colonial Spaniards left at Awatovi. In 1938 the excavation crew discovered "walls of non-Indian type" in the northeastern part of the site, "behind the seventeenth-century pueblo." Early the following season, Brew wrote, "we excavated the entire structure, having no idea of its nature beyond the fact that it was not Hopi. Both the ground plan and wall structure were unlike anything else on the site, Indian or Spanish. No internal evidence of function [that is, no artifacts or features] appeared. As in Father Porras' church [Church 1], floors and wall plaster were absent."

Once more Ross Montgomery came to the rescue. "With customary ready cooperation, he hastened from Los Angeles upon receipt of our telegram, measured and studied the ground plan and walls for three days, and produced a tentative solution." Brew summed it up: "In his letter to the King of Spain, Father Garaicoechea, after his visit to Awatovi in 1700, had recommended a detail of soldiers to protect the Awatovians from the other Hopis. Our foundation was obviously the beginning of the building which was to house them and their mounts. Montgomery's conceptual assignment of room functions included an enclosed stable courtyard, stalls for horses, barrack rooms, feed storage room, saddlery, and smithy."[35] Garaicoechea's hint of looming conflict among the Hopis proved prescient when Awatovi's neighbors so devastatingly attacked it the following winter.

A Scientific Legacy   187

The excavated foundation of the barracks and stable area found north of the historic Hopi rooms, 1939.

The excavation of the Franciscan mission ruins at Awatovi and the subsequent report published by Montgomery, Smith, and Brew still constitute one of the most complete and detailed investigations of Spanish mission archaeology and architecture in the Southwest—and one of the greatest accomplishments of the Awatovi Expedition.

For all its many successes, the Awatovi Expedition, like nearly every other archaeological project before or since, saw some of its lofty goals go unfulfilled. Its publishing record, the ultimate measure of a project's success in the academic world, was good, but it hardly met the timetable Donald Scott laid out in his 1939 report to the Smithsonian Institution: "The excavations were completed in five years, according to plan. A similar goal has been set for the final reports. The Peabody Museum expects to have the full results of the Awatovi expedition in the hands of students of the prehistory of the Southwest by the end of 1944."[36] As we have seen, that plan proved overoptimistic when many of the staff answered the call to war service or turned to the demands of jobs and school.

Nevertheless, the Peabody published 11 reports between 1942 and 1978, covering most of the major categories of finds at Awatovi and the other sites on Antelope Mesa—the natural environment, the pottery, the stone and bone tools, the kivas and their wall paintings, and the Franciscan mission. Other important parts of Brew's original, ambitious publishing plan never materialized. Although Volney Jones prepared more than one report on aspects of his botanical study, they were never published.[37] As I mentioned earlier, only one report ever appeared on any of the small sites, Daifuku's dissertation on Site 264. Most unfortunately, Brew never wrote the summary he planned, "integrating the various parts and fitting the Jeddito area into general Southwestern History."[38] That project gave way to Brew's myriad responsibilities as museum director and as an active participant on the world archaeological scene.

The Awatovi Expedition, unlike Fewkes's earlier excavations on Antelope Mesa, was never planned to excavate burials or look for a cemetery. The Peabody's interest in Awatovi lay in village and mission life. Nevertheless, when the crew found burials while excavating rooms, they carefully excavated and preserved them. In 2000 the Peabody Museum staff completed an inventory of the human remains and funerary objects from the Awatovi site, produced in consultation with the Hopi Tribe as required by the Native American Graves Protection and Repatriation Act (NAGPRA) of 1990. The collections continue to be cared for at the Peabody, and future disposition of the culturally affiliated human remains and funerary objects will be at the discretion of the Hopis, as stipulated by NAGPRA.

Today, it is required by law that archaeologists first consult with the descendants of any Native American groups whose graves they want to excavate. Only with tribal permission and an agreement about how the remains are to be handled and eventually reburied may excavation proceed. Failing to engage in such consultation is not only illegal but also considered unethical in contemporary archaeological practice.

The Peabody Museum's NAGPRA inventory of the Native American remains from Awatovi lists both males and females, ranging in age from a fetus and a few infants to a few males more than 50 years old. Most of these burials were found just above or underneath the floor of Church 2. Some of the deceased had been buried with grave offerings, which, interestingly, usually included both aboriginal items such as Hopi pottery and *paaho*, or prayer sticks, and Spanish-influenced artifacts such as wool textiles and Christian religious objects.

A steady trickle of dissertations and journal articles over the years attests to the importance of the Awatovi collections, but much remains undone. None of the wood or basketry artifacts has yet been studied, and someone could still analyze the data from the survey of Antelope Mesa and from the small sites test-excavated there. Much of the vast ceramic collection still begs for examination, too. Especially important is the pottery from the Western Mound, representing late precontact life at Awatovi, and that found in the rooms where Hopis lived from 1629 to 1680, during the Spanish presence.

The site of the village of Awatovi has been a source of unique information for both archaeologists and the Hopi people. It has the potential to reveal a great deal more, especially about the way Hopi culture did and did not change during its seventeenth-century encounter with Spaniards and their religion. In 1964 the site was designated a National Historic Landmark, meaning that it holds special significance among the many sites in the Southwest and the nation because of what it has revealed about pre-contact Hopi village life, about the Spanish missionary intrusion, and about the after-math of this religious and cultural contact.

Jo Brew's intention in 1935 was admirable: to conduct an interdisciplinary project based on the unique circumstance of continuity in Hopi country from the unwritten past through written history and on into contemporary life. He displayed innovative thinking when he encouraged John Hack to research modern Hopi agricultural prac-tices in Tallahogan Canyon, in order to compare his data with information from the precontact site. Hack's study of Hopi coal-mining sites was a first, and the collection of animal bones was relatively new in an archaeologist's bag of tricks as well. Having an ethnobotanist collect both modern plants and archaeological plant remains was unusual for the time. Anna Shepard's technological studies of clays used in pottery making were not unique but added greatly to the interdisciplinary pack-age. Watson Smith's study of the kiva murals was the first such detailed research. Another first was the study of the mission complex by an architectural historian, and its quick publication profoundly influenced the development of historical archaeology as a discipline.

The magnitude of the Peabody's interdisciplinary effort is highlighted in a memo from Brew to Scott, written in January 1939, in which Brew listed 21 institutions that had cooperated in the Awatovi research. In his preface to Hack's first publication, he mentioned six additional organizations. For decades the Awatovi Expedition served as an example of what a research project should be. It not only set a standard for future research but was far ahead of its time. Southwestern archeologists still consult and cite its publications. In 1973 two well-known Southwestern archaeologists wrote: "Awatovi . . . stands as one of the best digs in the Southwest . . . [with] careful planning, capable supervision, excellent staff, and fine laboratory analysis and catalogu-ing work. . . . It stands out as a model."[39]

Archaeologically speaking, other Southwestern sites had kivas with murals, and other sites had Spanish missions. But as archaeologist Raymond Thompson told me in 1989, it is the fact that *Franciscan Awatovi* and *Kiva Mural Decorations at Awatovi and Kawaika-a* were published relatively quickly and in such great detail,

Victor Mindeleff's 1884 drawing of a man standing by one of the friary walls (top), and Mott Davis standing by what may be the same wall in August 1991.

demonstrating such exemplary research, that gives the site special meaning in the annals of Southwestern archaeology.

It seems significant to me, too, that a Spanish greyhound trotted along with a caravan from Mexico all the way to Awatovi, a trip of many months and perhaps 2,000 miles. And there are the bones of the little cat found in a room in the mission complex, surely brought there as a companion to one of the friars, perhaps carried in a cage of some sort on the back of a horse or in a wagon.

The emotional force of Awatovi is extraordinary. As Jo Brew summed it up in 1980, Awatovi's "spectacular location and the ancient dignity of its massive and lonely remains spur the imagination. But added to those elements is the long story of its early growth, its transformation from an Indian pueblo to a major outpost of Spanish faith and power, and finally its grim and tragic death. As one of the largest and most important sites in the southwest it has beckoned the archaeologist and the historian for a century or more. To have had a part in its exploration, or even just to have been there, is to have shared a spiritual invigoration that is not readily forgotten."[40]

The site has held and continues to occupy a special place in the minds and hearts of all those who participated in the Awatovi Expedition. In 1975, the surviving staff and crew held a reunion at the site, on the fortieth anniversary of the beginning of the expedition. When Mott, Penny, and I visited Awatovi in August 1991, however, it was their first time back in 52 years. The sand road in from the highway was unchanged from when they had last traveled it, and the site itself was much as they remembered it. A wall of the mission friary still stood, some of the excavated walls in the Western Mound were still exposed, and pieces of broken pottery littered the ground. We took photographs from approximately the same place Victor Mindeleff had made a pen-and-ink sketch in 1884. The stone walls were slowly collapsing, the adobe walls disintegrating.

The camp area, Penny and Mott observed, had changed. The old juniper trees had grown and new ones had taken root, so it was difficult for them to remember where the tents had stood. They found it especially moving, though, to discover the cement steps of the cook shack still in place.

In one dramatic but necessary change, we found the site of Awatovi fenced and guarded by the Hopi Tribe. No one may visit it without permission and the accompaniment of a staff member from the Hopi Cultural Preservation Office. In its most significant role of all, Awatovi stands as a silent reminder to the Hopis of an important time and extraordinary events in their history.

Staff and Crew of the Awatovi Expedition

The following is an alphabetical list of the Awatovi Expedition staff and crew as identified in the various Awatovi series publications, with the addition of their dates of service. The last names of the Hopi men are always written in English in the field records. The publications give both the English and, where known, the Hopi last names. English surnames are given in parentheses. Married names of women on the staff are given in brackets.

THE STAFF

Charles A. Amsden, Southwest Museum, excavation supervisor of Site 4/4A, 1937–1939

Madeleine Amsden, Los Angeles, Calif., general assistant, 1937–1939

Edward Pierrepont Beckwith, Garrison-on-Hudson, N.Y., photographer, 1937

E. Boyd, Santa Fe, N.M., general assistant, 1938–1939

George W. Brainerd, University of California at Los Angeles, general assistant, 1937

J. O. "Jo" Brew, Peabody Museum, director of the Awatovi Expedition, 1935–1939

Kirk Bryan, Harvard University, consultant in geology, 1936–1939

Robert Burgh, Boulder, Colo., surveyor/topographer, 1935

Thomas Campbell, University of Texas, excavation supervisor, 1937

Helen "Haych" Claflin [Spring], Belmont, Mass., general assistant, 1938–1939

Katherine Claflin [Weeks], Belmont, Mass., 1936, 1937(?)

William H. Claflin Jr., Belmont, Mass., general assistant, 1936–1939

William H. Claflin III, Belmont, Mass., supervisor of area survey, 1936–1939

C. Burton Cosgrove, Peabody Museum, excavation supervisor, 1936

Harriet Cosgrove, Peabody Museum, field supervisor of pottery analysis, 1936–1939

E. Mott Davis, Harvard University, general assistant, 1939

Penrose Davis [Worman], Peabody Museum, artist, 1939

Fred Eggan, University of Chicago, general assistant, 1937–1938

Charles Foote, Miami, Mo., camp assistant, 1938–1939

Carlos García-Robiou, University of Havana, photographer and cartographer, 1938–1939

John T. Hack, Harvard University, physiographer, 1936–1939

Edward T. Hall, Denver University, dendrochronologist, 1938–1939

Jay Hooton, Cambridge, Mass., general assistant, 1938

Harry Hornblower II, Boston, Mass., general assistant, 1939

Marion Hutchinson [Tschopik], Peabody Museum, secretary, 1937

J. Robert Jones, University of New Mexico, surveyor/topographer, 1939

Volney H. Jones, University of Michigan, ethnobotanist, 1936–1937, 1939

J. A. Lancaster, Pleasant View, Colo., assistant director of the Awatovi Expedition, 1935–1939

John M. Longyear III, Peabody Museum, excavation supervisor, 1937

Kenneth D. MacLeish, Washington, D.C., general assistant, 1937

James O. McKenna, Winslow, Ariz., agent, 1935–1939

Jack Mineer, Keams Canyon, Ariz., general assistant, 1937

Ross G. Montgomery, Los Angeles, Calif., architect, 1937–1939

J. C. Fisher Motz, Reading, Pa., surveyor/topographer, 1937

Dorothy Newton [Inglis], Peabody Museum, general assistant, 1937

Evelyn Nimmo [Brew], Peabody Museum, cataloguer, secretary, 1938–1939

Homer N. Phillips, University of New Mexico, surveyor/topographer, 1936

Erik K. Reed, National Park Service, physical anthropologist, 1938

Wilmer "Chi" Roberts, Jeddito Trading Post, Ariz., agent, 1935–1939

Donald Scott, director, Peabody Museum, in charge of "petrographs" (rock art), 1936–1939

Louise Scott, Cambridge, Mass., general assistant, 1936–1939

Anna O. Shepard, Denver Museum of Natural History, ceramic technologist, 1938

Watson Smith, Peabody Museum, in charge of kiva paintings, 1936–1939

Alden B. Stevens, Kunkletown, Pa., surveyor/topographer, 1935, 1938

Marian Stevens, Kunkletown, Pa., general assistant, 1938

Lindsay C. Thompson, Blanding, Utah, cook, 1935–1939

Don Watson, Mesa Verde National Park, general assistant, 1936

Richard P. Wheeler, Harvard University, in charge of stone and bone, 1936–1937

Harold P. Winchester, Harvard University, excavation supervisor, 1938

Richard B. Woodbury, Harvard University, in charge of stone and bone, 1938–1939

THE CREW

First Mesa

Patrick Coochnyama (Williams), 1937–1939
Randolph David, 1936–1937, 1939
George Dewakuku, 1937–1938
Walter Edwards, 1939
Luke Hovelo, 1937–1939
Roland Hunter, 1936
Erik Lalo, 1936–1938
Dana Namoki, 1936–1939
Gibson Namoki, 1935–1939
Gilbert Namoki, 1936
Max Namoki, 1939
Sylvan Nash, 1935–1939
Kenneth Polacca, 1936
Evans Poleahla, 1937–1938

Second Mesa

Woody Blacksheep (Navajo), 1935
Cecil Calvert, 1935
Emory Coochwikvia (Dennis), 1936–1939
Douglas Coochwytewa, 1939
Vincent Edward, 1935
Larry Gallegos, a Hispanic who was married to a sister of the Dennis brothers, 1939
Fred Kinsley, 1938–1939
Elwood "Hoppy" Letayhouyuoma (Dennis), 1936–1939
Arthur Masaytewa, 1937–1939
Mancho McLean, 1939
Leland Naquahitewa (Dennis), 1935–1939
Milton Pakurza, 1936
Everett Pohuhoyma (Harris), 1935–1939
Jacob "Jake" Chong Poleviyuma, 1935–1939
Emerson Sesumptewa, 1936
Alec Siwinmtewa (Dennis), 1935–1939
Chester Talashoyuwema (Dennis), 1938–1939
Joe Thomas, 1935

Notes

1 Awatovi's Turbulent History

1. Watson Smith, *Painted Ceramics of the Western Mound at Awatovi* (Cambridge, Mass.: Peabody Museum, Harvard University, 1971), 6.

2. Pedro de Castañeda de Nájera, "Relación de la Jornada de Cíbola," in Richard Flint and Shirley Cushing Flint, eds. and trans., *Documents of the Coronado Expedition*, 1539–1542 (Dallas: Southern Methodist University Press, 2005), 396.

3. Some scholars have suggested that the village Tovar visited might have been Kawaika-a, a pueblo a mile east of Awatovi. For discussions of the identification of this village, see J. O. Brew, "The History of Awatovi," in Ross G. Montgomery, Watson Smith, and John Otis Brew, *Franciscan Awatovi* (Cambridge, Mass.: Peabody Museum, Harvard University, 1949), part 1, page 5, and Eric K. Reed, "Kawaika-a in the Historic Period," *American Antiquity* 8, no. 1 (1942): 199–120. Both writers suggest that Kawaika-a had already been abandoned by 1540.

4. Castañeda de Nájera, "Relación," 396.

5. The quotation is from Brew, "History of Awatovi," 7.

6. E. Charles Adams, "Passive Resistance: Hopi Responses to Spanish Contact and Conquest," in David Hurst Thomas, ed., *Columbian Consequences*, vol. 1, *Archaeological and Historical Perspectives on the Spanish Borderlands West* (Washington, D.C.: Smithsonian Institution Press, 1989), 80–81.

7. Ibid., 81.

8. Carroll L. Riley, *The Kachina and the Cross: Indians and Spaniards in the Early Southwest* (Salt Lake City: University of Utah Press, 1999), 110.

9. Brew, "History of Awatovi," 9.

10. Ibid.

11. J. O. Brew, "Names and Spellings: Awatovi, Tusayan, Moqui, and Hopi," in Montgomery, Smith, and Brew, *Franciscan Awatovi*, 11.

12. Brew, "History of Awatovi," 18–19.

13. Adolph F. Bandelier, *Final Report of Investigations among the Indians of the Southwestern United States*, Part 2 (Cambridge, Mass.: Archaeological Institute of America, 1892), 371–372.

14. Brew, "History of Awatovi," 22–23.

15. Peter Whitely, *Bacavi: Journey to Reed Springs* (Flagstaff, Ariz.: Northland Press, 1988), 21–22. See also Harold Courlander, *Hopi Voices: Recollections, Traditions, and Narratives of the Hopi Indians* (Albuquerque: University of New Mexico Press, 1982), 55–60; Ekkehart Malotki, *Hopi Tales of Destruction* (Lincoln: University of Nebraska Press, 2002), 124–190; and Edmund Nequatewa, *Truth of a Hopi: Stories Relating to the Origin, Myths, and Clan Histories of the Hopi* (Flagstaff, Ariz.: Northland Press, 1967 [1938]).

16. Brew, "History of Awatovi," 20.

17. Translated by John P. Wilson in his "Awatovi: More Light on a Legend," *Plateau* 44, no. 4 (1972): 129.

18. E. C. Adams, "Passive Resistance," 88.

19. For detailed accounts of Spanish contact with Awatovi and other Hopi villages between 1540 and 1700, see Brew, "History of Awatovi," 3–40, and Montgomery, Smith, and Brew, *Franciscan Awatovi*, 112–125.

20. Victor Mindeleff, "A Study of Pueblo Architecture in Tusayan and Cibola," *Annual Report of the Bureau of American Ethnology* 8: 2–228 (Washington, D.C.: Smithsonian Institution, 1891), 49.

21. J. W. Fewkes, "A-wa-to-bi: An Archaeological Verification of a Tusayan Legend," *American Anthropologist* 6, no. 4 (1893): 363.

22. Ibid.

23. Ibid., 373. Excavators from the Peabody Museum in the 1930s found what Watson Smith believed to be the kiva Fewkes had partially dug. The last tree-ring date for this room was 1628, and Smith considered it "plausible to infer that [the kiva] could have been in use after 1680 and up to the final destruction of the village in 1700–1701." See Watson Smith, *Prehistoric Kivas of Antelope Mesa* (Cambridge, Mass.: Peabody Museum, Harvard University, 1972), 74–75.

24. A copy of this article is in Watson Smith's papers at the Arizona State Museum.

25. J. W. Fewkes, "Archaeological Expedition to Arizona, 1895," *Seventeenth Annual Report of the Bureau of American Ethnology* (Washington, D.C.: Smithsonian Institution, 1898), part 2, 517–539.

26. George A. Dorsey, "Recent Progress in Anthropology at the Field Columbian Museum," *American Anthropologist* (n.s.) 3, no. 4 (1901): 740.

27. Dennis Gilpin, personal communication, 2005.

28. Ibid. See also [Frances] Theresa Russell, "In Pursuit of a Graveyard: Being the Trail of an Archaeological Wedding Journey," *Out West* 24–25 (1906): 39–49 ff.

29. Walter Hough, "Archaeological Field Work in Northeastern Arizona: The Museum-Gates Expedition of 1901," *Report of the U.S. National Museum for 1901*, 279–358 (Washington, D.C.: Smithsonian Institution, 1903), 333.

30. James H. Gunnerson, *The Fremont Culture: A Study in Culture Dynamics on the Northern Anasazi Frontier, Including the Report of the Claflin-Emerson Expedition of the Peabody Museum* (Cambridge, Mass.: Peabody Museum, Harvard University, 1969), vii.

31. J. O. Brew, "Introduction," in J. O. Brew, ed., *One Hundred Years of Anthropology* (Cambridge, Mass.: Harvard University Press, 1968), 18.

32. Samuel J. Guernsey, *Explorations in Northeastern Arizona: Report on the Archaeological Fieldwork of 1920–1923* (Cambridge, Mass.: Peabody Museum, Harvard University, 1931), iii.

33. Noel Morss, *The Ancient Culture of the Fremont River in Utah: Report on the Explorations under the Claflin-Emerson Fund, 1928–29* (Cambridge, Mass.: Peabody Museum, Harvard University, 1931), iii.

34. Ibid.

35. J. O. Brew, *Archaeology of Alkali Ridge, Southeastern Utah, with a Review of the Prehistory of the Mesa Verde Division of the San Juan and Some Observations on Archaeological Systematics* (Cambridge, Mass.: Peabody Museum, Harvard University, 1946), 3.

2 Awatovi, 1935

1. Watson Smith, "One Man's Archaeology," *Kiva* 57, no. 2 (1992): 152.

2. William H. Claflin, *The Stallings Island Mound, Columbia County, Georgia* (Cambridge, Mass.: Peabody Museum, Harvard University, 1931), 1–3.

3. Ibid., 3.

4. J. O. Brew, "The Excavation of Awatovi," manuscript of lecture presented at Southern Methodist University, May 7, 1975, 2.

5. Ibid. The couple's surnames are spelled variously in the documents.

6. *Boston Sunday Globe*, March 3, 1982.

7. Claflin, *Stallings Island Mound*, 14.

8. Gunnerson, *Fremont Culture*, 23.

9. Jenny L. Adams, *Pinto Beans and Prehistoric Pots: The Legacy of Al and Alice Lancaster* (Tucson: University of Arizona Press, 1994), 36.

10. J. O. Brew, "Donald Scott, 1879–1967," *Teocentli* 71 (Oct. 1967): 1.

11. Ibid.

12. William W. Howells, C. C. Lamberg-Karlovsky, Evon Z. Vogt, Gordon R. Willey, and Stephen Williams, "Faculty of Arts and Sciences—Memorial Minute [for J. O. Brew]," *Harvard Gazette* 8 (Feb. 1990): 9.

13. Richard B. Woodbury, "John Otis Brew, 1906–1988," *American Antiquity* 55, no. 3 (1990): 452–459.

14. A.V. Kidder, diary, August 1939, Harvard Archives, Widener Library.

15. A permit is still necessary but now falls under the authority of the Archaeological Resources Protection Act of 1979 as amended.

16. J. L. Adams, *Pinto Beans*, 35–36.

17. See Adams, *Pinto Beans*.

18. Ibid., 36.

19. Smith, "One Man's Archaeology," 157.

20. Brew to Scott, November 16, 1935.

21. Burgh published an article about some of the pottery: "Ceramic Profiles in the Western Mound at Awatovi, Northwestern Arizona," *American Antiquity* 25, no. 2 (1959): 184–202.

22. J. O. Brew, "The First Two Seasons at Awatovi," *American Antiquity* 3, no. 2 (1937): 126.

23. Ibid., 125.

24. Donald Scott, specimen list in "Preliminary Report of the Peabody Museum Jeddito Expedition of 1935," manuscript report submitted to the Smithsonian Institution by the Peabody Museum of American Archaeology and Ethnology, Harvard University, Cambridge, 1936.

25. Brew, "First Two Seasons," 125–126; Smith, *Prehistoric Kivas of Antelope Mesa*, 41–46.

3 Getting Ready

1. Cory D. Breternitz, personal communication, 2003.

2. Much of my information about the Cosgroves comes from Carolyn O'Bagy Davis, *Treasured Earth: Hattie Cosgrove's Mimbres Archaeology in the American Southwest* (Tucson: Sanpete Publications and Old Pueblo Archaeology Center, 1995).

3. Harriet S. Cosgrove and Cornelius B. Cosgrove, *The Swarts Ruin: A Typical Mimbres Site in Southwestern New Mexico* (Cambridge, Mass.: Peabody Museum, Harvard University, 1932). Facsimile edition published by the Peabody Museum Press, 2005.

4. Smith, "One Man's Archaeology," 160.

5. J. O. Brew, "Preliminary Report of the Peabody Museum Awatovi Expedition of 1939," *Plateau* 23, no. 3 (1941): 40.

6. Smith, "One Man's Archaeology," 126–133.

7. Smith, *One Man's Archaeology* (privately printed, 1984; copy in the Arizona State Museum), 98.

8. Smith, "One Man's Archaeology," 155–156.

9. J. O. Brew, "Foreword," in Smith, *Prehistoric Kivas of Antelope Mesa*, x.

10. Some of Beckwith's aerial photographs of Awatovi have been published. See John Hack, *The Changing Physical Environment of the Hopi Indians of Arizona* (Cambridge, Mass.: Peabody Museum, Harvard University, 1942), plates 1 and 8, and Smith, *Painted Ceramics*, figs. 5a and 5b. A few other enlargements of Beckwith's pictures of the camp and the site of Awatovi (but no negatives) are in the Peabody archives.

11. Richard B. Woodbury, *Sixty Years of Southwestern Archaeology: A History of the Pecos Conference* (Albuquerque: University of New Mexico Press, 1993), 21.

12. Raymond H. Thompson, introduction to chapter 4, "D-Shaped Features: The Kiva at Site 4," in Watson Smith, *When Is a Kiva? And Other Questions about Southwestern Archaeology*, ed. Raymond H. Thompson (Tucson: University of Arizona Press, 1990), 81.

13. Smith, "One Man's Archaeology," 164.

14. Marjorie Vasey, an artist at the Peabody for a short time, aided Smith with his publication about the kiva murals. She was never in the field at Awatovi but is listed as a staff artist in Smith's 1952 publication. Another important contributor to the project after the fieldwork ended was Cordelia Galt, an editor at the Peabody. She is listed as part of the permanent staff of the Awatovi project and undoubtedly had much to do with the preparation of the reports for publication.

15. J. O. Brew, "Preface," in Hiroshi Daifuku, *Jeddito 264: A Report on the Excavation of a Basket Maker III–Pueblo I Site in Northeastern Arizona with a Review of Some Current Theories in Southwestern Archaeology* (Cambridge, Mass.: Peabody Museum, Harvard University, 1961), x.

16. Ibid., ix–x.

4   New Awatovi

1. Smith, *One Man's Archaeology*, 162.

2. Baxter's account, "Archaeological Camping in Arizona," in Curtis M. Hinsley and David R. Wilcox, eds., *The Southwest in the American Imagination: The Writings of Sylvester Baxter, 1881–1889* (Tucson: University of Arizona Press, 1996).

3. Hinsley and Wilcox, *The Southwest in the American Imagination*, 154–155.

4. Ibid., 163–164.

5. Ann Axtell Morris, *Digging in the Southwest* (Garden City, N.Y.: Doubleday, 1933; reprinted 1978).

6. Barbara Kidder Aldana, "The Kidder Pecos Expedition, 1924–1929: A Personal Memoir," *Kiva* 48, no. 2 (1983): 244. Two accounts of archaeological camps associated with

University of Arizona field schools—very different situations from Awatovi—convey wonderful memories of camp life, including long-lasting friendships, Fourth of July parties, and some great cooks. See Emil W. Haury, *Point of Pines, Arizona: A History of the University of Arizona Archaeological Field School* (Tucson: University of Arizona Press, 1989), and J. Jefferson Reid and Stephanie Whittlesey, *Grasshopper Pueblo: A Story of Archaeology and Ancient Life* (Tucson: University of Arizona Press, 1999).

7. Dick Woodbury has pointed out an interesting similarity between Smith's proposed building and that illustrated in Agatha Christie's archaeological novel *Murder in Mesopotamia*, first issued in 1935 and still in bookstores.

8. Crosby to Brew, October 8, 1936.

9. Brew to Scott, July 23, 1937.

10. Morris, *Digging in the Southwest*, 208–210.

11. Neil M. Judd, *Men Met along the Trail: Adventures in Archaeology* (Norman: University of Oklahoma Press, 1968), 94.

12. Ibid. As recently as 1993, a book called *Practical Archaeology* recommended finding a good secondhand Ford or Chevrolet pickup if one were traveling to a remote field site—especially in a third world country—because parts were more likely to be available and more mechanics would be able to fix problems. See Brian D. Dillon, "The Archaeological Field Vehicle," in *Practical Archaeology: Field and Laboratory Techniques and Archaeological Logistics* (Los Angeles: Institute of Archaeology, University of California at Los Angeles, 1993), 39–62.

13. Brew to Scott, September 11, 1936.

5   Life in Camp

1. Davis, *Treasured Earth*, 103.

2. Ibid., 100.

3. Alden C. Hayes, "Archaeologists at Pecos," in Marc Gaede and Marnie Gaede, eds., *Camera, Spade and Pen* (Tucson: University of Arizona Press, 1980), 22.

4. Smith, "One Man's Archaeology," 167.

5. Reid and Whittlesey, *Grasshopper Pueblo*, 52.

6. Julian Hayden, "A Camp at Kiet Siel," in Gaede and Gaede, *Camera, Spade and Pen*, 102.

7. Katharine Bartlett, *Teocentli* 20 (Dec. 1935).

8. There were four of the original Awatovi staff at the Peabody's camp in 1951, which was the last season of the Upper Gila Expedition: Jo and Evelyn Brew, Wat Smith, and Lin Thompson. It seems probable that Wat and Lin cooked up the idea (if you'll pardon the pun) of sending Penny a batch of cinnamon rolls. Penny, who wanted to come to New Mexico for a visit, was inspired to write this poem—to my knowledge the only one she ever composed.

9. Smith, *One Man's Archaeology*, 137.

10. Alexander Lindsay, personal communication, 2000.

11. Smith, *One Man's Archaeology*, 164.

12. Smith, *One Man's Archaeology*, 166.

6   Mobs of Visitors

1. See Joan Mark, *King of the World in the Land of the Pygmies* (Lincoln: University of Nebraska Press, 1995).

2. Neil Judd, *Men Met along the Trail*, 95.

3. Emil Haury to Hester Davis, September 13, 1989.

4. Smith, *One Man's Archaeology*, 150.

5. These two drawings and another done by Kidder in 1947 during a visit to the Point of Pines field school, published in Haury's history of that project (*Point of Pines, Arizona*, xxii), are the only known Kidder cartoons that survive.

6. J. O. Brew, journal, August 1, 1939.

7. Watson Smith, "Victor Rose Stoner, 1893–1957," *Kiva* 23, no. 2 (1957): 1–3.

8. Smith, *One Man's Archaeology*, 189.

9. Smith "Victor Rose Stoner," 2.

10. Longyear retained a copy of this movie, and in 1990 the Arizona State Museum copied it on new film for its Awatovi archive.

11. Smith, *One Man's Archaeology*, 191.

12. Ibid., 123–124.

7 End of the Expedition

1. Smith, *Prehistoric Kivas of Antelope Mesa*, 77.

2. *Boston Sunday Globe*, March 7, 1982.

3. Woodbury, "John Otis Brew."

4. See, for example, Watson Smith, *Williams Ranch: A Frontier Mogollon Village in West-Central New Mexico* (Cambridge, Mass.: Peabody Museum, Harvard University, 1975).

5. Lucy Smith, privately distributed transcript.

6. Mitchell Reynolds to Watson Smith, November 7, 1988, Arizona State Museum Archives.

7. W. James Judge, "James Allen Lancaster," *American Antiquity* 61, no. 2 (1996): 267.

8. Smith, *One Man's Archaeology*, 144.

9. Ibid., 175–176.

10. See William R. Bullard Jr., *The Cerro Colorado Site and Pithouse Architecture in the Southwestern United States prior to A.D. 900* (Cambridge, Mass.: Peabody Museum, Harvard University, 1962); Smith, *Williams Ranch*; and Charles R. McGimsey III, *Marianna Mesa: Seven Prehistoric Settlements in West-Central New Mexico* (Cambridge, Mass.: Peabody Museum, Harvard University, 1980).

8 A Scientific Legacy

1. Smith, *Prehistoric Kivas of Antelope Mesa*, 127, 132.

2. Ibid., 127.

3. Brew, "Preface," in Daifuku, *Jeddito 264*, vii.

4. Richard B. Woodbury, *Prehistoric Stone Implements of Northeastern Arizona* (Cambridge, Mass.: Peabody Museum, Harvard University, 1954), 5–9.

5. Hack, *Changing Physical Environment*, 26.

6. See Fewkes, "Archaeological Expedition to Arizona," 580.

7. Frederick W. Hodge, "Hopi Pottery Fired with Coal," *American Anthropologist* (n.s.) 6 (1904): 581.

8. Katherine Bartlett, "Prehistoric Mining in the Southwest," *Museum Notes* (Museum of Northern Arizona, Flagstaff) 7, no. 10 (1935): 41–44.

9. John T. Hack, *Prehistoric Coal Mining in the Jeddito Valley, Arizona* (Cambridge, Mass.: Peabody Museum, Harvard University, 1942), ix.

10. Donald Scott, "Preliminary Report of the Peabody Museum Awatovi Expedition of 1938," manuscript report submitted to the Smithsonian Institution by the Peabody Museum of American Archaeology and Ethnology, Harvard University, Cambridge, 1939, 28.

11. Brew to Scott, August 21, 1937.

12. Scott, "Preliminary Report, 1938," 29.

13. Laurie D. Webster, "Effects of European Contact on Textile Production and Exchange in the North American Southwest: A Pueblo Case Study" (Ph.D. dissertation, Department of Anthropology, University of Arizona, Tucson, 1997), 267. According to Webster, the identifications of textiles and fibers given in Montgomery, Smith, and Brew, *Franciscan Awatovi*, 98, were taken from Leake's study.

14. Stanley J. Olsen, "The Faunal Analysis," in Stanley J. Olsen and Richard P. Wheeler, *Bones from Awatovi* (Cambridge, Mass.: Peabody Museum, Harvard University, 1978), 1.

15. J. O. Brew, "Preface," in Barbara Lawrence, *Mammals Found at the Awatovi Site* (Cambridge, Mass.: Peabody Museum, Harvard University, 1951), v.

16. Lawrence, *Mammals Found at the Awatovi Site*, 3.

17. Stanley J. Olsen, "The Dogs of Awatovi," *American Antiquity* 41, no. 1 (1976): 1–2.

18. Olsen, "Faunal Analysis," 19. Under Olsen's guidance, Regina L. Chapin-Pyritz completed a Ph.D. dissertation at the University of Arizona in 2000, titled "The Effects of Spanish Contact on Hopi Faunal Utilization in the American Southwest." According to Chapin-Pyritz's abstract, she used "ethnohistorical, ethnographical, and archaeological data, primarily the zooarchaeological collections, [as] a means of ascertaining what effects the introduction of Old World domestic animals had on Hopi subsistence strategies and bone resource utilization over time. . . . An intrasite comparison [was] conducted between the three major Awatovi sections: the Western Mound, the Hopi Village, and the Spanish Mission."

19. Donald Scott, "Preliminary Report of the Peabody Museum Awatovi Expedition of 1937," manuscript report submitted to the Smithsonian Institution by the Peabody Museum of American Archaeology and Ethnology, Harvard University, Cambridge, 1938, 26.

20. See Anna O. Shepard, "Technical Note on Awatovi Pottery," in Smith, *Painted Ceramics*, 179–184.

21. Ibid., 181, 184.

22. Ibid., 179.

23. Smith, *Painted Ceramics*, 605, 606.

24. Richard P. Wheeler, "Bone and Antler Artifacts," in Olsen and Wheeler, *Bones from Awatovi*, 37–74.

25. Ibid., 72.

26. Jeffrey S. Dean, Laboratory of Tree Ring Research, telephone interview, 2003.

27. Bryant Bannister, William J. Robinson, and Richard L. Warren, *Tree-Ring Dates from Arizona J: Hopi Mesas Area* (Tucson: Laboratory of Tree-Ring Research, University of Arizona, 1967), 13.

28. Ibid.

29. Haych Claflin's recollections were generously conveyed to me in a letter from her son William Claflin Spring in 2007.

30. For a detailed description of this technique, see Watson Smith, *Kiva Mural Decorations at Awatovi and Kawaika-a, with a Survey of Other Wall Paintings in the Pueblo Southwest* (Cambridge, Mass.: Peabody Museum, Harvard University, 1952), 39–46.

31. For a beautifully illustrated publication about this study, see Kelley Hayes-Gilpin, Emory Sekaquaptewa, and Dorothy Washburn, "Murals and Metaphors," *Plateau* 3, no. 1 (2006). This issue of *Plateau* is dedicated to Watson Smith, "whose scholarship did so much to preserve and interpret the ancient kiva murals at Awat'ovi and Kawayka'a, which have inspired contemporary Hopi artists and provided so much insight into the continuity of Hopi artistic tradition" (p. 5).

32. J. O. Brew, "St. Francis at Awatovi," in Stanley South, ed., *Pioneers in Historical Archaeology* (New York: Plenum Press, 1994), 39.

33. Ibid., 45.

34. Ibid., 30. For detailed descriptions of this special kiva, see Montgomery, Smith, and Brew, *Franciscan Awatovi*, 65–66, and Smith, *Prehistoric Kivas of Antelope Mesa*, 59–66.

35. Brew, "St. Francis at Awatovi," 45.

36. Donald Scott, "Preliminary Report of the Peabody Museum Awatovi Expedition of 1939," manuscript report submitted to the Smithsonian Institution by the Peabody Museum of American Archaeology and Ethnology, Harvard University, Cambridge, 1940, 26.

37. Richard I. Ford, a student of Jones's and later director of the Museum of Anthropology at the University of Michigan, has restudied the plant specimens and edited Jones's manuscripts. In 2007 he was preparing the material for publication (personal communication).

38. Brew, "Preface," in Hack, *Changing Physical Environment.*

39. Paul S. Martin and Fred Plog, *The Archaeology of Arizon*a (Garden City, N.Y.: Doubleday, 1973), 31.

40. J. O. Brew, "Excavation of Awatovi," in Gaede and Gaede, *Camera, Spade, and Pen* (Tucson, Ariz.: University of Arizona Press, 1980), 103–104.

Publications Related
to the Awatovi Expedition

The Eleven Published Reports of the Awatovi Expedition
Listed in Order of Publication

Hack, John T.

    1942   *The Changing Physical Environment of the Hopi Indians of Arizona.* Reports of the Awatovi Expedition 1. Papers of the Peabody Museum of American Archaeology and Ethnology, vol. 35, no. 1. Cambridge: Harvard University.

    1942   *Prehistoric Coal Mining in the Jeddito Valley, Arizona.* Reports of the Awatovi Expedition 2. Papers of the Peabody Museum of American Archaeology and Ethnology, vol. 35, no. 2. Cambridge: Harvard University.

Montgomery, Ross Gordon, Watson Smith, and John Otis Brew

    1949   *Franciscan Awatovi: The Excavation and Conjectural Reconstruction of a Seventeenth-Century Spanish Mission Establishment at a Hopi Indian Town in Northeastern Arizona.* Reports of the Awatovi Expedition 3. Papers of the Peabody Museum of American Archaeology and Ethnology, vol. 36. Cambridge: Harvard University.

Lawrence, Barbara

    1951   *Mammals Found at the Awatovi Site* (Part 1) *and Post-Cranial Skeletal Characters of Deer, Pronghorn, and Sheep-Goat, with Notes on Bos and Bison* (Part 2). Reports of the Awatovi Expedition 4. Papers of the Peabody Museum of American Archaeology and Ethnology, vol. 35, no. 3. Cambridge: Harvard University.

Smith, Watson

    1952   *Kiva Mural Decorations at Awatovi and Kawaika-a, with a Survey of Other Wall Paintings in the Pueblo Southwest.* Reports of the Awatovi Expedition 5. Papers of the Peabody Museum of American Archaeology and Ethnology, vol. 37. Cambridge: Harvard University. Facsimile edition, Cambridge: Peabody Museum Press, 2005.

Woodbury, Richard B.

    1954   *Prehistoric Stone Implements of Northeastern Arizona.* Reports of the Awatovi Expedition 6. Papers of the Peabody Museum of American Archaeology and Ethnology, vol. 34. Cambridge: Harvard University.

Daifuku, Hiroshi

    1961   *Jeddito 264: A Report on the Excavation of a Basket Maker III–Pueblo I Site in Northeastern Arizona, with a Review of Some Current Theories in Southwestern*

Archaeology. **Reports of the Awatovi Expedition 7.** Papers of the Peabody Museum of American Archaeology and Ethnology, vol. 33, no. 1. Cambridge: Harvard University.

Smith, Watson
   1971   *Painted Ceramics of the Western Mound at Awatovi.* Reports of the Awatovi Expedition 8. Papers of the Peabody Museum of American Archaeology and Ethnology, vol. 38. Cambridge: Harvard University.

   1972   *Prehistoric Kivas of Antelope Mesa.* Reports of the Awatovi Expedition 9. Papers of the Peabody Museum of American Archaeology and Ethnology, vol. 39, no. 1. Cambridge: Harvard University.

Gifford, James C., and Watson Smith
   1978   *Gray Corrugated Pottery from Awatovi and Other Jeddito Sites in Northeastern Arizona.* Reports of the Awatovi Expedition 10. Papers of the Peabody Museum of American Archaeology and Ethnology, vol. 69. Cambridge: Harvard University.

Olsen, Stanley J., and Richard P. Wheeler
   1978   *Bones from Awatovi.* Reports of the Awatovi Expedition 11. Papers of the Peabody Museum of American Archaeology and Ethnology, vol. 70, no. 1. Cambridge: Harvard University.

Other Works Stemming from the Awatovi Expedition

Brew, J. O.
   1937   "The First Two Seasons at Awatovi." *American Antiquity* 3, no. 2: 122–137.

   1939   "Peabody Museum Excavations in Arizona." *Harvard Alumni Bulletin,* May 5: 870–875.

   1941   "Preliminary Report of the Peabody Museum Awatovi Expedition of 1939." *Plateau* 23, no. 3: 37–48.

   1980   "The Excavation of Awatovi." In *Camera, Spade, and Pen: An Inside View of Southwestern Archaeology,* by Marc Gaede and Marnie Gaede, 103–109. Tucson: University of Arizona Press.

   1994   "St. Francis at Awatovi." In *Pioneers in Historical Archaeology,* edited by Stanley South, 27–47. New York: Plenum Press.

Brew, J. O., and John T. Hack
   1939   "Prehistoric Use of Coal by Indians of Northern Arizona." *Plateau* 12, no. 1.

Burgh, Robert F.
   1959   "Ceramic Profiles in the Western Mound at Awatovi, Northwestern Arizona." *American Antiquity* 25, no. 2: 184–202.

Campbell, Thomas N.
   1937   "The Masonry at Awatovi." Typescript on deposit at the Tozzer Library, Harvard University.

Chapin-Pyritz, Regina L.
  2000   "The Effects of Spanish Contact on Hopi Faunal Utilization in the American Southwest."
          Ph.D. dissertation, Department of Anthropology, University of Arizona, Tucson.

Hall, Edward T., Jr.
  1951   "Southwestern Dated Ruins VI." *Tree-Ring Bulletin* 17, no. 4: 26–28. Laboratory of Tree-
          Ring Research, University of Arizona, Tucson.

Olsen, Stanley J.
  1976   "The Dogs of Awatovi." *American Antiquity* 41, no. 1: 102–106.

Reed, Eric K.
  1942   "Kawaika-a in the Historic Period." *American Antiquity* 8, no. 1: 199–120.

Scott, Donald
  1936   "Preliminary Report of the Peabody Museum Jeddito Expedition of 1935." Manuscript
          report submitted to the Smithsonian Institution by the Peabody Museum of American
          Archaeology and Ethnology, Harvard University, Cambridge.
  1937   "Preliminary Report of the Peabody Museum Awatovi Expedition of 1936." Manuscript
          report submitted to the Smithsonian Institution by the Peabody Museum of American
          Archaeology and Ethnology, Harvard University, Cambridge.
  1938   "Preliminary Report of the Peabody Museum Awatovi Expedition of 1937." Manuscript
          report submitted to the Smithsonian Institution by the Peabody Museum of American
          Archaeology and Ethnology, Harvard University, Cambridge.
  1939   "Preliminary Report of the Peabody Museum Awatovi Expedition of 1938." Manuscript
          report submitted to the Smithsonian Institution by the Peabody Museum of American
          Archaeology and Ethnology, Harvard University, Cambridge.
  1940   "Preliminary Report of the Peabody Museum Awatovi Expedition of 1939." Manuscript
          report submitted to the Smithsonian Institution by the Peabody Museum of American
          Archaeology and Ethnology, Harvard University, Cambridge.

Webster, Laurie D.
  1997   "Effects of European Contact on Textile Production and Exchange in the North American
          Southwest: A Pueblo Case Study." Ph.D. dissertation, Department of Anthropology,
          University of Arizona, Tucson.

Suggested Reading

Adams, Jenny L.
  1994 *Pinto Beans and Prehistoric Pots: The Legacy of Al and Alice Lancaster.* Tucson: University of Arizona Press.

Davis, Carolyn O'Bagy
  1995 *Treasured Earth: Hattie Cosgrove's Mimbres Archaeology in the American Southwest.* Tucson: Sanpete Publications and Old Pueblo Archaeology Center.

Elliott, Melinda
  1995 *Great Excavations: Tales of Early Southwestern Archaeology, 1888–1939.* Santa Fe, N.M.: School of American Research Press.

Gaede, Marc, and Marnie Gaede
  1980 *Camera, Spade, and Pen.* Tucson: University of Arizona Press.

Hayes-Gilpin, Kelley, Emory Sekaquaptewa, and Dorothy K. Washburn
  2006 "Murals and Metaphors." *Plateau* 3, no. 1. Flagstaff, Ariz.: Museum of Northern Arizona.

Judd, Neil M.
  1968 *Men Met along the Trail: Adventures in Archaeology.* Norman: University of Oklahoma Press.

Mallowan, Agatha Christie
  1946 *Come, Tell Me How You Live.* London: Penguin Putman.

Morris, Ann Axtell
  1933 *Digging in the Southwest.* Garden City, N.Y.: Doubleday (reprinted 1978).

Riley, Carroll L.
  1999 *The Kachina and the Cross: Indians and Spaniards in the Early Southwest.* Salt Lake City: University of Utah Press.

Roberts, David
  2004 *The Pueblo Revolt: The Secret Rebellion that Drove the Spaniards out of the Southwest.* New York: Simon and Schuster.

Sando, Joe S., and Herman Agoyo, eds.
  2005 *Po'Pay: Leader of the First American Revolution.* Santa Fe, N.M.: Clear Light Publishing.

Smith, Watson
  1992 "One Man's Archaeology." *Kiva* 57, no. 2. Abridgement by B. Smith and C. Gifford of W. Smith's *One Man's Archaeology* (privately printed, 1984; copy in the Arizona State Museum).

Picture Credits

The members of the Awatovi Expedition produced extraordinarily rich visual documentation of their work and play, and the illustrations reproduced in this volume represent but a fraction of the photographic record. Unless otherwise noted below, all illustrations are housed in the archives of the Peabody Museum of Archaeology and Ethnology and are copyright © the President and Fellows of Harvard College. Where known, photographer, artist, and original place of publication are listed in addition to the Peabody Museum number. Many of the photographs in the Awatovi archive are undated. Hattie Cosgrove took some photographs in 1937, but most of hers and all of those taken by Evelyn Nimmo Brew and Carlos García-Robiou date to 1938 and 1939.

COVER:	For cover pictures, see credits below for pages 21, 31, 34, 50, 66, 81, 82, 88, 116, 118, 121, 141, 160, and 190.
FRONTISPIECE:	Photo by Mark Craig. 996-26-10/75391.
viii	2004.1.123.1.40.
xiv	Photo by Richard W. Hufnagle, USDA Soil Conservation Service.
1	Detail of photo on page 191 bottom by Hester A. Davis.

1 Awatovi's Turbulent History

2	From Jesse Walter Fewkes, *Archaeological Expedition to Arizona in 1895.* 17th Annual Report of the Bureau of American Ethnology to the Secretary of the Smithsonian Institution, 1895–96, by J. W. Powell, Director (1898): pl. 107.
4	Map by Deborah Reade.
5	Courtesy Arizona State Museum, University of Arizona.
7	Montgomery, Smith, and Brew 1949: fig. 34.
8	2004.1.123.1.92.
11	From Victor Mindeleff, *A Study of Pueblo Architecture: Tusayan and Cibola.* 8th Annual Report of the Bureau of Ethnology to the Secretary of the Smithsonian Institution, 1886–87, by J. W. Powell, Director (1891): pl. 3.
12	From Fewkes 1898: pl. 108.
14	Cat. no. 688, Kidder Collection, Archives, Laboratory of Anthropology, Museum of Indian Arts and Culture, Santa Fe.

2 Awatovi, 1935

18	Photo by J. O. Brew. 2004.1.123.7.
20	N35488.
21	Photo by Hattie Cosgrove. 2004.1.123.1.31.
23	Photo probably by Carlos García-Robiou. 995-11-10/99994.1.23.
27	Photo by Hattie Cosgrove. 2004.1.123.1.86.
28	Peabody Museum Awatovi Archive (facsimile).
29 left	Photo by Evelyn Brew. 2004.34.1.93.
29 right	Photo by Hattie Cosgrove. 2004.1.123.1.84.
30 left	Photo by J. O. Brew. 2004.1.123.1.5.
30 right	Photo by Hattie Cosgrove. 2004.1.123.1.62.
31	Photo by J. O. Brew. 995-11-10/99994.1.16.
33	Photo by Evelyn Brew. 2004.34.1.19.
34	Photo by Hattie Cosgrove. 2004.1.123.1.70.

35		2004.1.123.1.6.
36		Photo by J. O. Brew. 995-11-10/99994.1.13.
37		Peabody Museum Awatovi Archive. 995-11-10/99994.1.28.
38		Photo by J. O. Brew. 2004.1.123.1.4.
40		Peabody Museum Awatovi Archive. 995-11-10/99994.1.26.

3   Getting Ready

42		995-11-10/99994.1.35.
46		995-11-10/99994.1.15.
48		Photo by Evelyn Brew. 2004.34.1.139.
50		2004.1.123.1.99.
52 top left		2004.1.123.1.82.
52 top right		2004.1.123.1.64.
52 bottom left		Photo by Fred Orchard. 2004.1.123.1.47.
52 bottom middle		Photo by Hattie Cosgrove. 2004.1.123.1.94.
52 bottom right		Photo by Hattie Cosgrove. 2004.1.123.1.63.
53 top left		Photo by Hattie Cosgrove. 2004.1.123.1.87.
53 top right		2004.1.123.1.42.
53 bottom left		2004.1.123.1.43.
53 bottom middle		Courtesy Arizona State Museum, University of Arizona.
53 bottom right		Courtesy Arizona State Museum, University of Arizona.
54 left		Photo probably by Hattie Cosgrove. 2004.1.123.1.12.
54 right		Photo by Hattie Cosgrove. 2004.1.123.1.81.
55 left		Photo probably by Hattie Cosgrove. 2004.1.123.1.48.
55 right		Photo by Hattie Cosgrove. 2004.1.123.1.61.
57 top left		2004.1.123.1.13.
57 top right		Courtesy Arizona State Museum, University of Arizona.
57 bottom left		995-11-10/99994.1.14.
57 bottom right		2004.1.123.1.89.
58 left		Photo by Hattie Cosgrove. 2004.1.123.1.56.
58 right		Photo by Hattie Cosgrove. 2004.1.123.1.54.
59		2004.1.123.1.32.
61 top left		Photo probably by Hattie Cosgrove. 2004.1.123.1.88.
61 top right		Photo by Hattie Cosgrove. 2004.1.123.1.1.
61 bottom left		Photo by Hattie Cosgrove. 2004.1.123.1.15.
61 bottom right		Photo by Hattie Cosgrove. 2004.1.123.1.80.
62 top left		2004.1.123.1.714.
62 top middle		Photo by Hattie Cosgrove. 2004.1.123.1.82.
62 top right		Photo by Hattie Cosgrove. 2004.1.123.1.79.
62 bottom left		Photo by Hattie Cosgrove. 2004.1.123.1.59.
62 bottom middle		Photo by Evelyn Brew. 2004.34.1.82.
62 bottom right		Photo by Hattie Cosgrove. 2004.1.123.1.58.
64 left		2004.1.123.1.52.
64 right		2004.1.123.1.49.
65 left		Courtesy Arizona State Museum, University of Arizona.
65 right		Photo by Evelyn Brew. 2004.34.1.70.
66 top left		Photo by Hattie Cosgrove. 2004.1.123.1.60.
66 top right		Photo probably by J. O. Brew. Courtesy Arizona State Museum, University of Arizona.
66 bottom left		Photo by Hattie Cosgrove. 2004.1.123.1.55.
66 bottom right		Photo by Hattie Cosgrove. 2004.1.123.1.73.

4   New Awatovi

68		2004.1.123.1.18.
72		Peabody Museum Awatovi Archive. 995-11-10/99994.1.29.

73	Photo by Hattie Cosgrove. 2004.1.123.1.85.
74	2004.1.123.1.11.
76	2005.2.427.
77	Photo by Edward Beckwith. 2005.1.103.
78	Courtesy Arizona State Museum, University of Arizona.
79	Photo by Edward Beckwith. 2007.1.70.2.
80	2006.24.1.3.
81 top	Photo by Hattie Cosgrove. 2004.1.123.1.78.
81 bottom	Courtesy Arizona State Museum, University of Arizona.
82	Photo by Evelyn Brew. 2004.34.1.32.
83	2004.1.123.1.16.
84	2004.1.123.1.41.
85	2004.1.123.1.17.

5 Life in Camp

88	2004.1.123.1.45.
90	Photo probably by Carlos García-Robiou. 2006.24.1.2.
91 left	Photo by Hattie Cosgrove. 2004.1.123.1.68.
91 right	Photo by Hattie Cosgrove. 2004.1.123.1.72.
93 left	2004.1.123.1.67.
93 right	Photo by Evelyn Brew. 2004.34.1.16.
95	Peabody Museum Awatovi Archive. 995-11-10/99994.1.25.
96	Photo by Hattie Cosgrove. 2004.1.123.1.77.
97 top	Photo by Edward Beckwith. 2005.1.103.
97 bottom left	Courtesy Arizona State Museum, University of Arizona.
97 bottom right	Photo by Evelyn Brew. 2006.34.1.37.
98 top	2004.1.123.36.
98 bottom	Courtesy Arizona State Museum, University of Arizona.
101	2004.1.123.1.51.
102	Photo probably by Carlos García-Robiou. 2006.24.1.4.
103	2004.1.123.1.24.
104 left	Photo by Evelyn Brew. 2006.34.1.145.
104 right	Photo by Hattie Cosgrove. 2004.1.123.1.83.
107	Peabody Museum Awatovi Archive. 995-11-10/99994.1.18.
109	Photo by Hattie Cosgrove. 2004.1.123.1.76.
110	2004.1.123.1.23.
112	2004.1.123.1.90.
114	Courtesy Arizona State Museum, University of Arizona.

6 Mobs of Visitors

116	2004.1.123.1.44.
118	Photo by Hattie Cosgrove. 2004.1.123.1.71.
119	Peabody Museum Awatovi Archive. 995-11-10/99994.1.24.
120	2004.1.123.1.34.
121 top	Photo by Hattie Cosgrove. 2004.1.123.1.66.
121 bottom	Photo probably by Carlos García-Robiou. 995-11-10/99994.1.20.
122	Peabody Museum Awatovi Archive. 995-11-10/99994.1.19.
124	Courtesy Arizona State Museum, University of Arizona.
125	2004.1.123.1.30.
126	Courtesy Evelyn Brew and Alan and Lindsay Brew.
127	Courtesy Evelyn Brew and Alan and Lindsay Brew.
128	2004.1.123.1.50.
129 top	2004.1.123.1.26.
129 bottom	2004.1.123.1.35.
130	Photo by Hattie Cosgrove. 2004.1.123.1.53.

131	Photo probably by John Longyear. 2004.1.123.21.
134	Photo probably by Mott Davis. Courtesy Arizona State Museum, University of Arizona.
134 inset	Peabody Museum Awatovi Archive. Gift of Hester A. Davis.
136	Photo possibly by Chi Roberts. 2004.1.123.1.19.
140 left	Photo probably by Mott Davis. 2004.1.123.1.38.
140 right	Photo probably by Mott Davis. Courtesy Arizona State Museum, University of Arizona.
141 left	Photo probably by Mott Davis. Courtesy Arizona State Museum, University of Arizona.
141 right	Photo 2004.1.123.1.39.

7   End of the Expedition

146	Photo by Evelyn Brew. 2004.34.1.116.
149	Peabody Museum Awatovi Archive. 995-11-10/99994.1.27.
152	Photo by Evelyn Brew. 2004.34.1.103.

8   A Scientific Legacy

160	Photo by J. O. Brew. 2004.1.123.1.9.
162	Peabody Museum Awatovi Archive. 995-11-10/99994.1.32.
163	2004.1.123.1.93.
164	2004.1.123.1.91.
166	Photo by J. O. Brew. 995-11-10/99994.1.22.
167 left	Photo by Hattie Cosgrove. 2004.1.123.1.75.
167 right	Photo by Hattie Cosgrove. 2004.1.123.1.74.
169	Photo by Hillel S. Burger. 39-97-10/20419, 80270012.
170	Photo by Hillel S. Burger. 36-131-10/7843, T3620.
171 top	Photo by Hillel S. Burger. 37-111-10/9856, T3514.
171 bottom	Photo by Hillel S. Burger. 37-111-10/9855, T3495.
172	Serigraph by Louie Ewing from a drawing by Penrose Davis. Smith 1952: pl. D.
173	Serigraph by Louie Ewing from a drawing by Penrose Davis. Smith 1952: pl. A.
174	Peabody Museum Awatovi Archive. 995-11-10/99994.1.31.
175 top	Photo by J. O. Brew. 2004.1.123.1.3.
175 bottom	Photo by Hester A. Davis.
176 top	Photo by Hester A. Davis.
176 bottom	Photo by Hester A. Davis.
180	Peabody Museum Awatovi Archive. 2004.1.123.1.8.
182	Smith 1952: fig. 35a. 2004.1.123.1.20.
183 top	Serigraph by Louie Ewing from a drawing by Penrose Davis. Smith 1952: pl. B.
183 bottom	Smith 1952: fig. 35b. Photo probably by J. O. Brew. 98520106.
184 top	Smith 1952: fig. 35c. Photo probably by J. O. Brew. 98520107.
184 bottom	Smith 1952: fig. 35d. Photo probably by J. O. Brew. 98520108.
187	From Montgomery, Smith, and Brew 1949: fig. 35.
188	2004.1.123.1.27.
191 top	From Mindeleff 1891: pl. 5.
191 bottom	Photo by Hester A. Davis.

Index

murals, 49, 100, 182, **182, 183–184,** 185; records Nimmo-Brew wedding, **viii,** 138–139, 142–145

Smithsonian Institution, 13, 26, 187

Snake dances, 112, 114, 118, 125

Snob Hollow, 73–74

Soil Conservation Service, 128, **129**

Songòopavi. *See* Shongopavi

Southeastern Utah Expedition, 16, 21, 22

Southwest Museum, Los Angeles, 59, 106, 108, 156, 159

Spanish explorers and colonists, xvi–xvii, xviii, 3, 5–9, 165–166, 168, 177, 186–187

Spanish mission architecture, 186–187

Spoehr, Alexander, 128

Spring, Helen. *See* Claflin, Helen "Haych"

Stallings Island, 19, 20

Stevens, Alden B. "Steve," 27, 32–34, **34,** 35, 37, **42,** 54, 77, 86, **136;** and camera kite, 165, **167**

Stevens, Marian, 34, **42, 136**

Stone and Bone tent. *See under* New Awatovi

stone artifacts, 41, 179, **180**

Stoner, Father Victor Rose, 130–133, **130, 131**

Swarts Ruin, 17, 47

Talashoyuwema, Chester. *See* Dennis, Chester

Tallahogan Canyon, **xiv,** 3, 10, 20, 165, 190

Tawayesva, Jim, 157

Tewanyinima, Vivian, 20, **50, 96,** 148

Third Mesa, 3, 7, 50

Thomas, Joe, 29

Thompson, Eric, 117

Thompson, Lindsay "Lin" C., **viii,** 27, **33,** 67, **42, 124;** after Awatovi, 103; background of, 32; as character, 105; as cook, vi, 102–103, **104,** 117; Nimmo-Brew wedding preparations, 139, **141,** 143; on "Throne," 94, 96

Titiev, Mischa, 24, 128

Tobacco Clan, xvii

Tovar, Pedro de, xvi, 5, 6

transportation and roads, 26, 32, 80, 83–86, 96, 99–100. *See also* motor vehicles

Treasure Hill, 45, 47

tree-ring samples, 60, 63, 156, 179, 181. *See also* dendrochronology

Tsakpahu. *See* Chakpahu

Tschopik, Marion. *See* Hutchinson, Marion

Tusayan, 5, 10

University of Arizona, 60, 123; field schools, 101, 151, 199n6

University of New Mexico, Chaco Canyon field school, 92, 120

Upper Gila Expedition, 103, 159

U.S. Geological Survey, 56, 156

Vargas, Diego de, 8–9

Walpi, xvii, 7, 100

Water Clan, xvii

Watson, Don, 56

weather. *See under* Antelope Mesa

Webster, Laurie, 168

Weeks, Katherine. *See* Claflin, Katherine

Western Mound, 3, 24, 34, 41, 159, **166;** excavations in, 11–13, **12, 160,** 167; pottery from, 178–179, 189–190

Wetherill, John, 122–123

Wetherill Mesa Project, 179

Wheeler, Richard P., xix, 56, **57,** 75, 100, 136, 156, 178–179

Whiting, Al, 127

Williams (Coochnyama), Patrick, 194

Wilson, M. L., 128

Wilson, Seth, 143, 147–148

Winchester, Harold P., **42, 62,** 58, 63, 100, 194

women in archaeology, 92–93

Woodbury, Richard B., xxi, **42, 57, 98, 102, 112, 128;** after Awatovi, xix, 154; analyzed artifacts for Ph.D., 179; on carved awl, 179; on dance visits, 112, 114, 118; describes Wheeler, 56; on fate of the "Throne," 96; on food, 102, 105, 111; at Nimmo-Brew wedding, 145; on routine in camp, 100; studies stone, 164; on visitors, 120, 123; on weather, 86, 106

Worman, Penny. *See* Davis, Penrose

zooarchaeology, 168, 177

Zuni, 5, 6, 7, 9, 24